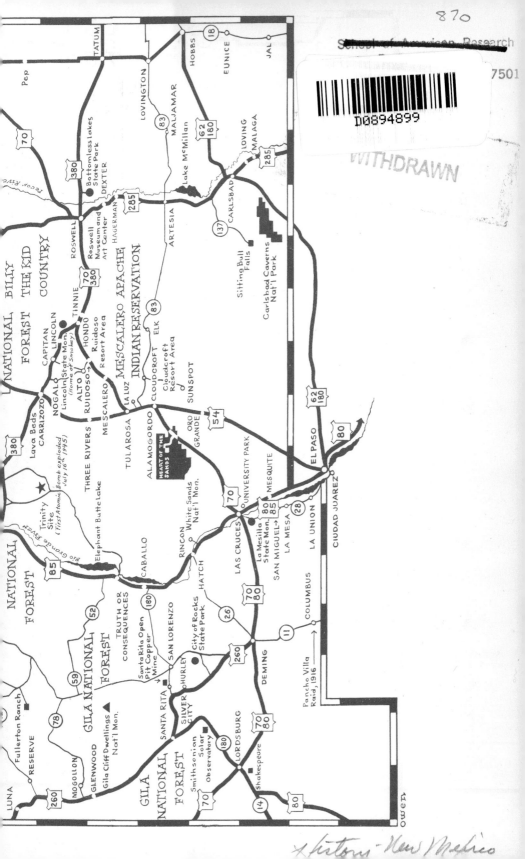

THIS IS NEW MEXICO

THIS IS
NEW MEXICO

edited by
George Fitzpatrick

HORN & WALLACE, Publishers

ALBUQUERQUE

Frontis color photograph by Dick Kent

Manufactured in the United States of America
Horn & Wallace, Publishers
Box 4204, Albuquerque, New Mexico

FOREWORD

For thirteen lucky years I have called New Mexico home. Inevitably this means that whenever I am anywhere else, its mysterious magic so haunts me that I long for the day when we leave the rush and tension of the great teeming cities and return to the old Ranch in the Pecos valley, seven thousand feet up in the Sangre de Cristo mountains. There the air is pure, and to breathe it is an exhilaration. The water is delicious, the sky unbelievably high and wide and of a deep, almost palpable blue.

One wakens in the shining spacious mornings feeling ten years old, and life is an adventure again. The remembered silence and the pleasant country sounds refresh the wearied spirit. Vision stretches gratefully to the far distant horizons. How good to see the great peaks and *mesas*, the fantastic towering rocks again, and the 2,000 year old pueblo ruins silhouetted against the spectacular sunsets. How fair is our valley . . .

Pine and *piñon* cover the red *adobe* land, and in the fall the aspens, and cottonwoods along the Pecos River, burn bright gold. In winter the forests are a white wonderland of Christmas trees. All year round the nights are crisp and cool, and the stars, startlingly brilliant, float in amethyst space and seem to bring heaven nearer to earth. If ever mortals could hear the music of the spheres, it would be in New Mexico.

We love our busy life at Forked Lightning, with the thirving herd of Santa Gertrudis on the range and the constant flow of guests at the old *hacienda*.

Here as everywhere, the human element is part of the fascination. Our friends and fellow-workers include Indian craftsmen, neighbors of Spanish-American descent from Pecos and other villages nearby and pioneer Westerners—merchants, cowboys, miners, sportsmen, ranchers, archeologists, artists and writers . . . a richly varied family bringing all the drama and romance of New Mexico's colorful past into its exciting present.

Where else in this world can you find such wide ranging contrasts of ancient and modern? Prehistoric remains and nuclear testing grounds; centuries-old Indian pueblos and modern motels; tribal Ceremonials at Gallup, *al fresco* Opera at Santa Fe; Spanish *santeros* and secret Penitentes in the mountains, the nation's most advanced space medicine center in Albuquerque; horse-drawn wagons on the country roads, air conditioned busses and crack trains on the new ways; sleepy-hollow hidden villages, boom-towns in the uranium, oil and gas fields; ageless caverns, mysterious rocks and relics from the first furnace of creation, and close by, the confident surge of today's descendants of the original *homo sapiens* as they build their streamlined homes and industries.

Possibly the March of Progress is more strikingly noticeable here in this ancient territory than elsewhere in the states. Romantics, of course, deplore the parking meters in the plaza at Santa Fe. (Me too . . . I even resent the automobiles!) They sigh to see the backyard hens and the family cow disappear in favour of the deep-freeze Instant Goodies at the up-dated country store. But some traditions stand firm. I doubt that factory cooked *pinto* beans, *tamales*, *tacos* or *chile* will ever displace the home-made kind. And although the lovely Mexican and Navajo costumes have to compete with the drip-dries and the bluejeans, they are still proudly worn by old and young. Junk jewelry glitters in the dime stores and factory-made souvenirs in tourist shops, but they will never oust the treasured silver and turquoise, the handcrafted leather and pottery. The Indian languages are still in use, and Spanish is everywhere current and familiar.

For this is characteristic of New Mexicans . . . they seem to know how to combine the best of old and new in a happy compromise. All around the countryside, for example, the small neat *adobe* house keeps its *horno,* its well and the outdoor plumbing, but nonchalantly sports a TV antenna on the roof and an automobile at the ol' hitching-post.

Ambition and enterprise are not lacking but the favorite toast among friends is still *"Salud, amor y pesetas . . . y tiempo para gustarlos."*

Most important of all, the Land itself changes not. Timeless, remote, and vast, it has absorbed all invaders from mastodons to missiles. Its beauty and power have inspired the artist, the writer and the mystic. The magic can hardly be communicated, but this rich anthology gives you, Dear Reader, a vivid glimpse of the Land of Enchantment.

It is an honor to write the Foreword. I only wish I had the skill to express my thoughts and dreams and wonder, but it is hard to speak of one's religion, or of one's love. And there is something of both in my feeling for New Mexico.

—GREER GARSON FOGELSON

CONTENTS

GLIMPSES OF HISTORY

AUTOGRAPHS . . . IN STONE
Evon Z. Vogt

EVON Z. VOGT came to New Mexico in 1905 and engaged in ranching. At about the same time efforts were being made to make El Morro a national monument. This was accomplished in 1906 when the Government set aside 240 acres to establish El Morro National Monument. Vogt had an abiding interest in El Morro and the inscriptions, and it was natural that he should be named as custodian of the Monument in 1917. As he put it, he "chaperoned" El Morro for about 20 years. He died in January, 1943. Mrs. Vogt still lives on the family ranch at Ramah.

Lighting a big black cigar, Charles F. Lummis settled comfortably under the reading lamp in our ranch living room and in his painstaking script began writing a tribute to the two places he loved so well—El Morro and Acoma.

It was past midnight. We had spent the evening listening to Lummis' tales of frontier days in the eighties. Finally the children got sleepy, then the rest of us. But for Charley Lummis the day had just begun.

Throughout the night, with his ever present black cigar, he labored at his writings.

He filled an entire page in the visitors' register from El Morro National Monument I had brought in for him from the rock. Then he worked on other writings until dawn.

When I awakened he had gone to bed. The big register lay open on the table.

This is what he had written:

Nowhere else does geology open to the layman so obvious, so dramatic, and so spectacular a page as in that region which I christened, 40 years ago, by the name it bears today—the Southwest. There is no other cross-section of earth building sequences as in the Grand Canyon; nor is there elsewhere on the earth such an exposition of earth-carving forces as the unique *Mesa* country of northwestern New Mexico, with its vast waves of red or fawn or grey Navajo sand-stone, breaking off in sheer and lofty cliffs; its lofty table-topped islands-in-the-air which are left in valleys to witness the far day when no valleys were, but one vast upland of triassic sand-stone; its "Monumental" erosion, prophesied by its jointing in an ancient uplift, sketched by frosts and ardent suns, turned, carved, chiselled, sand-papered by flood, rain, and wind. The world has many freaks, wonders of erosion; but it has nothing else to compare with this great area of water and wind erosion of the Navajo sandstone.

I believe there is no question that the two most interesting rocks in the world—counting their picturesque, intricate, and fantastic erosion and their historic associations,—are in this formation, Acoma, The Sky City, a pueblo still living as Coronado found it in 1540, east of the Zuñi Mountains or Continental Divide (whose up-humping broke the great sandstone blanket); and on the west, El Morro, *La Mesa Escrita,* Inscription Rock, "The Stone Autograph Album." So far as I can learn, no other cliff on earth records so much—or a tithe as much—of Romance, Adventure, Heroism. Certainly all other rocks in America, do not, all together, hold so much of American history. Oñate here carved his entry with dagger two years before an English-speaking person had built a hut anywhere in the New World, 15 years before Plymouth Rock.

No other description so brief has ever said as much, and Lummis meant every word of it. He loved the country so well he seemed a part of it.

To Lummis must be given credit for bringing the grandeur of the Southwest to the attention of the American public. His *Strange Corners of Our Country, Land of Poco Tiempo, Mesa, Canyon and Pueblo* and other books opened for readers new vistas.—A country that seemed to many a barren, desert land became clothed with new charm.

Lummis visited El Morro first in 1885, and the last time in 1926, with numerous visits in between.

Although Lummis popularized El Morro, the "stone autograph album" was really discovered for the outside world by Lieut. J. H. Simpson and R. H. Kern, who, with their orderly, W. Bird, and a Navajo trader named Lewis, visited El Morro on September 17 and 18, 1849 and copied the inscriptions.

Their report describing the inscriptions, the petroglyphs left by early Indians, and the great ruined pueblos on top the cliff, was published in book form in 1850 in *Reports to the Secretary of War, including an Expedition Into the Navajo Country.* Lithographs, some of them in color, made from Kern's sketches, illustrate the volume.

In ages past the Indians used the sand stone face of the castle-like rock to tell their story in petroglyphs. The *conquistadores,* seeking the *Seven Golden Cities of Cibola,* and blazing trails into new country, found the great rock sentinel on their path. Here they stopped to camp in a sheltered cove and left a record of their passing for others who followed.

Coronado passed there in 1540. No carved record of his expedition has been found, but like others inscribed during the next century it may have been obliterated.

The date and names of the Chamuscado party of the Rodriguez expedition of 1581 were noted by Bandelier and Cushing in the eighties, but they have since been effaced or obliterated.

The oldest inscription that still may be read is that of Don Juan de Oñate, the first governor and colonizer of New Mexico.

Over an old pictograph on the smooth face of the cliff Oñate carved his record:

"Here passed the Adelantado Don Juan de Oñate from the discovery of the Sea of the South on the 16 of April of 1605."

Seven years before, Oñate and his little band of colonizers had struggled across desert and mountain trails and had set up the first cross in the Indian Pueblo of San Juan. There they built homes, and, across the Rio Grande, started the first white settlement and capital of the new territory, San Gabriel. Five years later he founded Santa Fé and made it the capital.

In 1620 when the Pilgrims were establishing white civilization on the eastern coast New Mexico's fifth governor was recording his activities in stone:

"The captain general of the provinces of New Mexico for the King,

Our Lord. He passed by here on his return from the Pueblos of Zuñi on the 29 of July, 1620, and he put them in peace at their request, asking his favor as vassals of his majesty and anew they pledged obedience, all of which he did with sagacity, zeal and prudence as a most Christian-like (next word effaced) as a most particular and gallant soldier of un-ending and praised memory."

Some enemy of the captain general's seems to have scratched out one word and probably obliterated also the captain general's name.

There seems to be no doubt, however, that it was Don Juan de Eulate, who served as governor from 1618 to 1625. Prof. Lansing Bloom wrote me in 1929 from Seville, Spain, that he had traced the fact that Eulate left Mexico City for Santa Fé on December 31, 1617, and served as governor until Admiral Philipe Sotelo Ossario came in 1625.

Never knowing when they might be way-laid and killed by Pueblos or Apaches these parties of conquering and Christian-izing Castilians carved their records with great care, selecting the smooth surfaces that were rarely washed by rain. Thus, any searching party might know the date and direction of their expedition.

In the brief and quaintly indited lines, they left for all time a story of high courage and deeds of great accomplishment. The country between Acoma and El Morro and Zuñi is peculiarly adapted for surprise attacks. Any one who success-fully made the journey against the odds of enemies and un-friendly weather, uncertain feed and water, insufficient food and arms, could well be proud that he had successfully com-pleted the long *jornada*.

High on the south side of the cliff is the carved inscription of General De Vargas, who—at his own expense—came back after the Pueblo rebellion of 1680 to dispute the undisturbed rule of the *caciques*.

The general's message was brief and to the point:

"Here was the General Don Diego de Vargas who conquered to our Holy Faith and the Royal Crown all of New Mexico at his own expense year of 1692."

De Vargas mentions in his records camping at El Morro

in a *rincon como una naranja*—a cove like an orange—and gives thanks to God that there was water in the *pozo* or natural reservoir. There on a Sunday his priests said mass before proceeding to the Ojitos of Zuñi, probably the springs of Pescado, the Zuñi farming village, six miles west of Ramah.

In this cove where the old Spanish caravans unhooked their oxen and horse teams and camped there is still a large pine tree that grows high against the cliff. In those early days there were many more. The marks in the cliff 50 feet above ground where swaying limbs cut into the stone prove there was more shade then than now.

The first inscription you see after you leave your car fifty yards away under the giant pine is that of Lujan, who headed the expedition sent to Hawikuh to punish the Zuñis for killing their priest:

"He passed on the 23 of March of 1632 to the avenging of the murder of the Priest Le Trado. Lujan."

Hawikuh, 12 miles from Zuñi, chief city of Cibola when Coronado came in 1540, is in ruins today. This mission was founded by Governor Francisco Manuel de Silva Nieto, who, with his ten-wagon expedition, made the trip from Santa Fé to Zuñi in the summer of 1629.

The carved record of the journey is in iambic verse, with letters two inches high:

"Here passed the Governor Don Francisco Manuel de Silva Nieto who has the impossible overcome with his indubitable arm and his arm and his valor with the wagons of the King, our Lord. A thing which he alone was able to bring about. On the 9 of August, 1629. That it might be well to Zuñi passed and established the Faith."

At least twenty-seven parties of Spaniards camped at El Morro between 1605 and 1774. The phrase *paso por aqui* became a customary notation.

There are no dated carvings for the period between 1774 and 1849, but after Lieut. Simpson took news of his discovery to Santa Fe there seems to have been a recurrence of travel via El Morro, for names of a great many emigrants, ranchmen, soldiers, engineers and prospectors are carved on the sides of the cliff.

Last summer I made a list of these later travelers. There were 390 in all. Among these were H. L. Dodge, father of Chee Dodge and grandfather of Tom Dodge, Navajo Council chairman, dated 1849, '51, and '54; Col. E. J. Harwood, '67-'68; General R. L. Howze, '82; John Gunn, '84; General E. A. Carter, Lieut. McCook, D. D. Graham, first trader and agent at Zuñi, '82; Major J. R. Hughes, Franz Huning, John W. Conway, Santa Fé, 1873; Marmon Brothers, '81; Lieut. R. D. Hubbell, P. Gilmor, Breckenridge, Va., 1859; John Udell, first emigrant train; Isaac T. Holland, July 8, 1858; Pablo Castillo, 1873; Domingez, Compania Efe, '63; Julian Trujillo, '63.

R. H. Kern returned on August 30, 1851, with Dr. S. M. Woodhouse and Lieut. Sitgraves to conduct a reconnaissance of the Zuñi river country. The jay which Dr. Woodhouse discovered at El Morro and which has been named for him still finds there a happy home, unmolested in the little trodden coves.

Frequently new discoveries are made in the inaccessible ledges, great cliff wings, caves, lofty bastions of the *mesa*. Only last fall we found a prehistoric hand and foot trail leading up into a dark crevice to a hidden water hole a hundred feet above ground.

No one had thought to seek an interpretation of the petroglyph just below the trail. This consisted of two birds flying upward, a winding trail over an obstacle, and two hands and two feet traveling to a circle.

An old Zuñi one day showed us what it meant:

"Up high where the birds fly, by hand and by foot, over a difficult trail and a hard climb, one comes to a circle, indicating a reservoir."

Behind the ranger's cabin in a cleft in the cliff is another trail leading into a crevice so small that only children could be pushed up there—probably to be hidden by their mothers in time of danger.

These hand and foot holes are tiny, and as plain as if made yesterday.

El Morro is almost as isolated and as inaccessible as when

the *Conquistadores* first sought its shelter; yet three thousand persons yearly make the trip—sixty miles from Gallup and forty from Grants. Many are scientists, writers, artists, and some stay as long as a week to prowl the sylvan coves.

In 1906 the government set aside one hundred and sixty acres to establish El Morro National Monument. When a survey showed that the west line cut through the north ruin on top the cliff another 80 acres was added.

The Civil Works Administration project undertaken in 1934 made possible a mile-long trail leading past the inscriptions, the petroglyphs, through shady pine groves to the top of the mesa.

Sculptured in solid rock the trail takes one by easy flights, with ever changing views to the major ruin. Claimed by both Acoma and Zuñi this pueblo once had an estimated 1200 rooms and probably was abandoned some four hundred years before the first Spaniards camped at El Morro.

The trail from the ruin takes one over the top to provide a panoramic view that unfolds the surrounding region in clear majesty. Then past the somewhat smaller north ruin the trail switches back to the starting point.

Neither of the ruins has been excavated. What may be great treasures lies under the dust of centuries, to be unearthed only when a museum can be provided on the ground to preserve and display what is found.

THE TITLE OF DOÑA SOFIA
Beatrice Chauvenet

BEATRICE CHAUVENET first came to New Mexico in 1927. She has written articles and short stories for national magazines and in 1940 she received the Hopwood Award in fiction. Much of her professional life has been spent as an administrator of voluntary and tax-supported health agencies. She has taken time out to travel around the world and to lecture extensively in the United States and Great Britain in behalf of better international understanding. Her home is in Santa Fe.

It was Monday, June 3, 1895. Before the Court of Private Land Claims sitting in Santa Fe the most exciting case in its history was being tried. James Addison Peralta-Reavis and Doña Sofia Loreta Micaela de Peralta Reavis de la Cordoba (husband and wife) vs. The United States of America.

The plaintiffs asked the government to confirm their title to "a tract of land seventy-five miles from north to south and two hundred and twenty-five miles from east to west, in rectangular form, starting at the base of the Maricopa Mountain as the center of the west boundary." That western boundary was a line near Phoenix, Arizona, and the eastern boundary extended close to Silver City, New Mexico. Roughly twelve and a half million acres! Estimated value: some thirty-five million dollars!

Interest was at fever pitch. Hundreds of persons held possession of the land under homestead, pre-emption and mining laws. Yet if Peralta-Reavis could prove his title from the King of Spain, other claims would be invalid. Many owners, believing the government would lose the case, had already bought quitclaims. The Southern Pacific Company paid $50,000 for a right of way through the Peralta Grant. The

Silver King Mining Company gave $25,000 for a release upon its mining property. Individuals forked out anywhere from three to fifteen hundred dollars each to clear the title to their lands. Mr. Reavis and his wife lived in princely style on their expectations.

The government was ready with Matt G. Reynolds, attorney for the Land Court as Chief Counsel. Afterward he confessed that he was very, very nervous about the outcome. Summers Burkhart of Albuquerque was Assistant U. S. Attorney. Assisting were the experts who had looked into the original records, Severo Mallet-Prevost, a student of Spanish; Will M. Tipton, handwriting specialist, and Levi A. Hughes, business man of Santa Fe.

Two years earlier James Addison Peralta-Reavis had filed his claim before the Land Court. In proof he submitted certified copies of documents on record in Spain, Old Mexico, and the California missions, which gave him an unbroken chain of title to the Peralta Grant made by King Philip V in 1744 to the "Baron of Arizonaca."

Reavis showed that his wife, Doña Sofia, was the great-granddaughter of Don Miguel Nemecio Silva de Peralta de la Cordoba y Garcia de Carillo de la Falces, the original grantee. As indicated by his name Don Miguel was a nobleman of great distinction, holding among other orders such exalted titles as Grandee of Spain, Sir Knight of the Redlands, Gentleman of the King's Chamber with privileged entrance, and *of course* Baron of Arizonaca.

There were copies of the original grant with confirmation by various Spanish monarchs who followed Philip V. There was a genealogy tracing the lineage of Doña Sofia, accompanied by proper proof of the legitimacy and nobility of each heir. It was stated that Doña Sofia was the elder of twins born March 4, 1862, at the Bandini Ranch near San Bernardino, California. The parents and the male twin subsequently died, leaving the infant heirs to the guardianship of John A. Treadway, a Yankee. When the girl was twenty she entered into a "marriage contract" with Reavis.

Eminent attorneys who examined the great mass of evidence

gathered by Reavis during twenty years believed his case was valid, unbeatable. True, he had tried six years earlier to get the grant confirmed before Surveyor-General Royal A. Johnson of Arizona, and was turned down. However he had garnered more evidence in the meantime. Popular sentiment in New Mexico and Arizona was that his claim was just and would be confirmed.

The court was ready, with a full bench. The defendant was ready. But when the trial opened the plaintiff did not appear. Reavis had spent years and large sums of money in perfecting this claim, yet on the great day he was not in court.

After a brief consultation it was decided that the papers he had filed would be considered the plaintiff's statement of his case, and the government could proceed with its defense.

The government was ready!

Before a crowded court room Mr. Reynolds contended and brought witnesses to prove—

That the original Baron of Arizonaca was a mythical gentleman created by the fertile brain of Reavis. That the grant and all the papers relating thereto were colossal forgeries. In the archives of the City of Guadalajara was a book bound in cherry-colored leather, composed of twelve leaves of parchment, containing a coat of arms and alleged copies of the royal decrees in relation to the Barony of Arizonaca. All material portions of that book were declared forgeries.

It was alleged that James Addison Reavis had gone to Spain in 1885 at the expense of John W. Mackay of San Francisco, whom he had interested in his grant. There he spent nearly a year obtaining evidence in support of his claim.

Accompanying him as his ward was a young woman. In Madrid he went before the Charge d' Affaires of the American Legation and made formal declaration that she was his wife, by virtue of a marriage contract entered into in 1882. Reavis had been interested in the alleged grant long before he ever met "Doña Sofia." He recorded in Arizona various instruments which purported to show a chain of title that came down from the original Baron of Arizonaca through one George Willing, Jr., to Reavis.

Now the government asserted that he had originally hoped to obtain possession by virtue of those deeds, but finding the title dubious he had strengthened it by the simple expedient of producing an heir to the estate and making her his wife.

Furthermore, Reynolds contended Reavis was a fugitive from justice in Spain, having been detected trying to insert forged papers relating to the grant into the archives at Seville. He fled from Spain before being arrested but the government there officially branded the tampered documents fraudulent.

To cap the climax, "Doña Sofia" was declared to be really the daughter of John A. Treadway by an Indian woman called Kate who had borne her in Sherwood Valley, Mendocino County, California.

In summing up his case United States Attorney Reynolds declared that the most amazing thing about the whole monstrous claim was that there was "not a single, solitary genuine document, not one." He branded it a "persistent, intelligent and aggressive effort to perpetrate a fraud on the government. One of the greatest schemes ever attempted in this country or any other."

Government experts had been sent to Spain, to Guadalajara, to California, and they subjected the originals of Reavis' certified copies to close scrutiny. They declared that the language used by the King of Spain in the documents was very poor "American-Spanish," that changes had been made in the records with modern ink, written with a steel pen in a modern style of handwriting. They stated that California witnesses to the noble birth of Doña Sofia had repudiated their affidavits and that the records of San Bernardino Mission had once been loaned by a substitute priest to a Spanish agent who wanted to study them! In Mexican archives pages had been inserted which were not quite the same size as the original leaves of the book and the page numbering in documents relating to the Peralta grant was defective.

In short, Messrs. Mallet-Prevost, Tipton and Hughes, sleuthing for the government, had found plenty.

Apparently Reavis' elaborate proof had collapsed like a straw house before a hurricane. Yet, when all this damaging evidence had been presented, there came a wire from the plaintiff asking that the case be held open until he could reach Santa Fe from San Francisco. The Court obligingly waited a few days. Mr. Reavis appeared, coolly determined to save his great domain.

It was a dramatic moment when the tall, suave Missourian took the stand in his own behalf. He asked a postponement but was refused. After all, the case had been on the docket for more than two years. He attempted to have it dismissed without prejudice but the court ruled that the plaintiff could not ask such action. There was nothing to do but act as his own attorney, since for one reason or another all his eminent counsel had found urgent business elsewhere.

The ingenuity and persistence of the man were truly astonishing. As he testified, some facts of his life were brought to light.

Born in Henry County, Missouri, he entered the Confederate army at eighteen and served during most of the War Between the States. Afterward he went for a year to Brazil. Returning to St. Louis he worked as a street car conductor, retail clothing clerk, travelling salesman for a saddlery house and a dry goods establishment, finally drifting into real estate.

In 1871 a man named George M. Willing, Jr., came to his office and presented to Reavis a scheme for exploiting a large tract of land in Arizona. He had papers concerning a royal grant to one Don Miguel Peralta.

The two men entered into an agreement and started west. Mr. Willing went directly to Prescott, Arizona, where he died the night after his arrival under circumstances that were strange. When Reavis turned up later he obtained possession of Willing's personal effects, including the papers relating to the Peralta Grant. Subsequently he filed a deed from Willing to himself. On that title his original claim rested. Six or seven years later, however, when he was travelling on a train near Sacramento, his interest was roused by a young lady coming down from Woodland. "She was a Spanish beauty, and I was a young man," he testified. "I spoke to her, entered into a conversation, and exchanged cards before we left the train."

The young lady was Doña Sofia.

Before they were married, Reavis said, he learned she was the heir to the empire, title to which he had been searching for years.

Yet he filed before Surveyor-General Johnson his original claim to the grant by purchase from George Willing and did not mention the existence of this heir until nearly four years later. It seemed evident he did not marry Doña Sofia until he had lost hope of winning out on his purchase title.

Now, before the Court of Private Claims he accused the government of "hypnotizing, suborning, browbeating and coercing" his witnesses. He denied the forgeries. He repeated his original claims to the land and demanded that justice be given him. Doña Sofia appeared and ably supported his story. She broke only once. When she was asked to identify certain papers, she faltered and burst into tears. Then she confessed that she was an uneducated woman, having had less than three months schooling in her life. The spectators in the court room, including numerous ladies, felt a wave of sympathy for her.

The Court of Private Land Claims found the Peralta Grant utterly fictitious and fraudulent. It declared there was no such person as Don Miguel or any of his alleged heirs and that the plantiffs were in no way connected with the mythical Baron of Arizonaca.

Thus collapsed one of the most gigantic frauds ever attempted. No one discovered how much money Reavis had collected out of his grand scheme. His very greed was his undoing, because the government went to no such pains to look into the smaller grant claims.

In the criminal proceedings which followed, Reavis was his cool, masterful self. For a long time his wife stood up under a severe cross examination but at length she collapsed. The jury brought in a verdict against Reavis for trying to defraud the government. He was sentenced to two years in the penitentiary.

After serving his term John Addison Reavis returned to California. There the super-swindler sank into quiet oblivion and his "monstrous edifice of forgery, perjury and subornation" became merely a part of the archives of the Southwest.

THE HOUSE OF THE DONS
Ann Nolan Clark

ANN NOLAN CLARK's earliest writings appeared in *New Mexico Maga-zine* in the 1930's. She branched out into children's books and has made a spectacular success with her writing. Her awards included the New-berry Medal and, in 1961, the Catholic Press Association Journalism Award. Her two latest books are *Paco's Miracle,* published by Farrar, Cudahy & Straus, and *Desert People* published by Viking. When she is not visiting far parts of the western hemisphere for material for her books, her home is in Santa Fe. From 1930 to 1960 she was employed as an education specialist with the Bureau of Indian Affairs. She spent six years in Guatemala, Costa Rica, Ecuador and Peru.

Four miles west of Vegas Town on Highway 85 today's motorist may eat his lunch beneath the leafy canopy of huge old cottonwoods by the running waters of a little river. As background rise high gaunt walls of a fire-ruined *adobe* house, a second smaller *adobe,* the long low-roofed home of a sheep herder's family, and the shabby shell of a once proud barn.

Nothing much now to add spice to a picnic dinner.

Almost sixty years ago it was built to add spice to the social life of the nation.

When Don Trinidad Romero, returned from the turmoil of official Washington, walked over the quiet lands of his newly acquired El Puertecito Grant, he planned his home: a home which was to be a proper setting for his beautiful wife, his children, his career and his wealth.

Don.Trinidad was born at the family gold mine at Golden, New Mexico, in 1835, and the proverbial spoon in his mouth was of solid gold. He was educated by tutors and later at eastern schools, and by his twentieth year was a man of affairs, such early maturing being but customary of the times.

By 1879 he was a prominent stockman, owning many thousand head of sheep and cattle, had spent eighteen years freighting with mule team from Kansas City to Santa Fe, had been a member of the Territorial Legislature, had been Congressman, merchant and trader. He had traveled widely. When he set out to build a home he planned it to hold fittingly possessions gathered from the market places of the world.

El Puertecito Grant, four miles west on the Santa Fé Trail from Las Vegas, was once a part of San Miguel del Bado of the great Central District of Mexican sovereignty. The first settlers of this grant were the Benavediz family. Later it passed into possession of Leon Pinard, sheriff of San Miguel in 1873. Two years afterward, when misfortune overtook Leon Pinard, the land was deeded to his bondsmen, Don Trinidad and his partner-brother Don Eugenio Romero.

They planned magnificently, these two wealthy Dons of old. The house site itself was situated on a slight elevation overlooking the little river which trickled placidly on its way to join the bigger river of the town of Our Sorrowful Lady of the Meadows. Before even the foundation of the house was made the entire grant was fenced by stout stone walls built to last more than one man's life time. Seven miles of *acequia* was trenched and lined with stone. For fifty-six years this *acequia* has never ceased to carry a steady flow of water from the Gallinas River of Vegas Town to the ranch. In the old days there were three reservoirs, their outlines marked now by slight depressions only.

Rows of cottonwood trees were planted to surround the house and extensive gardens laid out. Cecilio Garcia recalls the place as "a paradise of flowers."

"Don Trinidad was one to live handsomely," he relates. "He had always the fastest horses, the finest carriages, the most beautiful house."

Cecilio Garcia lives now with his children's children in a little house at the end of a long back road beyond Romeroville.

He remembers well life at the great house when he worked there, with his father, head sheep herder for Don Trinidad.

"It has been fifty years," he told us in his formal, dignified Spanish, "since I worked for Don Trinidad, and during this time I also have been building a house to leave behind me. True, it has only three rooms as you can see, but it has been built to last, just as the great house of the Romero's was built."

The great house in the center of its paradise of flowers went up slowly; it took several years for its construction. There was much timber bordering El Puertecito Grant, and the Romero brothers had their own sawmill for all the rough lumber needed. From the Panderais sawmill at Rociada other lumber was hauled . The massive beams and the hard wood for panels and floors were brought by mule team from Leavenworth and Kansas City. The new home blended the cultural heritages of Mexico and Spain, the glitter of Washington and the wealth of the new, raw west.

By 1880 the house was completed, a square two-story structure built of *adobe*. There were a dozen large, lofty, high ceiling rooms paneled in walnut. The downstairs rooms had sliding doors opening into the spacious ballroom. There was a low, wide, curving stairway, a perfect entrance for the Spanish beauties who came tripping down it. The furniture was of great, heavy pieces of ornately carved wood. The piano, freighted in by ox team, still is being used in Las Vegas; and one of the beds, eighty-five years old, is for sale for forty dollars. The china closet was built at one end of the long dining room. It was ceiling high and its shelves were crowded with many piece dinner sets brought from a dozen foreign countries. One dinner service was of solid silver, a gift of Don Trinidad's grandfather who was from Spain. The table linens were of finest drawnwork, for the ladies of the household were dextrous needle women. Twenty chandeliers, with their hanging rainbow prisms, lighted the rooms. There were, also, the new-fangled lamps which when wound threw a luminous light. There is one such lamp left in Vegas today.

The kitchen was an enormous work room where various

servants, both Indian and native, were busy endlessly with the affairs of food. Old Spanish dishes, now almost forgotten, were prepared here; fruits and vegetables and meats were dried, and corn was ground; Indian herbs were hung from the supply room *vigas,* and on the shelves were tins and boxes of imported foods, the best that money could buy.

Outside work was as perfectly managed as tasks within. The sawmill, the sheep corrals, the cow barn, the stable had each its own corps of workers. The stable was a delight to all horse lovers. The harness shone like mirrored walls. The horses, too, were a delight to all connoisseurs of horse flesh. The Master's horse especially was outstanding. One of the belles of that day tells me, with an uncontradictable flash in her gay, black eyes, that Don Trinidad's horse could make the four miles to Vegas easily in fifteen minutes flat.

The children had their own horses and ponies as well as the grown-ups. There are many who still remember young Miguel's pony and cart.

Always there were many guests. There were five Romero sisters and three brothers besides Eugenio and Trinidad. The families of Lopez, Baca and C de Baca, Delgado, Jaramillo, Irrzari, Luna, Chavez, Otero, Armijo, Perea, Costillo, and Perez were but a part of the ever moving procession of visitors. Friends from the East and South, relatives from all over the Southwest and also from Spain and Mexico made almost continual *fiesta.*

Celio Garcia described the smart coaches drawing up to the *portal* with a flourish, the *cocheros* vying with each other in dashing arrivals, the gallant *dons* assisting the stately *doñas* and dainty *señoritas* to alight. The entire family came for these parties; the elders were accompanied by the children, the *dueñas* and nursemaids. Parties lasted for a week or ten days and often overlapped.

Food was lavish, always a mixing of Anglo and Spanish. There was always champagne. There was as often ice-cream, the freezers having been brought from the east and the ice from the family ice house in Las Vegas.

Talk around the table was both serious and gay, hint of

Indian troubles, the latest escapades of the Town's bad men (Las Vegas had many more sinners than saints it seems), the need of a school law, and ever and always the exciting railroad news, for by this time the railroad had reached Las Vegas and in February of 1880 had given to all men of affairs of the Territory a trip to the Missouri River in luxurious Pullman cars.

President and Mrs. Hayes and General Sherman had visited in the vicinity and had been feted in grand style. The Grants had come, too, and many others prominent in national life. A new breakfast dish called oatmeal grits was being tried out over the country and appeared on the Romero breakfast table at one party occasion. Croquet, a game for ladies, caused jesting comment about the tableboard.

There were plenty of things to talk about!

Doña Valeria Lopez de Romero, wife of Don Trinidad, told merrily of her Washington experiences. When she arrived there with her husband, who had gone as member of Congress, she found to her consternation that all Washington was speaking English, a tongue strange and terrifying to her Spanish ears. Doña Valeria was quite at a loss, but not so her husband, Don Trinidad. At once he employed an interpreter, with orders to stay constantly at her mistress' elbow so that not a word need be lost of all that was spoken around her. Likewise did the children's Spanish nursemaid have an interpreter at elbow for the so-English speaking Washington.

In the ummer of 1883 Tertio-Millennial was celebrated in Santa Fe for thirty-three days. Nothing in the new world had ever surpassed the regal pomp and splendor of this ceremony of the church. A cardinal came. Day and night the territorial elite held historical pageants, parades and processions, religious ceremonies, *bailes* and musicales in honor of church and State. The Indians joined in the festivities and representatives from all Southwestern tribes gave dance ceremonials. It was a superb, spectacular event.

Eastern visitors crowded the Romeroville Ranch for weeks before the event and were brought back afterward to be entertained for the remainder of the summer.

Never before had parties at Romeroville been so gay nor guests so appreciative. Night after night the great house was filled to overflowing. The stately Doña Julianita Romero de Baca showed me her memory book with yellowed newspaper clippings, faded pictures and pressed flowers, precious souvenirs of that gay summer. Sitting in the quiet, time-shadowed house with Doña Julienita, youngest sister of Don Trinidad and once the wife of the wealthiest man in San Miguel, wistfully fingering the treasures in her diary it was easy to become a part of that long ago gaiety.

It was easy to picture the downstairs of the Romero house thronged with eastern visitors. Anglo guests and the darker complexioned men of Spain. Among them moved the two brothers, Don Eugenio and Don Trinidad, hospitable, gracious, entertaining—the perfect hosts.

The long supper table glimpsed through the double doors of the long dining room was burdened with foods and silver. At one end of the ballroom sat the Las Vegas Orchestra, pridefully conscious of being the best in the Southwest. From windows opening out onto the *portal* came the soft strumming of Spanish guitar and violin of the *rancheros,* adding their bit joyously, for were they not a part of the great gay house?

Upstairs was delightful confusion as Doña Valeria and Doña Chonita directed their maids to assist the ladies in last minute touches to feminine toilettes. Sometimes the New Mexico belles wore the wide fringed, flower-patterned shawls and lace *mantillas,* heirlooms from the courts of Spain. At other times they were sedate in Paris frocks with proper polonaise, bustle and basque. Sometimes their raven tresses were demure with the curled bangs and chignon of fashion, and sometimes they were audacious and come-hither with the blood red rose.

The two Lopez de Romero sisters had their own precise little Frenchman hair dresser who coiffeured them as their fancy dictated. The five Romero sisters had also the French hair dresser and they also had their own filagree man who made into ornaments the raw gold brought to them from the family mine.

But so did all the belles of the day. Wealth was desired as the setting for beauty.

Little Doña Modestita Lopez de Delgado had made for her bracelets heavy with the gold of California, New Mexico, Arizona and Colorado. She had golden rings and brooches and chains as delicately made as the wing tips of butterfly or humming bird. Doña Modestita herself was very like a butterfly. Baby sister in a family of seven, she was married at fourteen and brought to her husband's house her family of numerous dolls and played with them there as happily as she had at her father's house at San Lorenzo *rancho*.

Another Spanish beauty, the petite Doña Carlota Jaramillo de Lopez had a wide golden girdle which she wore belted over her shawl-draped *mantilla* and a parrot brooch so lovely that it is still remembered wistfully.

So the ladies flitted about upstairs and patted and preened as ladies do, and at last were ready to come tripping down the wide curved stairs. It was then that the big house came into its own.

Beauty and gold!

Spain, Mexico, Washington and the virile West. Eastern visitors stared at such exquisite loveliness.

The party was on!

"But for truly magnificent living," one gentleman of the Old Town told me, "let me relate of the life of the house of Don Miguel Romero, father of Don Trinidad." Then he described the old Spanish house which still forms one side of the plaza of old Las Vegas.

This house had twenty-three rooms surrounding the *placita*. The *placita,* as in all typical Spanish houses was the heart of the home. Its *portal* was yellow-white and painted grapes and flowers festooned it. Here in the *plaza* the children played, the women worked and rested and laughed as the young men teased them. Each opening onto the *placita* were the rooms of the house. There was the family chapel, *el Zaguán,* the receiving room, and the common room for family meeting place, entertaining and *bailes*. There was the dining room, *la cocina,* the kitchen, the wine room and pantries.

"The little room" was used for sweets, those imported candies which Don Miguel had freighted in by ox team.

There were five sons and five daughters and five Indian servants.

When the sons married and brought new daughters-in-law to the household the grandmother, a true Spanish matriarch, took charge. From her specially built chair in the kitchen she directed the Indian slaves to assist the sons' new wives in learning household tasks. If, at the end of a year, the girls had learned to manage a house in proper Spanish fashion, a large home was built for them near by. It was furnished completely and Grandmother gave to each a present of a thousand dollars. The five daughters were treated in like manner, no difference being made between daughter and daughter-in-law.

And so ran life in Las Vegas, sister city to Denver fifty years ago.

Before 1886 Don Trinidad had tired of his hundred thousand dollar house and he and his brother moved away. Don Trinidad took his family to Wagon Mound.

Romeroville Ranch was sold to an Englishman named Cammell.

Cammell was a bachelor, a rather lonely figure, who collected guns and hunting dogs. He liked to entertain and was a great hand for poker. At one time or another all the young bloods of the Territory tried their luck at cards at Cammell's parties. His opening ball was a grand affair with rivers of champagne, but it missed the light frivolity of the parties of the Dons. The old ranch house was never again the same as when the two Lopez sisters were hostesses there to their husbands' guests.

Cammell made many improvements; the place took on the dignity of an English estate, but it had lost the gaiety of Spain.

Before 1887 Wilson Waddingham became owner of Romeroville. Wilson Waddingham was a jovial, hearty, hard headed business man who worked hard and played hard and lived completely. He and his wife Nannie came west from Connecticut and at one time owned the Bell Ranch.

Governor Mills was their son-in-law, and he and his wife lived at Romeroville after Cammell left. Governor Mills was a Mississippian and his wife a staunch New Englander. Their entertaining was rather quiet: conservative Connecticut tempering Southern hospitality.

Old timers tell with old timer twinklings of Governor Mills' white horse—a well behaved animal, it always knew the way back home from town even better than its master.

Romeroville became now a friendly farmhouse where the traveler was refreshed and the intimate received into his family. It was a home contented, conservative, conventional and completely American.

After the Mills family moved away the house belonged to Craven, Train, Carr and Crandall in as many years. Each one brought his own story and his own manner of living—all to become a part of the house of the Dons.

But the glittering gay eighties were gone and with them much of the gold that had made them glitter.

Somewhere during these years, so the story goes, Romeroville was lost and won back again in a night at cards.

Hard times came to the house at El Puertecito Grant. At one time a Texas Loan Company owned it; again it was the property of a Missouri Trust Company.

The Romeros never came back except as they were brought one by one to rest eternally in the family cemetery. Only newcomers came. It was a restless, discontented time.

The Ranch became a clubhouse for men. The near-by rolling hills made good golf links. Then it was a dairy and cows grazed placidly in Celio Garcia's "paradise of flowers."

An oil company leased the place and oil wells were drilled. Hobnailed boots and good strong pipes made headquarters at the ranch house. Another winter hay was stored in the walnut paneled ballroom and the wide curved stairs was a rendezvous for cats.

In 1905 came the thirteenth owner, the Montezuma Ranch Resort, formed by Doctors Brown and Seward of New York and J. V. Farmer, owner of a St. Louis Candy Factory.

Mr. Farmer's son, a doctor, was manager of the Ranch and

the clientele was made up of eastern tubercular patients. There was an exclusive waiting list.

Once again a new regime held sway in the old Romeroville Ranch house. Now all was hushed routine, half drawn blinds, disinfectants, rest hours and raw eggs.

Staid nineteen hundred had at last put the frivolous eighties in place!

Rubber soled shoes firmly trod the stairs where once had lightly tripped the red heeled dancing slippers of the Lopez and Romero belles. The antiseptic rustle of the starched uniforms of the nurses silenced completely all the little provocative ghost tinklings of the silken shawls of a gone-by year.

Tubercular invalids came, convalesced and went back to their Eastern treadmills. Doctor Farmer, himself, was cured and returned to his practice in St. Louis. Upon his departure the health resort was closed.

Then came a succession of renters. The last, about 1930, outfitted the place as a dude ranch. Tall tales and cow country drawls, ten gallon hats and silver spurs, Indian embroidered window drapes, Navajo blankets and Apache baskets gave the advertised atmosphere. Attractive booklets were mailed to prospective Westward trekkers. Panning gold as a part-time pastime for parlour bronc busters was one of the promised lures.

The tired old house gave up. It was too much. The end had come.

On a winter night in 1932 the electric lights went out. A fuse had blown. Ingenious Twentieth Century repaired the fuse immediately by putting a penny in the fuse box. The lights came on again. But not for long.

Fire!

Blaze burst out against the sky from the flame filled house. The huge old cottonwood trees that Celio Garcia had helped to plant so many years before turned into frenzied demons frantically beating their crooked, naked branches against the glare of the burning building.

For an hour and a half the massive beams, the walnut panels, the hardwood floors that had been hauled by mule team and oxen across the plains from Kansas more than fifty years before, crackled and burned. Crackled and burned in fury, then smouldered tiredly into charred remains.

The house of the Dons was gone.

House that has sheltered statesman, pioneer, wanderer, speculator, and invalid for more than a half a century burned in an hour and a half.

House of thirteen owners. Men of Spain, Mexico, France and England, Southerner and Yankee, Gentile and Jew had lived within the shelter of its walls and called it home. Burned to the ground.

A hundred thousand dollar house destroyed because of a penny in the fuse box.

There is no humane society for houses!

FIRST PRINTING IN NEW MEXICO
Margaret Abreu

MARGARET ABREU lives in Santa Fe and is a life-long resident of New Mexico. She has been a teacher and assistant State Superintendent of Schools (1930-34), and in 1934 she became the first woman accountant in New Mexico. From that year until 1956 she served as assistant State Comptroller. She has contributed a number of articles to *New Mexico Magazine* and is the author of a popular but now out-of-print booklet, *Food of the Conquerors.*

The first book and the first newspaper published in New Mexico were printed more than one hundred years ago. It was fitting that the first newspaper should be called *El Crepusculo De La Libertad..* It was a name teeming with portent and pregnant with meaning: *The Dawn of Liberty.*

The first book published, printed on the same press, was a spelling book.

In 1825 the first territorial assembly under the Mexican regime met and elected Santiago Abreu as delegate to the Mexican congress. While in Mexico Abreu negotiated for the purchase of a printing press in Chihuahua.

In 1832 Don Santiago Abreu became *jefe politico,* and it was not till after his term of office expired that he was able to bring the press into the territory. It was brought to Santa Fé in the spring of 1834, and New Mexico boasted the first printing press west of the Missouri River.

The press was operated by Ramon Abreu, a brother of Santiago. A printer, Jesus Maria Baca, who learned his trade in Durango, Mexico, came to the territory to do the printing for the Abreus. He later followed the press from one owner to another and gained the reputation of being not only the first but the only pri:.ter in the territory. The press was in operation in Santa Fe during the summer of 1834 printing circulars and other literature advertising lands the Abreus had for sale.

In 1835 when Albino Perez, the stranger from Mexico, and newly appointed *jefe politico,* issued his proclamation as, "A greeting to his fellow-citizens," incidentally and unequivocally announcing that he had taken over the reins of government, the footnote of his proclamation read, *"Imprenta de Ramon Abreu a Cargo de Jesus Maria Baca."*

In the summer of 1834 a Catholic priest, Father Antonio Martinez, apparently the only person in the whole territory with sufficient interest in education, decided to open a school in Taos. Books were needed and there was none to be had, so the *padre* decided to print his own. Negotiations were begun between Abreu and Martinez for the sale of the press. The teacher, however, was impatient, and not waiting for the sale to be completed, prepared and had published an elementary speller. It was a crude affair, of cheap paper and bound by hand with rawhide covers and tied with a leathern thong. Yet it had the impressive title of *Cuaderno de Ortografia,* (orthography note book), and was dedicated to the children of the Martinez family of Taos.

Pedro Sanchez, in a memoir in Spanish on the life of Father Martinez, writes that the priest bought a press in 1835, and at his own expense published books for the use of his pupils, printed pamphlets, syllabaries and vocabularies, catechisms, and other material on orthography, grammar, rhetoric, logic, physics and arithmetic, which he distributed free; and that he also published a newspaper, to which he gave the very appropriate name, *El Crepusculo De La Libertad.*

On November 29, 1834, appeared the first issue of *El Crepusculo De La Libertad.* It was a small sheet, eight by sixteen inches, printed in Taos, and although still owned by the Abreus, was published by Father Martinez.

A letter from Ramon Abreu to the *Ayuntamiento* of Santa

Fe transmitted a copy of the paper for their files. This letter, in translation, reads: "Very Worthy *Ayuntamiento,* I, Ramon Abreu, sub-commissary of the Territory (of New Mexico), respectfully and in due form present myself before your Honorable Body and say, 'That attentive to the highly esteemed letter of the Illustrious Mexican, Señor Licenciado Don Carlos Maria de Bustamente, the original of which I transmit, I request in proper form that your Honorable Body be pleased to order to be placed or to exhibit in its session hall a file of the periodical, *El Crepusculo De La Libertad,* and a copy of the notice with which the press was opened, which I have established in this city, all with the praiseworthy object indicated in the said esteemed letter; and also that in accord with the tenor of said letter the accompanying imprints be placed in the archives, with a certificate of the Secretary of your Honorable Body; being kind enough likewise to return to me this letter with whatever endorsement you may find proper to place on it, in order that, if it be in accord with my petition, it may accompany in the original, with the aforesaid letter, the documents to be exhibited in Santa Fe, January 17, 1835." This letter was signed by Ramon Abreu, (with rubrics), and the usual footnote attesting ownership of the press.

Since Spanish was the official language of the territory, and few could read, *El Crepusculo De La Libertad* was discontinued after the fourth issue. Father Martinez, however, continued to print his books. Abreu at this time was chief justice of the territory. This office he held until his death in the bloody revolution of 1837 when he, with his two brothers, Ramon and Marcelino, were cruelly tortured by their captors before being killed. In this revolution Governor Perez, very unpopular because he had been an outsider instead of a native born New Mexican, and because of radical changes in government, was killed, his head cut off and paraded through the the streets.

In November 1842, the printing press was sold to Donaciano Vigil, who published a weekly newspaper, *La Verdad (The Truth),* in Santa Fé every Thursday. It was quite varied in content. One copy contains an official report of Ute depredations in the vicinity of Abiquiu, where, owing to peculiar topography, wild tribes of Indians were freer to carry out their nefarious work. It also contained political gossip and social activities of the capital. One page is devoted to the ladies, with the art of coquetry and matrimony as chief topics.

Vigil edited *La Verdad* till January, 1845, when he sold the press to Governor José Chavez, who at government expense published an official periodical, *El Rayo De Nuevo Mexico.* This was a small sheet dedicated to political interests of the territory, and items of general interest.

In 1847 Messrs. Hovey & Davis of Santa Fé purchased the old press, and under the editorship of G. R. Gibson (since Baca knew no English) published a four page newspaper, The Santa Fé·*Republican,* whose motto was, "We Die but Never Surrender." It, too, was an ambitious periodical, "Devoted to Science, Agriculture, The Earliest News from the United States and the General Movement of the Army," according to one copy.

Then no more of the old press for a number of years. English had become the official language of the Territory of New Mexico. *The Daily New Mexican* of Santa Fé, in its issue of April 21, 1867, printed notice of the death of Jesus Maria Baca in Santa Fé at the age of 65 years. Two years later the old press comes into service again to print The Cimarron *News and Press,* published by the Maxwell Land Grant Cattle Company at Cimarron, New Mexico.

In the late sixties a rough element had come into New Mexico, mostly cow punchers and farm hands in the employ of settlers, cattle men around the Vermejo country, Elizabethtown, Cimarron and Red River. These boys—apparently with a lot of time on their hands—drank and raised merry hell in the little town of Cimarron. Their chief delight consisted in shooting up the town on Saturday, killing chickens, hogs, and making sober citizens dance at the point of guns.

One Saturday night, at a *baile,* their drunken celebration surpassed their usual atrocious behavior, and the Cimarron *News and Press* severely criticised their actions. The cowpunchers sobered up long enough to hear the complaint of their employers. Then they went on another spree, and expressed their resentment of criticism by breaking into the office of the *News*, chopping up the press of fame and romance and throwing the pieces into the Cimarron River.

Thus ends the story of the first printing press of New Mexico. And, as it rests in its stony grave, we think we hear the cold waters of the Cimarron murmur a *"Requiescat en pace."*

INTERVIEW WITH GENERAL SHERIDAN
Grant Maxwell & Fred Kirkpatrick

FRED W. KIRKPATRICK of Albuquerque, has been working as a journeyman printer for 52 years. For years it was his hobby to dig out little items of colorful historical interest from the files of old newspapers, many of which were published as fillers in the pages of *New Mexico Magazine*. It was in an old volume of the *Las Vegas Gazette* that he found the interview with General Sheridan, a little gem of frontier humor. Listed with Mr. Kirkpatrick as co-author is Grant Maxwell. The name is the *nom de plume* of a Santa Fe writer who has contributed to the pages of *New Mexico Magazine* on a variety of subjects.

General Phil Sheridan, the great Civil War cavalry leader, was a better general than he was diplomat. He was a difficult man for the newspaper reporters to interview, so they were none too kind to him in their stories. In the eighties during Indian troubles, General Sheridan was in and out of New Mexico frequently, but New Mexico reporters got little news from him.

A sub-head on a story of an interview in Albuquerque in 1885 reported that "He Gave Answers That Were Not Wholly Satisfactory."

The story referred to him as ". . . Little Phil who occupies some salaried position under the U. S. Government."

The Las Vegas *Gazette* in a story about him in 1880 described him as "a little hump-backed, bullet-headed Irishman with a bloated face. He seems as if he looked more in the bottom of a glass than on the plains of New Mexico for Indians."

The classic interview with General Sheridan appeared in

the *Gazette* also. There were six inches of headlines above
the story.

Here is the story in full:

FRISKY PHIL

Gazette Reporter Holds Interesting
Interview With the Hero of Winchester.

The Great Warrior Receives the
Newspaperman With Open Arms;
He Is More or Less Broken Up on
The Craft Anyway.

He Travels in a Special Military
Coach and Lives on the Fat of
The Land.

Sheridan Is Many Miles Away, But
the Champagne We Drank With
Him Lingers With Us Still.

We Feel a Little Puffed Up Over
Our Success Attending Our Re-
ception by Little Phil, But Man
Is Mortal.

May He Who Watches Over the
Sparrows of the Field Never Re-
move His Field Glasses From the
Diminutive Form and Great Soul
of Phil Sheridan.

General Phil Sheridan and staff
passed through the city yesterday in
an elegant private coach bound for
Washington.

The party is in excellent spirits as
the following will show.

Reporter—hat in hand and smiling blandly—"General, I am a member of the great daily press. I have

been deputized by the owners of the *Las Vegas Gazette* to propound to you a few interrogations.

"Where are you going, General? Where have you been traveling to, and what is your program in the future?"

General Sheridan replied thusly:

"It is none of your G―― d―― business sir."

THE "KINGDOM OF NEW MEXICO"
Fray Angelico Chavez

FRAY ANGELICO CHAVEZ is a priest, poet and historian. He has written poems, articles and stories in regional and national publications and a number of books, including *New Mexico Families, Clothed With the Sun, The Autobiography of an Ancient Statue, The Missions of New Mexico* (with E. B. Adams), *The Lady from Toledo* and many others. He entered the Franciscan Order in 1929 and was ordained to the priesthood in 1937 and has been assigned to a number of Indian and native village missions in New Mexico. During World War II he was with the U. S. Army at Guam and Leyte as an army chaplain. He later served in Germany.

Did you know that New Mexico once was a real honest-to-goodness kingdom? And for more than a hundred and sixty years? Even scholars who have seen the title in ancient Spanish documents have not been struck by its significance. But it's true. The official name and title for this section of the country was *"The Kingdom of New Mexico."*

But first let us clear up the origin of the name, "New Mexico." Most people think it was derived from our neighbor, Republic of Mexico. This is a stupendous error, though one easy to make. However, the name of New Mexico is more than two centuries older than that of Old Mexico. You see, when Hernan Cortes conquered the Aztec land south of us, which was given the name of New Spain, he found the great capital city of the Aztecs rich with gold and other treasure. The Spaniards called this city, and the beautiful valley in which it stood, the City and Valley of Mexico—after one of the Indian names for the city, *"Mexitli."*

Soon after, these Spaniards began to hear tales of a mysterious land to the far north which was wealthier than Mexico City itself. Some believed that it was the next step to the fabulously rich Kingdom of Cathy, or China. (You can see how very little of the North American continent was known in those days.) And so, long before they even came here, the Spanish explorers talked about this new rich land as *"La Nueva Mexico"*—the *new* Mexico. By and by explorers came, and they used names they had heard from the Indians, such as Cibola and Quivira. Others baptized the land with New Andalucia or New Granada. But the original fabulous name of "the new Mexico" stuck in spite of every attempt at new designations.

In 1539 Fray Marcos de Niza had called the land "The New Kingdom of St. Francis," a poetical and spiritual title. Forty-two years later, Fray Agustin Rodriguez and his two friar-companions, all of whom were martyred by the Indians, called the region a new Mexico because they expected to convert the natives by the thousands, as the Franciscan "Twelve Apostles" had done in the Valley of Mexico some decades before. Here we can see that New Mexico had a spiritual christening as well. While the soldiers hoped to find a new Mexico of gold, the *padres* hoped for a new Mexico rich with souls.

Thus it was that Cortez, Oñate, and others, vied for royal appointments as the first colonizer of this new Mexico. So convinced were they of eventually discovering great treasures, that these men impoverished themselves in their attempts. After Oñate got the royal appointment, and established the first colony of New Mexico in 1598, he almost lost the entire colony at San Gabriel on the Chama, because he spent most of his time wandering all over the great western plains, and also westward as far as the Gulf of California. Yes, he was seeking in vain for rich cities, or at least a passage to Cathay, which he had not found in the upper Rio Grande basin. After ten years he returned to New Spain, broken in spirit and in fortune. But the Spanish Crown continued the colony as the Kingdom of New Mexico.

But why a kingdom? We really don't know. This land was so far away, and hard to reach, from the populated centers of

New Spain, that it seems the eventual discovery here of vast treasures was still in the minds of the royal officials. The fable of New Mexico as a future source of great wealth would not die. And so it was officially made a kingdom. New Spain itself, with Mexico City as its capital, was designated as a vice-royalty, governed by a viceroy appointed by the King. Different sections of New Spain were called provinces, like that of New Vizcaya bordering New Mexico on the south. Though supervised in a general way by the viceroy, New Mexico was a separate entity, a *kingdom* governed by a governor and captain-general in the King's name. Therefore, the Kingdom of New Mexico did have a king, the King of Spain.

Although the hoped-for wealth of New Mexico never materialized, she kept the title of kingdom up to the year 1771. Countless official documents bear the title. What is more, the people themselves always referred to their land as "the kingdom," hardly ever as New Mexico. If they went to New Spain, or when they came back, they "left the kingdom" or "returned to the kingdom." They complained of having no medics or schools "in all the kingdom." As the years went by they boasted of their parents and grandparents as *conquistadores* "of the kingdom." One grandpappy of mine, in 1718, called it "this miserable kingdom."

When the Indian Pueblos rebelled in 1680, the people always referred to the calamity as "the Uprising of the Indians in the Kingdom" and "the loss of the kingdom." Even when they fled south to the country around El Paso del Norte, the *cabildo* or general council of the kingdom continued operating for twelve years as though it were still in Santa Fe. Then in 1692 and 1693, when Governor DeVargas restored the colony, the entire operation was called the "Reconquest and Restoration of the Kingdom." The DeVargas documents are replete with this phrase.

In 1771 Spain decided to reorganize her New World colonies. Then it was, apparently, that his royal majesty and his head treasurer looked at the maps and then into the account books, and began to wonder why New Mexico was still a kingdom. Up to now she had been a liability. It was then, for the first time, that she was annexed to the northern provinces of New Spain, and all were called *Provinces Internas,* or provinces of the deep interior. Chihuahua, a comparatively new city, became the main capital for all. Not that Santa Fe ceased to be a capital, but her governor lost the extra important title and power of a captain-general.

After a hundred and sixty-one years as a real Spanish kingdom, New Mexico lasted half a century as a minor Spanish province, for exactly fifty years later New Spain rebelled against the crown and became an independent republic. It was at this late date, 1821, that Old Mexico came into being, when the infant republic took the name of the ancient capital of the Aztecs and of New Spain. Automatically, New Mexico was included as the northernmost part of the Mexican Republic, and was given the official title of a department. As we know, she lasted only twenty-five years as a Mexican department, for in 1846 the United States of America took over.

If we keep in mind that in the beginning most of North America was a complete blank to Europeans, we will easily appreciate New Mexico's size in those times. She had no exact borders north, east, and west, for boundaries do not exist when there are no neighbors. In the first century, from 1598 on, New Mexico embraced all of what is now Arizona on the west. To the east she took in the southeast corner of Colorado, western Kansas, the Oklahoma and Texas Panhandles. This was by virtue of exclusive Spanish exploration, and is a conservative estimate, for they roamed as far as Nebraska to the north, and the Nueces River in Texas to the far southeast. The New Mexicans used and considered all this territory as their bison preserve. As there were no other European nations around to dispute their possession, no thought was given to boundaries. These vast expanses of land were considered, as we shall see later, as Provinces of the Kingdom of New Mexico.

Northward, the New Mexicans did not venture far beyond the San Luis Valley in Colorado, because of the cold frosted mountains, where they could easily be ambushed by nomadic Indians besides. The southernmost boundary was El Paso del Norte, for here they did have a neighbor, the sparsely settled

Spanish province of New Vizcaya. In this first century, El Paso del Norte had been founded and was considered part of New Mexico, for its first white settlers and officials were native New Mexicans. It was around 1692 that the crown decided it should belong to New Vizcaya instead.

During the following century, from 1700 on, the eastern great plains territory began to shrink rapidly as far as New Mexican possession was concerned. After the French occupied the entire Mississippi valley and delta, they began to venture westward in their trade with the Plains Indians. By this time the English settlers in the northeast had pushed the aborigines farther west, to swell the Indian population of the plains. These warlike Indians had acquired horses, from Spanish horses gone wild or which they had stolen, and they bartered skins and furs with the French for firearms. Hence the New Mexicans ventured east less and less because of the new equally armed and mounted warriors of the prairies. In fact, during this century they kept the New Mexicans hemmed inside the Rio Grande Valley, even raiding their settlements. At this time a buffalo hunt usually meant a costly Indian battle also.

Old Spanish documents of the period speak of the "Kingdom and Provinces of New Mexico." Scholars have wondered about the double term. But there is no puzzle to it. The kingdom proper consisted of Santa Fe and the other Spanish settlements along the Rio Grande, as well as all the Indian Pueblos that were missions and were supervised by a Spanish alcalde. The provinces were the unsettled parts, like those of the Quiviras, Wichitas, and Humanas to the east, and on the west the land of the Moquis, Navajos, and Cosninas.

FORGOTTEN ARMY POST
William S. Wallace

WILLIAM S. WALLACE has been librarian and archivist of Rodgers Library, New Mexico Highlands University at Las Vegas since 1953. His major research interests are the fur trade and explorations of the West before 1860.

Except for a few brief statements in the files of the War Department's Historical Section almost nothing was known of the old post at Las Vegas until James W. Arrott, of Sapello, presented Rodgers Library, Highlands University, Las Vegas, with copies of all existing Post Returns, Officers Rosters, and other documents concerning the post. Though little known, it was of great importance in its day and a number of eminent Americans began their careers there.

Even now the original site of the post cannot be definitely located. The War Department records give longitude and latitude readings for its location. The readings indicate it was located two or three miles from Las Vegas. But, two reasons seem to refute the early and inaccurate sextants of the 1840's in pin-pointing the post's location. First, it is known that the government leased existing structures, and secondly, Indian hostilities of that day would probably have made it unwise to locate a post of small size outside an inhabited area. This has been the case of similar posts at Albuquerque and Socorro, where posts were maintained within or adjacent to the local community.

Along with several other posts and forts in New Mexico the one at Las Vegas was part of a line of defense maintained in the late 1840's against the Indians. The short life of the post, when re-discovered through its old records, reveals a colorful and bloody moment in New Mexico history. Straddling the Santa Fe Trail at a point where travelers from the states and numerous bands of Indians passed, it managed to be a lively military center. There were never more than ten or twelve officers and about two hundred men stationed there at any one time. But what the post lacked in numbers of soldiers it managed to make up in engagements with Indians, trips of exploration, and subduing some of the rebellious citizens of the area.

Nuestra Señora de los Dolores de Las Vegas was the original name of Las Vegas. And here in February, 1848, Major J. B. Donaldson of the First Regiment of the Illinois Infantry Volunteers, with eight other officers and a total of 152 men, established the post. The Post Returns for that month show that there were 23 sick, one under arrest, 88 active privates, two buglers, two drummers, eight corporals, and six sergeants present. During the month five men died "ordinary" deaths.

From the beginning the post was very active. Both the civil and Indian populations of the area were restive. During preceding months a population not accustomed to the new United States control of the region had murdered American soldiers, and some of the ringleaders lived in Las Vegas.

In May of 1849, 1st Lt. and Brevet Captain Henry B. Judd in command of Company C of the 3rd Artillery, marched the seventy-five miles from Taos to Las Vegas, and a company of the Volunteers at the post moved out to positions on the Sapello river near Las Vegas. With the arrival of Judd's men and the manning of positions on the Sapello, it was evidently hoped that it would be easier to control the region. However, with Las Vegas offering the men of the post all the liquor, gambling, and other vices calculated to make discipline hard to enforce, things did not run smoothly. During May and June there were two officers absent without leave and ten enlisted men had deserted.

In September, 1849, the Illinois Volunteers were mustered out of service and they set out for St. Louis. This left Captain Judd with eighty-four men under his command. Judd was to remain in command of the post until April 19, 1850, when Captain and Brevet Lt. Col. Edmund B. Alexander of the 3rd Infantry assumed command. With but few interruptions, Alexander remained in command until the post was abandoned on July 25, 1851.

A sampling of the correspondence involving the post highlights a checkered record of its problems. Keeping the troops in order was a constant headache to the commander. In August of 1850 a sergeant deserted with his company's money and in October some of the troops tore up a Las Vegas gambling hall. Lt. Buford, who was officer of the day at the time the gambling hall was wrecked, was sued by the hall's proprietor for $500!

More important than escapades of the troops was the problem of protecting the travelers along the Santa Fe Trail. Typical was the gruesome discovery by two Americans at Wagon Mound. Sometime during the late Spring of 1850, a caravan including the mail from Fort Leavenworth was attacked by Indians. In May, two travelers on the trail, a Mr. Fields and a Mr. Adams, discovered eleven bodies "very much eaten by the wolves," near the base of Wagon Mound. The ground around the bodies was strewn with arrows and the contents of the mail bags.

Lt. A. C. Burnside (who will be mentioned again later on) was sent to investigate. From his official report we get a close glimpse of the bloody massacre:

"The trail of the marauding party was indistinct. We examined the *cañada* formed by the rising ground near the mound [Wagon Mound, New Mexico], and in fact all the ground in its neighborhood, and secured all the mail that could be found, which consisted principally of blank forms and a few private papers. From these facts I am led to the following conclusion, that the mail party with five or six other persons who had joined it, arrived at the Wagon Mound, either before the snow fell on the third of this month, or whilst the snow was still on the ground, for no tracks of any description could be seen; that the wagon with eight of the party started from Camp, two of the party, not of the mail carriers, mounted on American horses, remained at the fire for a short time, afterwards starting, were charged upon by the Indians, who were laying behind the small mound, at the foot of the Wagon Mound; their horses killed and themselves wounded, they ran to the wagon, and were assisted in getting in, by the main party, while in the act of doing this the party were charged upon by the Indians, thrown in a state of confusion, and finally all killed, within seventy-five yards of the wagon, on either side of the road . . . No signs were discovered of any Indians being killed. The attacking party were evidently in great numbers from the large number of arrows found on the ground; but the best evidence of it is the small space within which the whole party were killed. So large a party of Americans have never before been entirely destroyed by the Indians of that portion of the territory; and in fact ten Americans have heretofore been considered comparatively safe in traveling over the road, with proper care. . . . The party consisted certainly of not less than one hundred warriors. . . . No possible clue to the direction of the Indian trail could be found; and in fact the murder was committed so long before it was known, at least fifteen days that all pursuit would have been unavailing, could we have found the trail. No fresh signs of Indians were seen; but it was reported that a party had been seen by a hunter near Barclay's Fort [on the Mora river on the south bank of the Santa Fe Trail crossing], but not being able to learn anything positive on the subject I cannot say that the reports are correct. . . . Two of the party only were scalped, but all of them stripped. The principal part of the letter mail I think has been brought in. The Indians evidently thought the large rolls of blankets to be the most important; and consequently tore them open. I have brought in all that was worth picking up.

"The bodies were buried in a common grave; and the wagon

with all the rubbish was burned over it to prevent if possible the bodies being dug up by the wolves."

The Lt. Burnsides who made this report was one of three individuals stationed at Las Vegas who achieved national fame in the years to come.

The first mention of Ambrose E. Burnsides in the records of the post at Las Vegas appears on June 30, 1849. He was then a twenty-five-year-old 2nd lieutenant and he remained at the post until the end of August, 1850. This is the same Burnsides who later became a major-general during the Civil War and gained a short-lived fame as a military commander in the Union Army. More lasting fame, but for less doubtful cause, for him came through his popularization of the men's fashion of later years for long sideburns—still known as "burnsides."

Two other men who were to achieve fame and had served at the post at Las Vegas were Braxton Bragg and John A. Logan. Bragg was a Brevet Lt. Col. while he was at Las Vegas. During the Civil War he become a general in the Confederate Army and was in command during a number of that war's most memorable battles. John A. Logan was a 2nd lieutenant in the Illinois Volunteers at Las Vegas and his future fame was to come through political activities, as well as military ones. Besides becoming a major-general in the Union Army during the Civil War, he also helped to organize the Grand Army of the Republic, and became a United States Senator from Illinois.

Hardly less important than the post's dealings with the Indians was its operations in exploring portions of New Mexico little known in those days. Chief among such expeditions was that commanded by Capt. Henry B. Judd. Capt. Judd's notable journey came about when it became apparent that new and larger forts were needed to control the Indians of New Mexico; and various parties were sent out to look for possible sites for the new forts. One of these parties consisted of troops at Las Vegas. In the Post Return for Las Vegas during March, 1850, the following entry was made:

"Light company C. 3rd Arty., equipped as a cavalry, with a wagon train, left Las Vegas on the 5th of March on a tour of reconnaissance along the Rio Pecos. Having proceeded 200 miles down that River the Command returned to this Post on the 29th after marching nearly 400 miles in 14 marching days, the animals subsisting on half rations of corn, without grass or fodder. The objective now being the selection of a suitable position for a military Post."

Included in Judd's expedition was Robert H. Kern, a noted artist who was massacred several years later along with Captain John W. Gunnison by Utah Indians in the Sevier Lake area of what is now Utah.

Although Judd recommended that a post be established in the *Bosque Redondo* on this expedition his judgment was ignored. However, this journey did much to increase what was known of the upper Pecos Valley.

The beginning of the end for the post at Las Vegas came when the United States Government came to the conclusion that a series of posts scattered over a large area did not afford the protection that could he obtained by fewer but larger forts. Another factor was the high cost of garrisoning a large number of posts and the problem of maintaining discipline that resulted from having troops stationed in or near towns. It was therefore decided to build Fort Union, now the site of a National Monument, a few miles from Las Vegas just off Highway 85.

The first entry in the Post Returns for Fort Union gave notice of the end of the little post at Las Vegas and the beginning of an even greater era of military activity in northeastern New Mexico. In that first Post Return for Fort Union we find it stated that the commanding officer of Fort Union is Lt Col. Alexander with the additional statement that he, "Assumed command of this post, July 26th, 1851, relieved from command of post at Las Vegas, New Mexico, July 25th, 1851, by evacuation of that post."

SHALAM . . . "LAND OF CHILDREN"

Lee Priestley

LEE PRIESTLEY won the 1961 Zia Award as the outstanding New Mexico woman author of the year. She is author of numerous articles and several books. She is the wife of O. E. Priestley, publisher of the *Las Cruces Sun News,* and they have been residents of Las Cruces for the past 17 years.

Some ruined buildings near the Rio Grande and a remarkable book are all that survive physically of a strange experiment in communal and spiritual living.

Shalam, "Land of Children," was founded in the late 1880's in southern New Mexico by Dr. John Ballou Newbrough and a group of his followers who called themselves Faithists. The purpose in establishing the colony as given in OAHSPE, their sacred book, was "To take the babes the world will not have to a place where the world will not live . . . and make it a land of peace and plenty." The foundlings and orphans were to be reared there with no knowledge of sin to become world leaders and the nucleus from which a better race of men should evolve.

Behind the Shalam venture, which was to dissipate a million dollars and dislocate many lives before it failed, stand the controversial figures of Newbrough, Andrew W. Howland and Mrs. Frances V. Sweet. Their admirers and detractors alike agreed that they were remarkable people. They were called mountebank and charlatan or seer and prophet. Their colony was viewed variously as a confidence scheme, a congress of crackpots or a noble venture. Many refused them the smallest assistance; many others devoted their lives and fortunes to the service of their dream.

John Newbrough, founder of Shalam, was trained as a physician, a profession he partially forsook because of a hypersensitivity to pain and suffering. Instead he became a successful dentist in New York City. Much of the money he earned he spent in charities and benevolences. His interests ranged from inventing a cheaper composition for dental plates so the poor could afford them to the establishment of a farm for alcoholics whom, in advance of his day, he considered sick men.

With a young man's restlessness he had followed the gold rush to California in 1849. Successful there, he sent back bags of gold dust to his mother. In California the Doctor acquired a friend and a business partner in John Turnbull, a Scot. The two drifted to the gold fields of Australia, where they made another considerable fortune. Returning to the United States, the young doctor met and married his friend's sister, Rachael.

Practicing in New York City for twenty-three years, Doctor Newbrough observed at first hand the wretched condition of the poor and the shocking waste of youth. Much of his money went into his charities; more of his time and energy was channeled into a search for a way to remedy the world's ills.

Not surprisingly he was caught up in the wave of interest in spiritualism that swept the western world during the latter half of the nineteenth century. He traveled widely and studied many religions. His belief grew stronger that enlightenment would come to him through self-purification and concentration on inner powers. He made his vegetarian regime more austere by omitting milk and eggs, finally restricting himself to those foods which grew in the light of the sun. He lived for two years as a member of "The Domain," a spiritualistic colony at Jamestown, N. Y. but was troubled by the shortcomings and limitations of the belief.

For many months he rose at dawn when he believed the communion with unearthly powers was best achieved to make himself ready for a revelation. In his own words we are told how the revelation came: "I had been commanded by the spirit voices to purchase a typewriter, a new invention which writes like the keys of the piano. I applied myself to this invention with indifferent success. Then one morning lines of light rested on my hands . . . Over my head were three pairs of fully materialized hands, while behind me an angel stood with hands on my shoulders. My fingers played over the typewriter with lightning speed. I was forbidden to read what I had written and I obeyed. This same power visited me every morning. My hands kept on writing, writing for fifty weeks. The illustrations were made under the same control. Then I was told to publish the book which should be called OAHSPE, a Paneric word meaning Earth, Air, and Spirit."

To this book, called "the most notable example of automatic writing," Shalam owed its existence. The plan for the Land of Children was a part of OAHSPE. "We pray, but not one of us puts forth a hand to accomplish what we pray for," was part of OAHSPE's indictment of society. Doctor Newbrough believed he was called to put forth a hand.

He preached and practised the extraordinary rites set forth in his personal bible. He was peculiarly fitted for the role of prophet. Six feet four inches in height and of a handsome commanding presence "he possessed intense personal magnetism." Available evidence agrees that he was a proven medium and no mean showman. He was so persuasive that many attributed to him the powers of hypnotism. Certainly he drew to himself a band of devoted followers.

A group of converts established themselves at Woodside, N. J., with the fortunes of several invested in the venture. When it failed another group gathered at Pearl River, N. Y. Important among them was Andrew M. Howland, a Quaker of scholarly tastes and the possessor of a large fortune. He devoted himself and the money to his friend with complete and lifelong fervor. Here, too, came Frances Van De Water Sweet, the woman who was to become "the Mother of Shalam." Under the spell of Doctor Newbrough's high hopes she literally sold all she had to join the venture. Family silver, jewels, and fine linens were converted into money for Shalam.

In the summer of 1884 Newbrough and Howland set out to find "the unoccupied land beside the river" of OAHSPIAN prophecy. Spirits argued the virtues of the Rio Grande valley over other sites and led a blindfolded Doctor Newbrough to a wilderness of mesquite near present-day Dona Ana north of Las Cruces. Here, in a horseshoe bend of the capricious river was "the place the world would not live" that should receive "the babes the world would not have."

Andrew Howland purchased this tract which was a part of the Dona Ana Bend Colony Grant. Later other smaller tracts were bought from John D. Barncastle who had acquired them from the native settlers. The two founders admired the green cover on their land, overlooking the fact that it was a wet year, that the tract was far from established irrigation, and half encircled by a treacherous river. Here, they proclaimed, was the perfect place for their directed experiment in childhood.

In late October, 1884, Doctor Newbrough and twenty disciples, both men and women, pitched their tents on the tract. Only grim determination got most of them through the winter, unprepared as they were for life in a stark cruel land. They cooked over campfires and drank muddy water from the river. They slept on the ground, shivering with cold and fear of the desert denizens that howled around the tents, or in smaller sizes, lurked in clothing and shoes.

With spring came new hope—and a railroad car full of groceries purchased by Howland. Native neighbors helped them to build outdoor ovens and introduced them to native foods. More than two hundred workmen from Dona Ana began to build the great Fraternum that was to house them all.

Now twenty-two Faithists wrote their charter of fourteen articles incorporating "The First Church of Tae." The articles specified that the colony should be "humanitarian in outlook, agrarian in plan" and severely vegetarian in diet. "No meat, fish, butter, eggs, cheese or animal food might be used . . . except that milk might be given to children under six years of age." Under the Covenant into which they entered, property was held in common for the good of all and no person received more than food, lodging, clothes and attendance when ill. Profit motives were banned and certain professions were excluded. "Let not these come, the lawyer, doctor, preacher, or politician who desire to live by their wits." At least five orphans were to be adopted yearly.

Between 1885 and 1890 Shalam advertised for members through tracts, almanacs and newspapers. Those who responded were a various lot. Some were sincere, but there were also religious fanatics, adventurers scenting a chance for something for nothing, even a few mentally deficient. The colony could accommodate one hundred people but was seldom full. Many of the newcomers soon found little wish to practise the extreme self-denial demanded of them. Coming as disciples, they left as disillusioned and very vocal critics.

In the records of Dona Ana County two changes in Doctor Newbrough's personal life are now noted. In 1886 he was granted a divorce from his wife Rachael, stating that she objected violently to his beliefs. In 1887, the records certify that he and Frances V. Sweet were married by Faithist rites. "The Mother of Shalam" was a woman with great strength of character who became the temporal power in the colony.

With the first buildings finished, the first orphans came to Shalam. The first ten, all less than six months old, were brought from New Orleans. Other receiving stations were established in Chicago, Kansas City and Philadelphia. Neither race, color, parentage nor legitimacy concerned the Faithists. Nothing was placed on record regarding the foundlings who were given Oahspian names.

Those were the building years. Running water and baths refined the forty-room Fraternum. A library, gymnasium, a steam laundry complete with Chinese laundryman, and beautiful gardens were added. The Children's Home was large and complete, down to ten small bath tubs. The Temple of Tae, a circular building with a conical roof studded with stars was the scene of spirit manifestations and weird ceremonials. In the windowless Studio, Doctor Newbrough painted in trance. Using both hands at once he produced portraits of leaders and prophets each with the strange Star of Light on the forehead.

Doctor Newbrough labored mightily to organize his effort. Occupied with an influx of the incompetent and indolent, he found no time for the vital agrarian program. Teachers were imported soon so the education of the foundlings began.

Faithists divided education into the intellectual, the vocational and the spiritual. The children were taught first the use of food and hygiene to achieve bodily perfection. Then the five senses were trained by many forward looking devices. Visitors were amazed to hear choirs of babes with perfect pitch and intricate knowledge of harmony. Elaborate visual training made infants expert in the analysis of light and color. Each child was trained to a craft needful in an agrarian life. Naturally, spiritual education was given a maximum of time.

In the Spring of 1891 an epidemic of influenza swept the Colony. Many persons became ill and several died. Doctor Newbrough, who had exhausted himself in attending his patients contracted pneumonia and died on April 22. At his passing strange manifestations took place. Colonists testified that crashings and whirling air filled the rooms; spirits wailed, furniture and crockery skipped and leaped. After waiting for Andrew Howland to return from Boston, the founder of Shalam was buried in the small cemetery among the graves of children.

Andrew Howland who now inherited the burden of the Colony felt unequal to the great task. But how he tried! The native workmen crossed themselves when that striking patriarchal figure, beard and long hair flying, commonly dressed only in white trousers and sandals galloped the fields urging them to further labor. Only a demon, they felt sure, could contain such energy.

Howland proved himself far ahead of his time in the development of agriculture and husbandry. As a small army of workmen cleared off the scrub, he designed systems of irrigation with wooden troughs leading the water from an enormous reservoir. Staring at the water gushing into it from pumps powered by a sixty-horse boiler Mr. Howland said wryly that he had first filled the reservoir with silver. Thirty thousand dollars had been swallowed by the well alone before he stopped keeping accounts.

Three steam tractors pulling five plows apiece broke the virgin soil. Crops of corn, wheat, barley, sugar cane, beans and peanuts grew bountifully on the leveled fields. Exotic introductions such as nectarines, figs, and artichokes became acclimated and thrived. Looking forward to truck farming, a five-acre hotbed was constructed. Peaches, pears, apricots and plums flourished in the thirty-five acre orchard. The vineyard spread over thirty acres more.

Next a dairy herd brought by express from fine stock farms in Wisconsin and New York was added. Soon bottled sterilized milk was offered for sale in El Paso. A butter and cheese plant, powered by steam, utilized the surplus milk and cream. Five poultry experts brought from the east set up an elaborate chicken farm. A model apiary supplied honey, a much used article of food. Fifteen teams of horses and mules from noted stables opened the eyes of the natives to what good breeding could do. Neither labor nor expense was spared by the tireless Howland who worked eighteen hours a day, often on one meal of raw unsalted cabbage.

Whisperings and even attempted blackmail led Andrew Howland and Frances Newbrough to marriage. In June of 1893 they were joined by the Faithist rites before a group of witnesses that, strangely, included "John B. Newbrough." It is believed to have been not the spirit of the founder of Shalam but his son who was in the west surveying railroad routes.

Now that gossip and rumors of free love were stilled for a time (it is interesting to note that much of later derogatory material in print seems to stem from a single article) the work went on. To provide for new adherents who wished to retain family life and freedom to work their own land as they pleased, Levitica was founded. In twenty houses each set in its own acre two railroad coaches of families brought from Kansas City were installed. Hoping to make rural living attractive to the young and also to grow truck for market in El Paso, water, seeds and implements were put into supposedly eager hands.

The utopian plan of Levitica proved the beginning of the

end for Shalam. Gardens died of neglect while the Leviticans and the parasites who had attached themselves to the colony quarreled and committed nuisances the pacifist Faithists could not punish. After two years Mr. Howland chartered more railway cars. Providing each with a sum of money to tide him over, he sent the quarrelsome to the destinations of their choice. Soon thieves came by night to plunder the deserted houses. Then the river in flood swept away all that remained.

Now disaster came thick and fast. The river nibbled away fertile acres. Hot sun warped the wooden troughs spilling the precious water before it reached thirsty field and orchard. In midsummer drought the wells failed. Trees died and vines withered. When crops were bountiful no market could be found for the surplus. The butter and cheese project floundered on uncertain train service. Broilers died by the thousands through the carelessness of workmen. Fine stock was stolen or spirited away for breeding purposes. Young trees and vines disappeared overnight. Outlying buildings were stripped of windows and water pipes and often fired. Most ominous of all the seemingly inexhaustible flow of Andrew Howland's fortune dwindled to trickle.

The children were growing up now and not always along the lines hoped for. Picnickers fed the children ham sandwiches. Girls were enticed into the chaparral by the mouth-watering scent of rabbits roasting over camp fires. Then the boys who had built the fires helped to satisfy more carnal appetites. Two of the teenagers eloped. When the school at Shalam was forced to close and the remaining pupils sent to Dona Ana, supervision became impossible.

By 1900 ruin was upon Shalam. One by one the buildings were closed. The last few families left, some weeping and others cursing. The children grew more rebellious at the burden of added work. His fortune vanished, Andrew Howland peddled dairy products, candies, cookies and vegetarian foods in neighbering towns. One Las Cruces matron remembers a cooky called "U-Like-Ums" that seemed to be made of cornmeal and honey.

Mysteriously, and an unmistakable sign of doom to Shalam,

the Temple of Tae collapsed in 1900. Faithists believed it had fallen at the command of the spirit of Doctor Newbrough, lest it be defiled by the unworthy and wanton who now came and went in the failing colony.

Andrew Howland, as trustee for the children, petitioned the courts to set aside the various transfers of deed to the foundlings and return the property to him. He promised in return to place the children in proper homes.

Some of the twenty-five children under fourteen years of age went to orphanages in Denver and Dallas. A colored child, considered exceptionally intelligent was taken by Booker T. Washington. A Chinese child found a private home. The older ones went out to make their way in a strange and lonely world. At last only five were left with Mr. and Mrs. Howland to live frugally in a few rooms at the Home.

On November 30, 1907 Andrew Howland locked the door of the Children's Home for the last time. With tears and sobbing the last handful of the faithful mourned the failure of their experiment. And Shalam, the Land of Children, the colony born before its century was left to the slow destruction of time.

THE FIRST TERRITORIAL GOVERNOR
Calvin Horn

CALVIN HORN is an Albuquerque business man who has long been interested in history and historical research. For the past several years he has
been doing extensive research on the early governors of New Mexico.
The chapter on Governor Calhoun is the first carried by the Magazine
in the Governor series. He is a former President of the Historical Society of New Mexico and has lectured extensively on historical subjects.
He and William S. Wallace organized Horn & Wallace Publishers, a
couple of years ago, to re-issue out-of-print historical books which they
believe deserve a present-day audience.

The stage arrived late that February 26, 1851, evening in
Santa Fe. Only those expecting important letters braved the
falling snow, driven by a raw mountain wind that penetrated
even heavy woolens. Crowded about the stage at the *plaza* were
American traders, storekeepers, soldiers—even the dignified,
heavy-set Indian Agent, James S. Calhoun.

Everyone recognized sharp-spoken Calhoun, who for 20
months had represented Washington in Santa Fe. President
Zachary Taylor had appointed the Georgia business man as the
first Indian Agent in the military zone of New Mexico.

Calhoun waited impatiently for the stage driver to finish
watering his horses and open the mail pouch. He was anxious
for an answer to his December 28th letter to Luke Lea, the
Indian Commissioner in Washington. "The Utahs," Calhoun
had written, "seem to be perfectly quiet, and say they are waiting to ascertain what their Great Father, the President of the

United States, will do for them. Many of the Pueblo Indians inquire why it is their Great Father will not allow them to visit him."

The stage driver handed him two official letters. His heart lifted. With lighter steps, Calhoun hurried to his house to read the mail.

But the eagerly-awaited letter from Luke Lea said nothing of his request for Pueblo Indians to visit Washington. It brought only the "Annual Report" of the Indian Service. As usual, there were no instructions to this man who had been completely on his own since his appointment as Indian Agent in July of 1849.

In the quiet of his study, he opened the other official-appearing letter, glancing first at the signature. It was from Daniel Webster:

Department of State
Washington, January 9, 1851

Sir:

The President having, by and with the advice of the Senate, appointed you to be Governor of the Territory of New Mexico, I have the honor to enclose your commission. You will be pleased to inform this Department of the receipt of it, and, should it be accepted, of the name of the State or County in which you were born.

I am, Sir, respectfully,

Your obedient servant,
DANIEL WEBSTER.

James Calhoun, running his big hand through receding black hair, momentarily was thrilled by the new honor; yet he pondered whether to continue his New Mexico work, which had received so little Washington support; whether to accept the appointment as Territorial Governor, which would, perhaps, receive as little attention and assistance from Washington as the office of Indian Agent.

Calhoun sat at his desk, his square chin resting on the palm of his hand, reflecting the reasons he accepted appointment as

Indian Agent for New Mexico. He mused upon his former pleasant life in Georgia, and of the hardships and difficulties of life and work on the New Mexico frontier. There was so much to be done, and so little to do with.

Calhoun smiled as he thought of his appointment as Indian Agent for New Mexico by President Zachary Taylor. He and the President had soldiered together in the Mexican War, and because he admired and loved President Taylor and because President Taylor had insisted that he continue public service with him—he accepted the $1,500 a year position.

He had fulfilled the President's request. There was no reason to continue. President Taylor was now dead.

Calhoun remembered the serene life in Georgia, of his steamship line between Havana and the mainland, of serving as director of two banks and the Chattahoochee Railroad, of his political service in Georgia, three terms in the legislature, mayor of Columbus, Georgia, and then three terms in the State Senate.

Calhoun reflected on the past 20 months as Indian Agent. What reason was left to continue fighting Washington, wild Indians—and the local military commander—to help New Mexico?

Just when he decided to accept appointment from President Millard Fillmore as first Territorial Governor is not known, as no record could be found of his reply to the letter from Daniel Webster. If that answer were available, we would also know where he was born. History does not clarify the record as to whether he was born in South Carolina or Georgia. History also fails to tell us whether he was born in 1802 or 1803.

On March 3, 1851, one company of artillery and one company of infantry escorted James S. Calhoun to the Government House to become the first Territorial Governor of New Mexico. He opened his inaugural address: "An era in the history of New Mexico commenced this day. The problem as to the capacity of the people for self government is to be solved, preparatory to the assuming of a higher and more glorious position as one of the sovereign and independent states of the Union. . ."

Territorial Government of New Mexico, authorized by the

Organic Act passed by Congress the preceding September, replaced a confused, muddled situation which had existed in New Mexico since General Stephen Watts Kearny conquered New Mexico in the summer of 1846. General Kearny, acting only under military orders, took possession of New Mexico and set up a civil government based upon a series of statutes known as the Kearny Code.

Congress debated whether a military general had the authority to establish a civil government. It was argued that he exceeded his authority and powers "by establishment of temporary governments in some of the provinces."

President James Polk added to the confusion on July 24, 1848, by stating: "These temporary governments necessarily ceased to exist with the signing of the peace treaty with Mexico." President Polk continued: ". . . Until Congress shall act, the inhabitants will be without an organized government. Should they be left in this condition, confusion and anarchy will be likely to prevail." New Mexico was left in that condition until the appointment of James S. Calhoun as the first Territorial Governor.

Calhoun set a 90-day goal for the creation of the new territorial government, including elected representatives to sit in the first territorial legislature.

Calhoun appreciated his opportunity. He had the privilege of advancing government in 90 days equal to the full "six century story of freedom." He realized the people had never heard of the Bill of Rights or the Declaration of Independence. They only knew that the supply trains from the States were bigger and better than the ones from Chihuahua, Mexico.

During the 90 days formation period of the new government, Calhoun hoped to stop Indian murder and depredations. Being Governor, Commander-in-Chief, and Indian Superintendent, Calhoun felt he now had the needed authority. On March 18, he issued a proclamation to the people: "I recommend to all able-bodied male citizens of the Territory, capable of bearing arms, the formation of volunteer corps to protect their families, property and homes, and as Commander-in-Chief . . . will commission the officers of such companies . . ."

He wrote Indian Commissioner Lea four days later: "I seize the opportunity to inform you that Indian murders and depredations are almost daily occurring in this Territory, South and West of Santa Fe."

The following week he appealed directly to President Millard Fillmore: "Until the Apaches and Navajos are completely subdued, we can neither have quiet or prosperity in this Territory. You are aware that our Treasury is empty, and that we are without munitions of war."

Two days later, he appealed to H. H. Stuart, Secretary of the Interior: "We need munitions of war of every kind. These we have not, and our Treasury is empty. Has Congress provided the means to aid us? If I had the means at this moment, I could, in a few months, secure a lasting peace with the Indians of this Territory, and locate them within fixed limits . . ."

With the precision of a military commander, Calhoun started work on the four necessary steps to form a democratic government, where none existed.

Step One: A Census Had To Be Taken. On March 12, Calhoun ordered the first census. He employed six census takers. He promised to ask the Territorial legislature for an appropriation to pay them. A month later the census was complete, with 56,984 citizens counted in the new territory.

Step Two: Apportioning 13 Senators and 26 Representatives Among The Eight Counties. Governor Calhoun allowed his secretary, David W. Whiting, the opportunity to work out the apportionment. David Whiting wrote in his diary: "The districts of Taos, Rio Arriba, Valencia, and Socorro have the largest surplus; the odd senators were accorded to them. The counties of Rio Arriba and Valencia having the largest surplus, the odd representatives were accorded to them." In the House of Representatives, Taos and Rio Arriba had five representatives each; Santa Fe and San Miguel, three each; Valencia and Socorro, also three each; and Santa Ana and Bernalillo, two each.

Step Three: Elections For The First Territorial Legislature. Governor Calhoun set the election for May 19, 1851. His secretary wrote after the first election: "Received complaints from

several sources that the election has been illegally carried on
. . . soldiers having voted, and that not only once, but often
three or four times, teamsters and others not residing in the
territory . . . were allowed to vote; and even lads not over 14
years of age were allowed to take the oath and drop their tickets
in the ballot box."

Step Four: Convening The First Territorial Legislature.
Governor Calhoun set June 2 as the date to convene the legislature, which was the final 90 day act, and last step. However, on
Monday, June 2 a majority of the legislators failed to appear.
The following day, June 3, the legislature organized. Calhoun's
address was read to the legislature. It was one of the most timely
addresses ever delivered to a legislature, either in 1851 or 1957.

With the Governor's address and the working of the legislature, American democracy came to New Mexico.

Calhoun discussed the issues of his day, issues that still are
with us in New Mexico: "There is nothing more corrupting
or dangerous to the liberties of the people, than frauds committed under the assumed guise of personal rights . . . it is
our solemn duty, so to guard the rights of our citizens, that is,
the people of the Territory, that their own votes shall reflect
their own purposes . . . I suggest the propriety of a law which
shall require each voter to register his name prior to an
election."

"Humanity shudders at the thought of capital punishments,
but I am not prepared to recommend their entire abolition
at this time. The day is near at hand, I trust, when you will
be prepared to substitute an effective remedy for such punishments."

He recommended prescribing by law the regulations under
which pardons may be granted. "The subject of commuting
punishments is an important one, which I commend to your
consideration."

"The serious evils of gambling," he continued, "are daily
seen, and if it could be accomplished, its entire prohibition
would contribute immensely to the peace and happiness of
society.

"The subject of education will not fail to command a full

share of your consideration. Unless the people are educated and enlightened, you may, in vain, expect a sound morality to prevail, can neither be stable or prosperous . . . I recommend you to memorialize Congress, and respectfully ask for such an appropriation as will be equal to what has been granted to other territories for schools."

His finest words were 100 years too soon: "Dependence and degradation are inseparable, and poison the very foundation of honesty, truth and virtue. If these assumptions are true, should not wise legislators, seek to remedy the evils consequent upon poverty. . . . Let us, at the very commencement of our career in self government take special care of the weak and the innocent, and secure to them the means of an honest and virtuous independence, the surest shield of probity and morality."

Calhoun, perhaps unwittingly, projected himself into the acrimonious slavery controversy of the day, and became the center of a bitter storm of newspaper comment and national charges and counter charges as result of urging the Legislature to pass a law preventing the entrance of free Negroes to the new Territory.

This was used in a political way to make his life miserable from then on. But in the meantime, he also suffered physically in the summer of 1851—from catarrh and jaundice—and he requested permission for a vacation.

By the end of August, 1851, he had given up any hope of a vacation. Calhoun appealed to Luke Lea and to Daniel Webster concerning political battles, Indian trouble, and lack of cooperation from the military. A petition was circulated in the territory concerning his opposition to the election of Captain A. W. Reynolds, assistant quartermaster, as a delegate to Congress. ". . . the whole power and influence of his office (governor's) has been prostituted from what was its proper end and aim. . . ."

Governor Calhoun, weakened by an attack of scurvy and worried over Indian murders and depredations pleaded with Daniel Webster in a February 20th, 1852 letter: ". . . if such outrages continue much longer, our Territory, instead of becoming settled with an industrious and thriving population, will be left a howling wilderness, with no other inhabitants than the wolf, and the birds of prey hovering over the mangled remains of our murdered countrymen."

Calhoun wrote to Luke Lea the first part of April concerning conditions and differences with Colonel Sumner. "I further assert that the lives of the citizens of the Territory are in eminent danger if Colonel Sumner insists in carrying out his views to withdraw his main force from the Settlements for the purpose of making a campaign in person to Apache country . . . I have deemed it advisable for every American female to leave the country with as little delay as possible. . . ."

He appealed again to Colonel Sumner on April 7, as he prepared to evacuate the women and children from Santa Fe: "You are perhaps advised of my weak, feeble, and almost hopeless condition, and I feel that I am speaking almost as a dying man —yet I feel desirous of doing all in my power to promote the public weal."

Governor Calhoun, being a methodical and foresighted man, during the month of April hired native carpenters to build a coffin. By the end of the month his coffin was finished.

In addition to his illness, lack of cooperation from the military, no help from Washington, and New Mexico political charges, he was attacked nationally by the press and in the halls of Congress. The *National Era,* an anti-slavery newspaper with the largest circulation in the Nation, smeared on February 26: "Governor Calhoun of New Mexico is no better than an infamous kidnapper. Gangs of traders, with licenses bearing his name, authorizing them to purchase Indian children, as slaves, for the benefit of persons in New Mexico, have lately been driven out of the Territory of Utah."

Congressman Phelps of Missouri accused Calhoun of protecting New Mexicans in the perpetration of the murder of Americans from the States.

The charges upon charges proved a burden too great to carry, the more so because they were untrue—and it was a broken hearted man who was helped into the stage on May 6, 1852, in Santa Fe, to begin the vacation and the visit to Washington and his home, which had been so long delayed.

As part of his entourage were his two daughters and sons-in-law, his secretary, five Pueblo Indians, a military escort of 20 men—and the coffin he had ordered a month earlier.

As he left New Mexico, he could look back on many achievements. The accomplishments of James S. Calhoun, New Mexico's "Purple Heart Governor," included his concern that a real democratic government be created in New Mexico. Under his direction the first Territorial Legislature, acting without a Constitution, passed an Act called "The **Rights** of the People." This consisted of twenty sections enumerating the rights of the citizens: "All political power is inherent in the people and all free governments are founded on their authority, and instituted for their benefit, and they have at all times the inalienable right to alter, reform, or abolish their form of government in such manner as they may think expedient." Also ". . . it shall be the duty of the Legislature to enact the necessary laws to protect equally all the religious denominations . . ." On and on for twenty sections.

Governor Calhoun won the respect and confidence of the native New Mexican people and the Pueblo Indians for himself and thereby for the United States Government. He won the allegiance of former Mexican citizens for the United States.

Governor Calhoun worked for three years attempting in vain to win the friendship of the blood-thirsty Apaches, Comanches, and Navajos. In failing to win their friendship, he learned to understand them and knew the necessary means of controlling them. He long advocated placing them on reservations. The United States Government took his recommendations years later, possibly when it was unnecessary.

By traveling constantly in New Mexico, he knew the Territory well and did an excellent reporting job by telling Washington the exact state of affairs in the Territory. He constantly informed Washington of the measures and means required to take care of his number one problem, that of protecting the people and their livestock.

It has been said correctly that Governor Calhoun in New Mexico "surely did his best to make bricks without straws."

The hardships of the trail added physical agony to a suffering body and an anguished mind—and the great courage that had helped him face enemies as cruel, and tasks as great, as any man's was not enough to see him safely across the plains.

Some place on the plains of Kansas, he died. His companions placed his body in the coffin, and he was carried to Independence, Missouri.

Only a mortuary at the eastern end of the Santa Fe Trail officially recorded his passing:

"The corpse of Governor Calhoun, who died on the road from Santa Fe to Kansas was bro't in for burial. . . ."

Today this first Territorial Governor of New Mexico lies in a pauper's grave—unhonored, unsung—unknown but to a few historians and an occasional student of history. The body was prepared for shipment by an Independence, Missouri, funeral home. When the remains reached Kansas City, they were in poor condition. The steamboat company refused to accept the body. As a consequence, it was found necessary to bury the body in the old cemetery there. The only available place for the burial was near the slave burying ground. Later, the graveyard was turned into Shelley Park. The property was high above the street level and in grading the streets a number of bodies were exposed. Friends and relatives removed a number of bodies. The bodies of the others were placed in large boxes and interred in pauper's graves. Among these were the remains of Governor Calhoun.

HORSES & MEN

DON QUIXOTE OF THE SIX-SHOOTER
J. Frank Dobie

J. FRANK DOBIE is one of America's greatest story tellers. He has been a teacher and lecturer, and has authored 17 books on such subjects as cattle drives, outlaws, range animals, lost mines and buried treasures. Some of his best-known books are: *Apache Gold and Yaqui Silver, Coronado's Children, Vaquero of the Brush Country, A Texan in England.* Domino Records recently produced a long-playing record of Dobie Tales. Mr. and Mrs. Dobie live in Austin, Texas.

After all these years the populace still regards Billy the Kid and other bad men of his kind as representative cowboys—even if a little extreme. Billy the Kid, it is true, rode well, stealing from John Chisum, who had him hired, and then from any owner whose cattle or horses were stealable. That he was a good hand, interested in his work—as all good hands at any business must be—has never been intimated. His reputation is based solely on his efficiency as killer and thief.

Sam Bass rode up the trail with a herd of cattle. At the end of the trail he helped rob a train, and the rest of his short life was spent in evading officers of the law—until they shot him. Before he went up the trail he had done odd jobs, stolen horses from the Indians, and made something of a reputation at racing "the Denton mare." He did very little cow work, and probably no real cowman would have cared for his services.

You can go up and down the list of the more noted bad men

of the West—Billy the Kid, Sam Bass, John Wesley Hardin,
Ben Thompson, the Daltons—and while you will find most of
them associated sporadically with cowboy life, you will hardly
find a dyed-in-the-wool, straight-out cowboy among them.
Of course, there were plenty of tough *hombres* among both
range owners and "hired men on horseback." More of them
shot to hold what they had than shot to get what they held.
Like other moral lines, the line between good range men who
shot bad men and thieves, and bad men who rode the range
was not always distinct; it often wavered. Many a cowboy
was like the one in the song who says, "I know I've done
wrong." But here I am talking about conduct, while Clay
Allison of the Washita waits impatiently to ride and shoot.

Clay Allison is not to be classed as a gun man, either on the
side of the law, like Wild Bill Hickok, or outside of the law,
like John Wesley Hardin. Yet he was emphatically a man of
guns. He was not a bad man in the sense that that term has
come to have. Yet he seems to have killed more men than
many a bad man made his reputation on. Charlie Siringo
credits him with having killed eighteen; others say he killed
only nine or ten. All agree that everybody he killed
deserved killing. To quote from my old-time trail-driver
friend, Bob Beverly, of Lovington, who has supplied me a lot
of data on this character, Clay Allison was "a gentleman
killer." He was strictly a range man; he hated cow thieves,
and nobody ever accused him of being one. He was quixotic
in standing up for his rights, and he was quixotically independent in interpreting what constituted his rights. The
more whiskey he drank, the more rights he possessed; and
sometimes when he came to town he bought a great deal of
whiskey. He was generous with it, however, even insisting on
his horse enjoying a fair portion.

Born in Tennessee, he was about twenty years old when the
Civil War started. Of course he joined the Confederates.
Once, it is told, he was captured as a spy and sentenced to be
shot. But he slipped the handcuffs off over hands that were
remarkably small, and lived to fight many other days. He
never was reconstructed, and in maturer years was described

as looking the part of a Southern plantation gentleman. In his prime he was six feet, two inches tall, erect, weighing around 180 pounds, always neatly dressed. When he came to town he rode either a pure white or a coal black horse. After the War he went west, ranching in Colorado, New Mexico and Texas. He had made "the reputation that comes when fellers shoot" before he located on the Washita River in the Texas Panhandle, late in the 70's. He was well known in the Indian Territory and in Dodge City, where he had a notable run-in with Marshal Wyatt Earp. He died in New Mexico about 1884.

The episode in his career that has been most often related —with many variations—was his meeting with a desperado named Chunk Colbert at the Clifton House, a stage stand, in northern New Mexico. He did not know Chunk, but Chunk knew him. Chunk wanted fresh laurels to add to his reputation. Killing Clay Allison would put the biggest kind of feather in his cap. He did not conceal his ambition. Yet he was wary, and Clay was wise.

Not long after the two met, Chunk complimented Clay Allison's horse and proposed a race. The challenge was accepted, and, to Clay's chagrin, his horse was beaten. Chunk seems not to have been becomingly reticent over the victory, and Clay slapped his jaws. Night came and then bed time, and still no gun had been drawn. When Allison went down to breakfast next morning, he found Chunk already seated at the table. With a polite salutation, he sat down directly opposite him. He had reason to think that Chunk's six-shooter was in his lap, under a napkin. A plate of scrambled eggs was set before each man. Chunk requested Allison to pass the salt, which was off to one side. When Allison reached for it, Chunk raised his six-shooter, but he fumbled the shot, and before he could shoot a second time he had a bullet between his eyes. It is related that Clay Allison finished his breakfast and walked out—to make proper funeral arrangements.

No preacher or priest was within reach, but Allison insisted on a Christian funeral. Finally he found a young man named Bill Robinson who had an Episcopalian prayer book that his mother had given him. He agreed to read the proper prayer over the corpse provided the nickname of "Parson" or "Preacher" was not fastened to him. He was new in the country and did not want to get tagged with any such name.

Clay Allison readily agreed to this. At the funeral he got up and said: "Friends, mourners and others, Bill Robinson here is going to give the late Chunk Colbert a decent Christian burial. This is on condition, however, that nobody will ever allude to him as Parson, Preacher, or any other such name. Now, I want you all to understand this and to realize that I am under obligation to see that his request is complied with."

Nobody ever violated the request. Edgar Beecher Bronson, in his book *The Red-Blooded* tells another story of Clay Allison's religious proclivities. I am sure that the language ascribed by Bronson to Allison was not in character, for Allison, according to all accounts, used correct English. The story is probably more of what might have been than what was; but it is a sample of many Clay Allison stories.

One morning, as Bronson tells, Clay Allison walked into the Lone Wolf Saloon at Pecos City, liquored, laid two pistols within handy reach on the bar, and remarked to Red Dick, the bartender, that he intended to turn the saloon into a church for about two hours and that during the services he wanted no drinks sold or cards shuffled.

Then, standing at the door, one of the six-shooters in hand, Mr. Allison began to usher in the congregation. All passers were stopped. Merchants, railroad builders, gamblers, cowboys, freighters—they all knew Clay Allison. When fifty or sixty souls had assembled, he closed the door and faced about.

"Fellers," he began, "this meeting being held on the Pecos, I reckon we'll open her by singing *Shall We Gather at the River?* Of course we are already gathered, but the song sorter fits. Now turn loose."

The result was not encouraging, for not many of the audience knew any hymn, much less this one. However, Mr. Clay Allison of the Washita was not fazed.

"The next in order," he said, "is a prayer. Everybody down!"

To quote Edgar Beecher Bronson, "Only a few knelt. Among the congregation were some who regarded the affair as sacrilegious, and others of the independent frontier type were unaccustomed to dictation. However, a slight narrowing of the cold blue eyes and a significant sweep of the six-shooter brought every man of them to his knees, with heads bowed over faro lay-out and on monte tables.

" 'O Lord!' began Allison, 'this yere's a mighty bad neck o' woods, an' I reckon You know it. Fellers don't think enough o' their souls to build a church, an' when a pa'son comes here they don't treat him half white. O Lord! make these fellers see that when they gits caught in the final round-up an' drove over the last divide, they don' stan' no sort o' show to git to stay on the heavenly ranch 'nless they believes an' builds a house to pray an' preach in. Right here I subscribes a hundred dollars to build a church, an' if airy one o' these yere fellers don' ante up accordin' to his means, O Lord, make it Your pers'n'l business to see that he wears the Devil's brand and earmark an' never gits another drop o' good spring water.

" 'Of course, I allow You knows I don' sport no wings myself, but I want to do what's right ef You'll sort o' give me a shove the proper way. An' one thing I want You to understan'; Clay Allison's got a fast horse an' is tol'able handy with his rope, and he's goin' to run these fellers into Your corral even if he has to rope an' drag 'em there. Amen. Everybody git up!' "

The sermon that followed had to do with Jonah in the belly of the whale. After seeing that all hands were raised to signify belief in this Bible story, Clay Allison had Red Dick pass the hat for money to build a church. The contributions were generous and general.

In the region of Pecos, Texas, Clay Allison did another good deed. Riding into a cow camp one evening, he noticed that a young man who had a crippled arm and hand seemed very nervous. He learned that this youth had had a falling out that afternoon with another cowboy over a maverick yearling, each claiming it. They had agreed to shoot it out the next morning at a certain spot between two cow camps, the opponent's camp being over a hill. Allison told the cripple that he could never get his gun out in time and that he would take his place. So the next morning Clay Allison rode forth. He was well known to the second party of the quarrel, and when this second party galloped up, raising his gun to fire, and saw who was opposing him, he wheeled so rapidly to ride in the opposite direction that he dropped his gun. He left it behind.

In the old town of Cimarron, New Mexico, Allison did many of his bold deeds. Here, in the St. James Hotel billiard room he killed Pancho Griego, who while pretending to fan himself with his hat was working to get his six-shooter out of the scabbard. Mace Bowman was sheriff here and wanted to take Allison into custody. This was against Allison's principles. Finally they agreed to put their six-shooters on the bar of the saloon that constituted the main part of Lambert's hotel, each man to turn his back on the other, walk twenty-five steps, wheel, rush back to his gun and shoot. Allison specialized in odd duels. One time, as the story goes, he and his adversary agreed to dig a grave jointly, then to stand up at either end and shoot it out, the victor to cover up the other. The result of this duel was another Christian burial at which Allison was master of ceremonies. But he was crippled from a bullet that he had accidentally put into his own foot; sometimes he used his rifle for a crutch. Only on a horse was he without handicap, and it seems odd that he should have agreed with Mace Bowman to make the footrace.

He won the race, however, and his pistol was pointed straight when Bowman stuck out his chest, hit it with his fist, and said, "Shoot, you blank of a blank." Still holding his gun steady, Allison replied, "Mace, you are too brave a man to kill." The two shook hands, and the law was satisfied.

Considering his cavalier career, Clay Allison's end was pure irony. In Toyah, Texas, on a spree, he heard that two men named Joe Nash and Jake Owens were trying to get possession of his water over the New Mexico line and had made talk about him. He got a buggy and team from the livery stable and started out to find them. After driving about twenty miles, he came, at dark, to the camp made by a freighter for the Hashknife outfit. He knew that the Hashknives were working the range and he supposed that Joe Nash and Jake Owens were probably with them. The freighter said they were; moreover, he knew where the chuck wagon was camped.

Nothing would do Clay Allison then but for the freighter to get in his buggy, drive to the Hashknife camp and warn Nash and Owens to prepare to meet their God. The freighter got back about daylight next morning, having driven all night and delivered the message. There was no road to travel, just a direction, sometimes a trail, across the prairies. The wagon was going the same way as Clay Allison for a good part of the distance.

After the four mules had been hitched to the loaded wagon, Allison proposed that he tie his buggy horses, so that they would lead, to the back of the wagon; that the freighter lie down on the load and get some sleep, and that he (Allison) get in the seat and drive. Perhaps the freighter was entirely willing; perhaps Clay Allison still had enough whiskey in him to make his arguments persuasive. Anyhow, the freighter went to sleep and Clay Allison went to driving. Before long, one of the front wheels hit a clump of salt grass, causing such a jerk and lurch that Allison was thrown off the wagon and almost under it. This scared the mules and they gave a lunge that pulled one rear wheel over Allison's head, crushing the skull and killing him instantly.

He was one range man exceedingly deft with a six-shooter who was not a bad man. Other men much less interesting have had whole books written about them. He seems more of a story-teller's character than a biographer's. The most delicate points of the code of the West could be drawn from his career.

POET ON HORSEBACK
Lewis D. Fort

Louis D. Fort was a close friend of Eugene Manlove Rhodes. He was
born in New Orleans and worked on the *Mobile Register* and *New
Orleans Times Democrate,* before moving to New Mexico in 1899. After
about 10 years in New Mexico, he moved eastward again and finally
settled in Memphis, Tennessee, where he operated an advertising
agency for many years. He died in 1953.

Going over some old letters recently I found one from a man
—to use the *Reader's Digest* descriptive appellation—who was
"My Most Unforgettable Character." The letter was signed
by my old true and tried friend, Gene Rhodes. I do not think
it necessary to state to a New Mexico reading public that
Eugene Manlove Rhodes, which was his full name, was New
Mexico's best beloved literary son. The letter in question was
dated Tesuque, Mar. 3, 1927, and it read in part as follows:

"Dear Lewis:
For several years Houghton-Mifflin Co. have been demanding publicity
of me. I sent Mr. Ferris Greenslet a wire: "My jewels were stolen last
night"—but they are still unsatisfied.
I am sending this under cover to Mr. Dale Warren with the suggestion
that you, who lived with me for two work-a-day years, could—if you
would and if Mr. Warren wished it—write a short and vivid skit—not
so much about me, but about that weird way of life, which was compact
of hardship, privations, mirth and laughter.—The boys who rode with
me in my youth are not given to letters; and as a further disqualification,

they are mostly dead. What is more—you saw us from the outside looking in—which is what we could not do for ourselves.

I have always had a loathing for synthetic publicity—and methinks I have lost by it. But whatever you had to say would be spontaneous and not built up, etc., etc.

Yours as ever
Gene."

When I received this letter I made one attempt after another for several weeks to write the little skit he asked for. But each effort that I made only served to convince me that I was incapable of doing justice to my subject. I was both humiliated by my failure and chagrined by my inability to measure up to his expectation of the spontaneous bit of writing that he credited me with being able to do. And now after a lapse of sixteen years I find myself again attempting to relate something of "that way of life" in which I first knew him—which was as he so well described it "compact of hardship, privations, mirth, and laughter."

When I first heard of Gene Rhodes I was working for an Englishman, T. G. Martin, on his ranch in the Glorieta mountains. There I had formed a pleasant friendship with a boy who was working on the Valley Ranch. This boy, whose name was Crispin, told me of a certain ranchman named Rhodes whose ranch was located in the San Andres mountains 35 miles east of Engle, a station on the Santa Fe Railroad. Crispin related that he was the best bronco buster in southern New Mexico, wrote poetry of a high order, and was as genial and likeable as he was fearless and valorous. The chronicles of his many valiant bouts formed a veritable saga of Doña Ana County and adjacent territory, which was destined to figure later as the scene of those stories and books which Bernard De Voto, one-time editor of *The Saturday Review of Literature,* said: "Are the only embodiment of the level of art of one segment of American experience. They are the only body of fiction devoted to the cattle kingdom which is both true to it and written by an artist in prose. Surely that is a great deal: to have given fiction its sole mature expression of one era in our past, one portion of the experience that has gone to make up America."

So vivid and intriguing was Crispin's word-picture of Gene that I was immediately fired with an intense desire to meet this young ranchman who was the perfect composite personalization of all of my dreams of the West—that West which I had long yearned to know intimately at first hand by way of participation in its picturesque activities in the great open spaces of mountain and plain. Since coming to New Mexico I had learned to handle a rope with some degree of efficiency and to keep my seat fairly well on a bucking bronco. I therefore felt I could make application as a cow hand without betraying my tenderfoot background. I decided to write and ask Gene for work on his ranch. As it was early spring I knew the season for taking on help was in my favor. His reply was a bit noncommittal, but he wrote if I should be in his neighborhood I might drop by and see him. With the confidence of youth I decided to leave a perfectly good job and gamble on getting one with Gene.

Having no horse of my own to carry me to the San Andres I shipped my saddle by express to Engle and boarded a southbound train. Gene was absent from his ranch on a trip of several days somewhere, but had instructed one of the boys of his outfit to meet me at Engle with a horse to ride. As I knew something of the hazing accorded a tenderfoot by the average ranch personnel of those days I had been careful to wear my boots, work clothes, etc., so that my appearance could in no wise betray my city origin.

Besides himself Gene's outfit consisted of three boys approximately the same age as myself. All three were skilled cowpunchers and good bronco busters. In coming among them my chief concern was to win their friendship and regard to the extent of being on an equal footing with them. It was nearly a week before Gene returned so I was able to make a fairly good start with the trio before he arrived. In Gene, however, I was distinctly disappointed. No one introduced us, and there were no formalities of getting acquainted beyond a slight nod in my direction when he rode into the corral. That night at the supper table he directed neither remark nor question to me. I determined to hide my feelings over his taciturn reception and to discover if possible its cause. Accordingly in the succeeding days I took advantage of every opportunity to make myself unobtrusively useful wherever I could. A week passed during which the question of my possible hire was not mentioned by either of us. At last a day arrived when I felt that I could and should bring matters in some way to a head. The other three boys were absent and Gene and I were alone, seated under a tree in the yard mending some harness.

"Guess I'll be moving on," I ventured by way of leading up to some sort of understanding between us. To my remark he made no reply.

"As you know I have no horse, could you lend me one and let one of the boys ride to Engle witn me to bring him back?"

"I reckon I could spare Steve for a day. When are you going?"

"Tomorrow, if it's all right with you."

We both fell silent while the work of mending the harness was continued. Suddenly there flashed into my mind words of Omar Khayyam, which on the impulse of the moment, with no thought of the consequences of uttering them, I quoted musingly, for they so perfectly expressed my predicament:

> "And this was all the Harvest that I reap'd—
> I came like water, and like wind I go."

With a startled whimsical gleam in his gray-blue eyes Gene looked up at me as he repeated the succeeding lines:

> "Into this Universe, and Why not knowing
> Not whence, like Water willy-nilly flowing;
> And out of it, as Wind along the Waste
> I know not Whither, willy-nilly blowing."

As he ended the quotation we both smiled understandingly.

The ice was broken. The depths of an enduring friendship had in those few moments been sounded. Shyly at first, but with growing enthusiasm we each in turn probed with delight the other's knowledge of literature, finding accord of taste in those pathways in which we both had been wont to seek and find mental stimulus and delight. When we finally arose from the work our hands had been doing Gene, like an awkward schoolboy, threw an arm across my shoulder and exclaimed:

"Look here Lewis I am not lending you any horse to ride away from this ranch tomorrow, nor any other day soon. Why man alive! I've been praying for years for someone like you to show up. Oh Lewis, don't leave me now that you've come!"

There was a child-like pathos in his plea which was so sincere that its ludicrousness was entirely overshadowed by the earnestness of his appeal. His inner life, which he had no one to share, was totally at variance with that of the personnel of his immediate environment. It therefore followed that he saw in me the possibility of an understanding soul to whom he could turn for a communion of spirit that he had long been denied. Thus in those few moments of naive declaration was begun a friendship of forty years standing which only his death brought to a close.

Gene's brand was the numeral 61, which was borne by some eight hundred head of horses and about two hundred and fifty cattle. His main dependence for a livelihood was that of breaking horses and selling them for cow ponies. And there was always a good market for 61 broncs. Headquarters of the ranch was in a deep cañon about midway of the San Andres, now known as Rhodes Pass. Passage through the mountains to and from the ranch was equally boulder-strewn eastward toward Tularosa and westward toward Engle. In fact so rough and uninviting was the Pass in those days that it was rare indeed that anyone ever ventured a trip across the San Andres by that route. Added to this difficulty of access there were no adjacent ranches in the mountains save one some thirty miles distant, with practically no means of communication between. Owing to the problem of transportation, the dwelling house and all that pertained to it was primitive and crude to a degree, both the building and its furnishings being fashioned by hand from such material as nearby nature grudgingly offered. The one bunk-room of the house was used for sleeping quarters only when we were driven indoors by rigorous mandate of the weather. Otherwise our "tarps" were unrolled at sundown and spread for occupancy on the unyielding earth of the yard. Breakfast was over usually at daybreak, and the rider of the "night horse" at that time had rounded up and brought to the corrals enough horses for the work of the day. So that the first streaks of dawn found us all in readiness for our respective assignments either in the corrals or out upon the range.

As before mentioned Gene enjoyed a widespread reputation for fine horsemanship. Many were the times I have seen him emerge from the most hazardous and hair-raising experiences with wild broncos which he had essayed to ride the first time they were under saddle. Despite daily encounters with many horses of various dispositions his record stood for a long period of years of having been thrown but three times. He was kind and patient with all horse flesh, no matter how cantankerous their behaviour. And he rarely failed to make good saddle animals of all he took in hand for that purpose. He was an avid reader and rarely mounted a horse for a ride of any appreciable distance without a book to read as he rode along. The Springfield (Mass.) *Republican* he considered the best edited daily in the country, and he was a regular subscriber. *The Congressional Record,* which he always read from cover to cover, he depended upon to keep him posted on matters of national import. He had one of the most remarkable memories of anyone I have ever known. One could repeat to him a line or two from almost any of Shakespeare's plays, and he could not only quote the lines which followed, but he could go on repeating the text for several succeeding pages. Equally remarkable was his memory of much that is best in English verse. To me he was first a poet, and secondly a writer of fiction, for it was always my feeling that had he given himself over to the writing of verse he could easily have reached a position of first rank as an American poet. This for the reason that the writing of poetry was with him a seemingly effortless procedure. I recall especially an example of an equisite little poem he wrote which he called *Little Next Door,* which he composed early one morning seated atop a stepladder in a little orchard adjoining my home in Roswell where he was on a visit to me. Often when a strenuous day of horse breaking in the corrals was at an end, and we were all gathered in a group under the stars in our respective "tarps" for the night, he would humorously weave the episodes of the day into a song, which he would sing to us improvising without pause as he sang.

In the early days of our friendship he began to gain recognition as a writer of Western fiction. I recall one short story in particular which he submitted to *McClure's* Magazine, called "His Father's Flag," about which the editor-in-chief wrote him that it had been read by every member of the staff with intense enthusiasm. In fact he stated "not in many years has a story been received at this office which has been given such uniform praise, but—" and then he made request for several minor changes in the manuscript. These changes Gene was unwilling to make, so he requested the return of the story. Two years later the same editor wrote Gene and asked for the manuscript again, which he published word for word just as it was originally written.

Gene Rhodes was not only an "unforgettable character," a rare good poet, and a spinner of yarns of high degree, but he was the embodiment of all of the finest traits that dear old New Mexico has ever held to her rugged breast, in those days when "hardship, privations, mirth, and laughter," were the privilege and the joy of life in many of those almost inaccessible nooks like the 61 Ranch.

TITAN OF THE RANGE
Agnes Morley Cleaveland

AGNES MORLEY CLEAVELAND lived during a part of the wild and woolly days of the New Mexico frontier. The daughter of W. R. Morley, Santa Fe Railroad engineer who built the road across Raton Pass, she lived as a child in Cimarron, and was exposed to a lot of the drama of that early period. When her father died, her mother bought a ranch in Datil in a remote area of western New Mexico and took the children there to live. The dramatic story of their lives is told in Mrs. Cleaveland's book, *No Life For a Lady*. She lived for many years in Berkeley, California, but after the death of her husband, returned to New Mexico and lived until her death on March 8, 1958 on a part of the old Morley ranch in Catron County.

Stories of Ray Morley will probably be repeated so long as any remain alive who knew him personally or know anyone who did! Since my book *No Life for a Lady*, a story involving the Morley family, appeared, I have been deluged with the query "Why didn't you put in your book about the time that Ray . . ." followed by some anecdote about him; about the time he dyed a small bunch of sheep scarlet, as visual evidence for tourists who always wanted to know if the red in Navajo rugs was a "natural" color; the time he started a gold rush in Magdalena by a show of ostentatious mystery in locking a bag of pebbles in the bank's vault; the time he testified before a formal Congressional Committee that he was the founder and President of the Loyal and Fraternal Order of Busted Bankers; the time he sponsored a "Cowthieves Ball" and printed on the invitations, as the Committee of Arrangements, the names of men against whom he had suits pending in the courts (they came); the time he and brother-in-law Tom Reynolds roped the mountain lion and brought it in alive, being careful themselves to present no rear elevation to the audience until they had put on their other breeches; the time —but the list is endless.

Some of the tales are undoubtedly aprocryphal and unfortunately more of the kind will probably arise as times goes on for Ray Morley was of the stuff of which tradition is made.

When the editor of *New Mexico* Magazine asked me to do a short article about Ray I realized that the task carried with it the obligation to avoid as much as possible the coloring which a personal relationship tends to give to such a story and try to look at him completely objectively. I'll try.

Ray was an amazing combination of gentleness and rugged strength. The sight of blood made him ill and yet he underwent an abdominal operation without flinching and without anesthetics. He was as tenderhearted as a child and as implacable as a granite cliff when he felt he was right.

Of course only the Recording Angel can audit the books of any man's life and it is not for me to attempt to take over that function, especially in as complicated a case as Ray's. I would probably give him so many black marks for failure to be on time for appointments that all of his undeniable virtues would be hard pressed to even up the score. The hours I've waited for that man! And when he finally showed up my blast of righteous indignation would usually boomerang against the jocular good nature of his explanation, "Met a fellow. Had to talk to him." He had to talk to everybody, and he left everybody feeling that a brisk but pleasurable breeze had swept away some of life's drabness and petty annoyances, or possibly more serious troubles.

Two Stanford sorority sisters of mine returned from a transcontinental motor trip in the early days of automobiling with a report of the most memorable incident that had befallen them on a trip that was regarded as nothing but adventure itself.

They had driven into a blinding sandstorm on the San Augustin Plains and gotten off the road. It was in those days of unsurfaced roadbeds and very easy to mistake the sand off to the side for the sand that presumably was the highway.

Anyway the two girls found themselves hopelessly stalled and too far off the line of travel to expect immediate help. They were close to panic when through the violently swirling curtain of sand loomed a figure, a broad shouldered, bewhiskered figure who struggled with the wind as he moved toward them. His appearance scarcely tended to allay panic in two city bred girls. They clutched one another and waited.

"You folks in a jackpot?" the oncoming figure bellowed to be heard above the howling wind.

Not being sure what he meant and genuine embarrassment tinging her uneasiness one of the girls made a megaphone of her hands and screamed, "Is this the usual weather out here?" Remember she came from California where there are but those two kinds of weather, "perfect" and "unusual."

Ray cupped his hands and yelled back, "No this isn't usual weather. Usually the wind blows."

Afterwards the girls who hadn't yet discovered that it was my brother whom they were talking about reported that the absurdity of the reply instantly restored their confidence. And great was their gratitude when after an hour's work Ray had extricated them from the sand and got them back on the roadway. When in a lull in the blowing gusts of sand he had caught sight of a stalled automobile off the road it hadn't occurred to him to pass it by without investigating. While he protested organized and pre-planned helpfulness as apt to miss its mark no one was quicker than he to offer man-to-man assistance where it was manifestly needed.

But if there was one quality in Ray which stood out beyond others it was, I think, his love for New Mexico. It was undoubtedly his ruling passion. Father and Mother had loved it before him and had given their all to it, so we children, Ray, Lora (Mrs. Tom Reynolds of Datil) and I came honestly by our addiction to New Mexico, but it is Ray of the two generations who will without question leave the imprint of his personality and character most permanently upon it.

While from a strictly material standpoint he may be thought to have failed (in the face of conditions where the cards were stacked against him) in the long view it may not be thus regarded, for in Ray was epitomized many of the qualities which made the early West what it was—a foundation upon which a later generation could build with the assurance that the foundation was sound: Self-reliance, courage, willingness to face life as a job to be done and not a frosted cake to be eaten, wresting fun out of almost every situation or deliberately creating funny ones, and beyond and above all else the acceptance of one's fellow man as an equal, provided—and this was the test—he would pull against the collar and not let the traces on his own side go slack.

We did not ask in those early days who were a man's forbears, what the size of his bank account (if any); we asked, "Will he make a hand?" If reassured on that score we conferred upon him the badge of honor, of social equality "He'll do to take along."

It is not, I trust, too vainglorious for a sister to say that Ray would do to take along—even in the face of those maddening waits for him before we got started.

THE BEEFSTEAK TRÁIL
N. Harry Champlin

N. HARRY CHAMPLIN is a Presbyterian minister. When "The Beefsteak Trail" was written he was a Sunday School missionary, assigned to the Reserve, N. M. district, a large area of mountains and plains in western New Mexico. He spent his boyhood in Oneida, N. Y., and studied at the University of Michigan, Southwestern and Western Theological Seminary, Pittsburgh. While attending the seminary he met the future Mrs. Champlin and they were married after he finished his studies. He has served a pastorate in Alaska and is now in Centralia, Washington.

The tired cow puncher snuggled into his bedroll and pulled up the tarp. In a weary voice he called out to me: "Better wrangle the horses, Preacher, before they get too far away." With a finality that invited no discussion he pulled the tarp over his head. And probably was asleep instantly.

That cowboy deserved some sleep. It was 3 a. m., and it had been a long hard day on the trail.

A tenderfoot, on my first trail drive, I wondered how in the world I was to go about the business of wrangling the horses. Finally I filled a *morral* with oats and started out after the stud that I rode that day. I figured out that if I could get him into camp the others would follow. But I hesitated to take off their hobbles for fear they would wander off in the wrong direction. I let my horse smell the oats, then started for camp. He followed as best he could with his front feet hobbled. But looking over my shoulder in the pale moonlight he seemed always to be right on top of me and twice as big as ever. I stepped lively to keep out of his way, but he came on in huge leaps. So finally I put the *morral* on him and tried to lead him, but the hobbles hindered him, and fearfully, I crouched under him and took off the ankle cuffs. Eventually we arrived in camp, with the other horses dutifully hobbling along behind. The boys got up soon after 4 o'clock, so all was well. We were ready for the next leg of our hundred mile drive from the home range near Reserve to the railroad at Magdalena.

Our herd numbered 60 when we started. It had increased to 225 by the second day as we picked up cattle from a few ranches along the way. These ranches threw in their cattle with ours to save the expense of driving a small number to the railroad. And we, in turn, helped make up the expense of the drive by taking along the extra cattle for a small fee. Since that drive I've been speaking rather possessively of the cattle, giving the impression they partly belonged to me. But so they seemed before the drive was over, though actually I did not own so much as a hair on the back of one of them. I took part in the drive more from a desire to know about and be a part of one than for any other reason. And since my job is that of a Sunday School missionary covering some 10,000 square miles of territory, most of which is cattle country, the cattle drive seemed the best way I knew of to be initiated into the great and perhaps over-romanticized art of cow punching.

The first morning in camp at the darkest hour before dawn Bob awakened me. For breakfast we had beefsteak, expertly cooked in smoking hot fat; sourdough bread, delicious, baked in a dutch oven; *pinto* beans and hot coffee. After breakfast we fed the horses. Outfits which provide several horses for each mount do not bother to feed them. They graze when not being ridden.

My mount consisted of a much too tall stallion, who would embarass me by raising his head out of reach whenever I tried to put the bit in his mouth. I had never bridled a horse and was half afraid of the things anyway. Finally one of the boys came to my aid and bridled it for me. Realizing my ignorance he went right ahead, much to my relief, and also saddled the brute. And now—it was time to mount. I couldn't reach the stirrup, so they told me to stand on my bedroll to mount from there. But as soon as I found the saddle the horse backed up, and regardless of my pulling on the reins he kept on backing, stepping on my suitcase, smashing one side, and finally knocking the pot of beans over, spilling nearly all of them. The boss yelled, "Give him the reins!" I loosened my hold and the horse stepped forward.

We rounded up the cattle that had been left in the pasture overnight. They were there only as a result of previous weeks of hard riding and "cutting" from the main herd. We drove through timber land, over *mesas,* up and down canyons and across the headwaters of Apache Creek. Here we watered the stock and the horses in the refreshing mountain-spring water.

The "chuck-wagon" had gone on ahead following round-about roads and trails. I for one was glad to see it along about noon. We got down for dinner: beefsteak, sour dough bread, beans, and coffee. The chuck wagon consisted of a pick-up truck loaded with our bedrolls, feed for the horses, food for their riders, and a supply of wood. A coffee-can full of oats, put in a *morral* made of burlap and hung from the horse's head by a piece of bailing wire, was the fare of each mount. A few minutes rest and we were off again, the cattle having grazed in the interim. Once more my horse had to be bridled by one of the boys, though I tried a dozen times to do it myself. I did manage to do one important thing that morning. I learned to mount from the ground without having the horse back out of my reach. Before stirrups were invented at the beginning of the seventh century riders vaulted upon the horses. I would have given up right there.

We alternately drove and grazed the cattle until about seven o'clock when it had become dark and quite chilly. The cattle were left to themselves in the hope they would "bed down" for the night. Camp was set up between them and the back trail that we might intercept any homesick cow on its way back home. Supper was a repetition of beefsteak, sour dough bread, beans and coffee. When supper was over

I estimated that I had consumed ten cups of coffee that day —considerable for one used only to one cup a day, at breakfast time. By 8 o'clock the experiences of that first eventful day found me completely undone. My bedroll was unrolled and I crawled in. I slept in the longies the boss gave me the night before when he saw the briefs I was wearing. (I was still wearing that same suit of longies 10 days later!) That satisfied, deadened feeling of the weary was within my grasp when the worst happened! "Get up. We're driving the cattle." The cattle were moving. It was useless to keep them milling in a circle and they decided to drive them down the trail a little farther. My rest consisted of a mere twenty minutes when they all pulled out and left me to pack up the belongings and bring the chuck wagon along. About that time I was beginning to wonder into what kind of racket I had maneuvered myself. My shivers soon turned to perspiration as I juggled the heavy bedrolls and camp equipment onto the truck. After the herd was overtaken I drove on a couple of miles and made camp. Then I built a fire, put on a pot of coffee for the boys and went to bed for the second time that night. I was conscious of the fact that the cattle and the cowboys arrived some time later.

It was three a. m. the next morning before the last boy was on his way to bed. I was left on guard to see that nothing happened to the cattle and to take care of the horses. It was then that H. B. told me to wrangle the horses before they got away. After my early morning wrangling escapade, horses lost their terribleness. And better still, after the second day out I was blessed with a cowpony that really merited the name of cowpony. He taught me more about cowpunching in one afternoon than I thought there was to know. Just let a calf or any head of cattle get by him and he was after it at a high gallop. I could bridle and saddle him from the start, and somehow even knew enough to tighten the cinch after the leather thawed out and stretched a bit. I admired that pony and was fond of him. They say if you want to teach a horse anything you have to be smarter than the horse. In this case the horse must be conceded the honors.

The second day at noon found us rounding over the Great Continental Divide at an elevation of seventy-five hundred feet. From now on the trail led over the rolling San Agustin plains. Here we entered the "driveway." Ever since cattlemen first came into this country and drove their cattle to the nearest railroad for marketing this particular strip of land has been used as a driveway. Originally just a well-marked trail through the wide open spaces, it gradually became fenced, but the cattlemen insisted upon their right to the driveway. Today the driveway stretches from the Divide for fifty-eight miles northeast through Horse Springs to Datil and east to Magdalena, the shipping point. During the last four years the boundaries of the driveway have been fenced and extra watering places provided by the Division of Grazing. The "driveway" varies in width from a few hundred yards to five or six miles. At some point near the end of the drive our herd passed another of more than three hundred head belonging to the three McCarty brothers from Reserve. But we did not see them until they trailed us into town the last afternoon.

If we were to water the cattle each day it was necessary to cross an oil-surfaced highway between Datil and Magdalena a total of three times. The pavement offered no trouble but the white center stripe was like a stone wall to some of those wild cattle that had spent their short lives in the mountains. When we crossed the first time all but a dozen head made it okeh, but that dozen could not be forced across for shouts nor water. We shouted and raced around, and got them all in a huddle, but when they came up to that white line they ducked to one side or the other or under the horses' necks. A twelve hundred pound bull started across the highway, came up to the white line, put his front paw on the line and smelled the other side, but could you get him to cross? No, sir! When we tried to force him across he would duck under the horse's neck and was away. My pony was after him at a gallop. The bull ducked back and the pony stopped in his tracks leaving me suspended in the air for a few seconds until gravity caused me to find the saddle again. After a thrilling little rodeo of our own we finally had six head left on the wrong side of the road and decided to put them in a nearby corral for the night.

Next day we brought the main herd back across the highway. But this time we had a system. We covered a sizeable stretch of the highway with sand, got the whole herd of cattle in a huddle right up to the road, everyone shouted at one time and the boy from Datil rattled a tin can with a rock in it. All this commotion caused a stampede of bellowing, frightened cattle across that road that even Selznick would appreciate. A couple of cows up against the white line decided a bit late to turn back. They were knocked down for their fickleness by the force of the herd and crossed the highway with their feet in the air. There were, however, no casualties.

One of the reasons for wanting to take part in a drive was because it is becoming the common practice to haul the cattle to the railroads in huge truck-trailers that can carry about ninety steers in one haul. But the old timers say that as long as there is feed on the "driveway" cattle will be driven to the railroad. The truckers, however, are doing a bigger business every year. One should really say "herded" to the railroad instead of driven, since the idea is to get them there in as good condition as when they left their home range. By this method it is often possible to improve the stock en route. It was my impression that the purpose of a drive was to get the cattle to market as quickly as possible even if you had to run them. However, in these drives, wherever the feed is good at all, the cattle are left to graze by the hour only being driven on when they are ready to lie down. But while they are grazing they are always kept headed in the same direction down the trail.

The buyers know these cattle are in good condition when they reach the end of the drive so they write into their contract that the cattle must stand a twelve hour shrink in the pens before they are weighed. Most cattle are sold according to weight, rarely by the head. Most of these range cattle are fed sixty to ninety days or so in the corn belt country before they are turned over to the packers and become juicy beefsteak on our dinner table. Or, in the case of the bulls, bologna or corned beef. Nowadays everything is used from the hoof to the end of the tail but most of the choice meat is consumed in the East. When a rancher has his stock trucked to the railroad, he realizes less than the rancher whose cattle are driven. Cattle in trucks cannot, of course, graze and during the whole trip are more or less "choused about" as the cattlemen say.

When a totally uninitiated starts out with an outfit to help in the long drive he is given the job of driving the drags. In any herd of cattle there are natural leaders. What a striking comparison there is between cows and people. As there are leaders, there are likewise those who insist upon bringing up the rear. The leaders do not have to be driven, merely pointed in the way they should go. The cowboy who rides fairly close to the front of the herd does the pointing. And as the boss aptly put it, "Few men and no boys can point a herd of cattle." I tried it only once. The cowboys who ride up and down the sides of the herd have the job of flanking them. Even though the leaders are given the direction there are always some revolutionaries in every herd that are continually wandering off. As soon as they start off their own trail they are followed by a fair portion of the remaining herd. If progress is to be made "towards the slaughter" they must be driven back into the herd by the flanking cowboys. The rear is made up of the sore-footed cattle, the skin and bone specimens, and the lazy "all brawn and no brains" bulls. It fell to my lot to drive these drags.

At first I felt like putting a bullet through the slow-pokes and butchering them then and there. I was thoroughly bored with moving at a snail's pace and always being the tail-end of the procession. Sometimes I would be a half mile behind the leaders. In a herd of a thousand head I am told they sometimes spread out over five miles of trail. As day after day went by, however, and mile after mile was left behind I gradually became accustomed to the various personalities of these drags and with familiarity came not contempt but sympathy. That potent word "sympathy" when exercised towards stock can change disgust into defense. One big bull weighing about fourteen hundred pounds, but looking like at least a ton of beef, reminded me of Walt Disney's creation.

He was the most ferocious character in the herd and had his horns tipped, that is the ends sawed off before the drive started so he could not cause too much damage. Ironically, he developed sore feet the first day, was always in the rear, and would lie down whenever he had a chance. I named him "Ferdinand" and the boss was calling him "Ferdy" the last few days. We called one leather bag of bones with a plump little calf at her side "Big 6." The scars on her side seemed to form that brand. Most of the brands were distinct but hers were just a jumble. She would never walk straight ahead or even in the general forward direction as a dutiful cow should. She had to walk twice as far because she would always turn to one side or the other. And of course she was the slowest thing in the herd. When we wanted her to move along faster we put our horse's shoulder against her flank and gently spurred the horse. Sometimes my pony would get into the spirit of the occasion and bite at her. "Big 6" was my pet plague at first but I soon became reconciled to her limitations. This job of driving the drags is a fine proctor of that noble virtue patience. It is bound to "kill or cure" any impatient soul who has the temerity to attempt it.

When the cattle were not penned at night, which was the usual case, it was necessary for all hands to take turnabout standing guard. One night I had the graveyard shift which includes midnight. I was solely responsible for the whole herd of cattle and the horses. The cattle were in a right-angle of the fence line. The moon was bright enough for me to see any movement of them over the back trail. Cattle have the habit of shifting their positions at midnight, so they told me. Perhaps that is the origin of the tale that Christ was born at midnight and cattle always pray at that time. They started moving at a quarter of twelve. I had been standing around the campfire toasting my shins for nearly an hour when I looked up to see a yearlin' steer coming down the fence line headed for home. It had been cut off from its mother who was left behind, which is bad at such a time. In the next half hour I sent that little steer scampering back into the herd four times. Twice I experienced the danger of running a horse at night on the plains. Twice he stepped into prairie dog holes but luckily recovered each time in good order.

Soon my guard was over so I 'roused the next guard and crawled into bed. By morning youth had asserted itself and the young steer was missing. One of the boys found its trail where it had made a wide circle of the campfire a good two hundred yards away. Mal rode the back trail after it about ten miles but gave it up. Later, the owner reported that it had returned home the same afternoon having covered some thirty miles.

Sleeping each night on the ground in a bedroll is not exactly like reposing upon a Beautyrest mattress. Cold nights and frosty mornings cause many a shiver but it is a healthful experience nonetheless. It is a constant coldness to which one becomes accustomed. And for once in my life I could understand what a native meant when he said he liked to hear the coyotes howl at night. The first time I heard a person say that I figured he must be slightly "teched in the head." Brought up in the state of New York and coming directly out here, the shrill yipping of a pack of coyotes in the darkness of the night was an eerie and hair-raising experience. But after spending eight or ten nights in the wide-open plains country, it gave one a neighborly feeling to hear a lone coyote bark its greeting from a few hundred yards distant. They are really quite harmless and are more attractive than a police dog when seen in their natural habitat. Cooping them up behind bars gives them that pale, drawn, and carniverous appearance.

The first Sunday night on the trail I was too tired to think. But when the next Sunday night rolled around I had an experience the like of which would be coveted by many of my fellow clergymen. After the day's drive, the cattle left to graze or bed down, the horses fed, and supper over, the boys sat around the campfire. They used their saddles as back rests and I sat upon a dutch oven covered with a saddle pad close to the fire. In the glow of the campfire I opened my Testament and preached what was intended to be a short sermon since the boys were tired and needed sleep. But after ten minutes I was interrupted by a question from one of them, and a twenty minute discussion followed on the mysteries of God, and life here and hereafter. It was the first time these boys ever heard a sermon in a cow-camp, but it was a unique and satisfying experience, too, for me.

We were on the trail eleven eventful days and nights from the time we left the ranch until the cattle were in the pens alongside the railroad tracks. Having been with an outfit that long one could easily appreciate the tension of that last night in camp when the cattle were in good shape and had just a few miles of the trail ahead of them. A whole year's earnings were tied up in those bawling, grazing, or bedded cattle. Any unusual commotion might cause a stampede, and many head might be stamped to death or lost, with the remainder losing many valuable pounds before they could be quieted down. Such things have happened. But our herd entered the pens in good order ready to be shrunk, inspected, weighed, culled if necessary, and loaded into the waiting stock-cars.

Another successful drive over the beefsteak trail had become history.

THIS SUN-LOVED LAND

SUN AND SANCTUARY
John L. Sinclair

JOHN L. SINCLAIR by good fortune had a claim to native American citizenship, for his mother accompanied his father, a Scottish sea captain on a voyage to New York at the time of his birth. Reared in Scotland and educated in England, he did not return to the land of his birth until he was 21. In 1923 he came to Roswell and got a job as a cowboy. He had tried writing as early as 1930, but collected mostly rejection slips until 1936 when he made his first sale for one dollar to *West,* a pulp magazine. His first article sale was made to *New Mexico Magazine* the next year. He has written dozens of short stories and articles and two novels, *In Time of Harvest* and *Death in a Claim Shack.* For many years he has been superintendent of Coronado State Monument at Bernalillo.

A couple years ago, I performed one of the few worthwhile accomplishments of my life—I helped a man find serenity. It was a glorious afternoon here at Kuaua (the Coronado State Monument, near Bernalillo), and the *bosque* across the Rio Grande was a blaze of color, the Sandia mountains a rich cobalt, the sky a deep egg-shell blue, and the air was vibrant with health. The tourist thousands had dwindled to a few hundred a month, and all was peace. I found the man knit-browed and studious, full of geography, as he peered at the large relief model map of New Mexico we have in the museum here. He looked up to greet me with a sad smile.

"May I help you with the map?" I asked him, as I ask thousands of tourists in the course of a year.

"No," he said. "I don't think anyone can help me. I'm looking down at the most painful disappointment of my life."

"New Mexico?" I said. And he nodded affirmatively.

I detected the symptoms, so I reached for the pointer I use on just such cases as that. "Boosterism" is the most repulsive word I know; yet if the reputation of New Mexico was at stake I was determined to do my best at defense.

He explained the reason for his "disappointment." He had come here the year previous, from an eastern state celebrated for its commerce and industry, for a population well into the millions, and a thorough lack of sunshine. He had retired from a dismal post, one that he'd held onto with long-sufferance— ever hopeful of the day to come when the freedom of retirement should enable him to fulfill his dream . . . New Mexico of the *Magic Southwest!* Time and elbow room. Broad plains and sweeping deserts, mountain peaks meeting the clearest blue; lush valleys peopled with colorful folk, domiciled in homes as earthy as themselves; clean high-altitude air—far from the commonplace, *"where seldom is heard a discouraging word"*—no clash or turmoil; all peace and serenity. In such an environment, thought this young man of sixty-one years, there was no barrier against living to be a hundred.

But, what had the dream turned out to be?

A city, just like home. Perhaps not as cloudy, and far less smoky, yet another commercial hub—but, of course one with a superb mountain view. The dreamed-about *mesas* were here, all right, but they were *outside* the city limits; and what does it matter if the East Mesa and the West Mesa are separated by the Valley of the Rio Grande, one of the really *great* rivers of the earth? . . . Clean desert air—well perhaps. . . . Center of a vast Indian world—poppycock! Who ever heard of an Indian riding a pick-up truck? . . . This Albuquerque is as typically-American as Dayton or Kalamazoo . . . And to him downright disappointing.

For instance, it has an uptown and a downtown, a few near-skyscrapers, luxurious hotels with chefs of the same calibre. Parks, shopping centers, and subdivisions unsprouted, sprouting and sprouted; drive-in movies, stands featuring foot-long hot dogs, a civic symphony and auditorium, an airport that is almost an Idlewild, a medical center on a vast acreage, and—at last reckoning—a couple hundred thousand folk making a living, uniformed to the American pattern of life, come from all parts of the nation, seeking something and finding it, engaged in all manner of social and commercial activities, such as appearing at the symphony ball and helping keep up with nuclear competition.

But no Mexican *peons* dozing under monstrous *sombreros*.

No burros being packed and whacked down Central Avenue.

No nothing—nothing but the eternal job of converting a desert into an Empire.

Progress, boom, bustle and haste.

"Why did you select Albuquerque? I asked the man at the map. "People who choose to live in Albuquerque have a purpose other than listening to the mockingbird, or feeling the zephyr, or basking in stillness. They usually come to compete with others at the task of making some money."

"You ask why?" said my friend at the map, with a shrug of the shoulder. "Where else?"

Of course, where else? . . . Roads led to Rome and Samarkand, and a Trail brought traffic to Santa Fe. Everyone knows of Santa Fe, and isn't Albuquerque one of the fastest growing cities in the nation? And there is Taos—and in recent years Los Alamos and Alamogordo, because of a certain substance, have become world renowned. . . . Where else? . . . Where is sun, where is sanctuary?

For a man of this one's taste—whose palate was kin to mine— I could suggest other and far less boomish communities, such as Reserve or Encinoso, Fence Lake or Hachita, Rociada or Llaves. There before us lay the square of plaster and cardboard, the cracks and bumps that were the canyons and mountains of New Mexico in relief—scale, one inch to the mile. With the pointer in my hand I could identify havens of quietude high among the mountain crags, or a half-dozen acres surrounded by hundreds of square miles of economically-worthless sun-blessed land, and sanctuaries where the heaven-sent downdraft forbids even the intruding drone of an airplane, where sheer remoteness from the hubs discourages the subdivider and his bulldozer. There are lonely roads to the back of beyond—narrow, steep—with bends too sharp to allow the passing of a semitrailer truck, and as for a speeding motorist with an irate state policeman in pursuit, well . . . New Mexico offers impossibilities as well as possibilities. There are temples of nature amid pine or sagebrush, where peace of mind, heart and soul is the fare; where the rasping voice and the shoving elbow is not.

"All right," said the man, looking up with a twinkle in his eye and the seriousness of the movement vibrating all around us. "Your name is Destiny. Think it over for a minute. Then put the tip of your pointer on the spot that was made for me. You're supposed to know New Mexico. Now put your knowledge to a practical purpose."

I looked up at the man and down at New Mexico. Then, like the headsman who raised his axe slightly above the alabaster neck of Anne Boleyn, I lifted my pointer and let it fall—on a place in the solitudes I both know and love.

"Thanks," said the man. "I'll drive down and take a look at it tomorrow. Then, if I'm still disappointed, I'll just try California."

At parting, I reminded him that "trying" California could be a fate worse than death. I expected to get a Christmas card from him later, one postmarked Pittsburgh, but didn't. I forgot all about him for nearly two years; then, in the spring I walked into the museum to find a tourist looking down at the map. It was my old friend of the heart-bowed-down-by-weight-of-woe countenance. He wore the same eye-twinkle, however, and he said: "Say, you wouldn't sell me that old pointer of yours, would you? . . . Just for a souvenir—the piece of wood that blazed my trail."

And did he find it, his sun and sanctuary? He found it and more.He bought some land and built a house—a rock fireplace too, and the well he drilled is as sweet as the Waters of Shiloh. He has a garden and a freezer, and the super market is no longer his source of supply. There's a cracker barrel grocery two miles down the road. For summer sound he has the song of the birds and the talkative pines and the dramatic thunder of the mountains; in winter, when the ground is white, he has a crackling fireplace and a high-fidelity sound system that does wonders with the New York Philharmonic. Where he lives there's cool shadow; or the bath of sunlight can be attained by walking a few feet. He is one of the happiest, unmolested men in the world; and terrifically busy—busy at the business of living to be a hundred years. For the tonic of the solitudes is composed of divine ingredients, all contributing to longevity.

It sickens me when someone says: "Where can we go? This State is filling up with people so fast that we who love space are slowly but surely being cramped out of it." That, of course, is nonsense. For there are plenty of spots in New Mexico useless for the economically-minded and each a perfect paradise for bird-watchers. New Mexico has an area of 121,666 square miles, and human preference tends toward close settlement. Even the ten largest towns are mere blisters on the body of a territory vast as this. And there are few Jim Bridgers among the newcomers. Sparsely-settled places, awesome deserts and high mountain canyons can be quite terrifying to people fresh off Eastern and Middle Western city pavements, and are to be met only on a Sunday afternoon drive. In spite of atoms and electricity, civilized man is still a little afraid of the dark.

Here at Kuaua, we are but twenty-one miles from the core of New Mexico's largest city; and a brief half-mile to a heavily-traveled paved highway. Yet ours is one of the longest half-miles in the world. Brief but thick, and beyond the armor of it come to us the sounds of the hubbub. They disturb us little, for they are other men's business. My wife and I are Dwarfs of Tradition who must bend to the Giant of Progress—but we bend at a distance. The sounds we hear are the hymns of people concerned with progress, and who love to build, and improve, and get ahead, and thrive by it. And there lie the blessings that New Mexico has to offer, and in abundance—Sun and Progress, and Sun and Sanctuary.

Our choice goes to sanctuary, yet the reason for our being here at Kuaua at all gives us to know that we are helping with progress. From beyond the half-mile strip of access road, to this our home, because it is a State Monument and of intense archaeological interest, come thousands of the tourist horde. Here we look upon the face of the world—upon its pock marks and beauty spots. Those of a certain sort we treat as ships that pass in the night; others we'll remember with love for the rest of our lives. Many envy us for the elbow room we enjoy, for the divine panorama of the Sandia Mountains, and even for the mud house we live in.

Sanctuary can be found anywhere under the sun, for it is all a matter of mind. The language of the Divine is silence. His Light the light of the sun. New Mexico, after a little looking around is accomplished, will show itself to be a quiet, sun-blessed land.

NEIGHBORS TO THE SUN
Irving F. Hand

IRVING F. HAND entered the United States Weather Bureau in 1912, and was in charge of solar radiation investigations for the Bureau with headquarters at the Harvard Blue Hill Observatory, Milton, Mass. His work included supervision of 27 Weather Bureau and cooperative solar stations in the United States and Alaska and research projects relating to radiation. His article, *Neighbors to the Sun*, grew out of solar investigations made at Albuquerque. He has written numerous articles of a scientific nature for a variety of magazines.

New Mexico has considerably more than the average amount of sunshine in the United States. Owing to its mean elevation of 5700 feet and comparative freedom from large manufacturing industries, the atmosphere is much more transparent to the solar rays than that in large cities. This is an important factor from the health standpoint, for smoke is one of the chief robbers of the so-called health-giving, or actinic radiation which prevents rickets and allied diseases.

That the clearness of the atmosphere and prevalence of sunshine in New Mexico are well recognized is evidenced by the fact that both the U. S. Weather Bureau and the Smithsonian Institution maintain apparatus for solar measurements in the State. The Weather Bureau, while it has a score or more stations well distributed throughout the country for the measurement of total solar and sky radiation, has only four stations for the more precise measurement of direct normal-incidence radiation from the sun, and one of these is at the local Weather Bureau office at the Airport in Albuquerque. The solar radiation intensities here are not only higher than at any of the other stations, but also are obtained more frequently because of the prevailing clearness of the weather.

The Astrophysical Observatory of the Smithsonian Institution maintains one of its two solar observatories in the United States at the top of Burro Mountain, near Tyrone, midway between Silver City and Lordsburg. At this station on clear days, measurements of practically all wave lengths of solar radiation from the ultraviolet out into the infrared are made; and by a rather complex system of calculation, the amount of radiation that enters the outer limits of the atmosphere is determined. This value is termed the "Solar Constant," although it is believed that the value is not strictly constant, but varies by a small amount. Attempts are being made to correlate these solar changes with weather in order to determine if forecasts of coming weather, particularly long-range forecasts, may be made with accuracy from solar observations.

Little thought is given to the radiation from the sun by laymen, who merely consider the sun as a source of light and heat during the day, have a recollection that with the shortening of days in winter, colder weather follows, and know that the sun is highly important for plant growth. Let us analyze solar energy and see how complex it is.

To begin with, the sun is the nearest star. Few people realize that, for the general consensus is that stars are seen only at night. The sun is so much nearer than any of the other stars that it appears tremendously larger and brighter, but it would look much like others if removed to a comparable distance. The light from the sun reaches us in about eight minutes, traveling at the rate of about 186,000 miles per second: the sun is approximately 93 million miles distant. Light from the next nearest star takes more than four years to reach us. The light from any star that we view at night started toward the earth many years ago, and it is conceivable that some of the stars now visible may have vanished centuries ago but that their light is still on the way.

Solar radiation as it reaches the surface of the earth after being filtered through the atmosphere, ranges in wave length from about twelve millionths to two thousandths of an inch.

The shorter wave lengths comprise the ultraviolet radiation, or that part which generates vitamin D; and it is interesting to note that at the higher elevations of cities like Albuquerque, many more times the amount of ultraviolet is received than through the smoky atmospheres of large cities. The visible radiation is but a small portion of the total solar energy penetrating to the earth, and in the solar spectrum is located just above the ultraviolet, being of longer wave lengths. Just beyond the visible is the infrared, or heat radiation. Solar radiation consists of electric waves, analogous to radio waves but of much shorter wave lengths.

Not only is sunshine valuable for its tangible benefits, but it also has beneficial psychological effects on patients in hospitals. Any physician will verify the fact that sunlight streaming into a hospital room cheers up the patients, and often this cheering effect on the mental attitude is the difference between life and death. The newer hospitals for the most part not only recognize this fact and design the rooms for the maximum benefit from sunshine, but also and for the same cheering effects attempt to design the rooms so that they are homelike, with a bit of color, rather than of the older pure white or dead-gray type, with white iron beds and standard uniform furniture so that each room looks like another. Sunshine, when not filtered too great a degree by a smoky atmosphere, is a powerful germicide, killing many bacteria which otherwise would persist under cloudy skies.

Often the question is asked, "What good are measurements of solar radiation?" Mention of a few direct uses may suffice. In the first place, as the sun is the primary generating cause of all weather, the amount and distribution of solar radiation received over the globe are of major importance in weather studies. Records of the amount of radiation received from day to day at various places have found many practical applications in illuminating engineering, heating and ventilating engineering, studies of plant growth and crop yields, biological and medical investigations, deterioration of materials under exposure to the weather, hydrologic engineering, power engineering, and a variety of military problems.

Intensive studies have been made of the possibility of direct utilization of solar energy for house heating; and at the Massachusetts Institute of Technology, a building with approximately the capacity of an average eight-room house has now been heated for two years from the sun alone with the temperature inside never falling below 70 degrees Fahrenheit. The summer solar energy is stored for winter use, by the absorption of solar radiation by a copper plate, blackened on top and covered with three layers of glass to prevent reradiation to the sky and loss of heat by wind. Beneath the copper plates are welded small copper pipes, and the heated water is stored in an underground tank which is thoroughly insulated. The experiment has shown that it would not be economically practicable so to heat a home in New England, owing to the northerly latitude and rather high percentage of cloudiness; but as every British Thermal Unit is accounted for, it is easy to calculate where such heating would be practicable and how large a plant would be needed. In a state adjoining New Mexico, an engineer heats his house by a very simple method. Having a square house oriented with the cardinal points, he has placed ordinary storm windows on the east, south, and west sides, the windows being set at a forty-five degree angle from the ground. Beneath the windows he has massed obsidian, or black rock of volcanic origin, which becomes heated by the sun during the day, and at night, through thermostatic control, a fan blows air over the heated rocks, thereby heating his home. Such a device is practicable only where the skies are very clear. Although this home is located in the desert, the temperatures at night often fall below freezing; and through this device, the engineer is the only householder in the neighborhood who does not have to resort to customary methods of house heating.

Dr. Charles G. Abbot, secretary of the Smithsonian Institution, has devised a solar cooker; the oven can be used for baking until two a. m., as the heated black liquid circulates around the well insulated oven drum. He also devised a steam engine, using the sun for generating the steam, and with its use operated a large radio station for a brief period.

Solar radiation data have been used in the study of the growth of tiny organisms at the bottom of Lake Erie. Oceanographers, both at La Jolla, Calif., and Friday Harbor, Washington, have found the data valuable in their work. Similar data have been used by growers of dates in California. Obviously the intensity of solar radiation, and especially the values of its several color components, are of utmost importance to paint and fabric manufacturers in order to determine the fastness of colors. The amount and distribution of the ultraviolet component of radiation are of importance to physicians. The amount and distribution of both the visible and the ultraviolet and, more recently, the infrared also, are important in the movie industry. Camouflage studies involve considerable use of solar data, not only of the visible portion, but of other portions as well. These are but a few of the practical applications of the studies being carried on at the Weather Bureau Office at the Airport at Albuquerque and by the Smithsonian Institution at the top of Burro mountain, 8,000 feet above sea level.

The amount of solar radiation reaching the earth, measured in comprehensible units, is an amazing quantity. Quite recently some studies were made in the deserts of a nearby state where the average radiation approximates that received in New Mexico. On an average clear day in August it was found that the daily amount of solar energy impinging upon the top and all sides of a cubical structure approximating a ten-foot cube, reached the surprising total of 191 kilowatt hours, or enough energy to maintain constantly for 24 hours 198 40-watt electric lamps. Or, expressed in different units, this energy is the equivalent in thermal units of 48 pounds of the best anthracite coal. The difficult part of direct utilization of solar energy for house heating, or for furnishing electric power, is the inability so far to improve very much upon Nature in converting the radiant energy for useful purposes. Nature, for example, through photosynthesis utilizes solar energy to promote plant growth, such as rapidly growing trees, which may then be cut for fuel; the efficiency is greater than in most methods so far devised by man.

There are paradoxes in radiation phenomena as in many other things. For example, odd as it may seem, on the coldest day experienced in Washington, D. C., for twenty years, the highest rate of radiation also was received. This is very simply explained by the fact that on exceptionally cold days, the atmosphere of necessity must be comparatively free of water vapor, which renders it very transparent to the radiation.

Radiation from the sun is the ultimate source of all except a practically negligible portion of the supply of energy that is essential for the maintenance of plant and animal life on the earth and for the operation of nearly all natural phenomena on the surface of the earth; in particular, the amount and distribution in time and space of the solar radiation which is intercepted by the earth are the prime generating causes of the physical activities in the atmosphere that determine weather and climate.

We must conclude, therefore, that if one places human life and well being above riches, there can be no doubt that sunshine is New Mexico's greatest asset.

YOU CAN CHOOSE YOUR CLIMATE
Cleve Hallenbeck

CLEVE HALLENBECK was one of the authorities on New Mexico weather. In 1941, after twenty-six years with the Weather Bureau in Roswell, he retired because of a period of illness, but continued his interest in the weather by writing about it until his death. His principal hobby was New Mexico history and he authored two published books on southwestern history, *Spanish Missions of The Old Southwest* and *The Journey and Route of Alvar Nuñez Cabeza de Vaca* and was co-author with Juanita H. Williams of *Legends of the Spanish Southwest.*

During the twenty-seven years I was in charge of the Roswell Weather Bureau office, I heard thousands of comments upon the climate, for people meeting the weatherman naturally begin talking about the weather.

Judging from those comments, the features of New Mexico's climate that most impress newcomers are: the rejuvenating coolness of the summer nights, the open, sunny character of the winter, and the peculiarly invigorating effect of the climate as a whole. And one comment that I heard perhaps oftener than any other was to this effect: "The people back home have the *craziest* ideas about the climate and country out here!"

According to climatological classification, New Mexico actually has nine types of climate, which is not generally recognized because each type merges into the next. In this state people are living and working at all elevations from 2,500 to 9,500 feet above sea level, and climate changes rapidly with elevation. Other factors being equal, the temperature falls more than three degrees for every 1,000 feet increase of altitude, and precipitation increases one to three inches in the same distance. Sunshine, humidity and wind also vary more or less with elevation. Hence the great variety of climate found in New Mexico can be understood.

Except California, no other state has so wide a range of *liveable* temperatures. Therein, such points as Elizabethtown, Chama, and Dulce are comparable to points in the lower Hudson Bay district of Canada; others, such as Columbus, Chamberino and Malaga are comparable to New Orleans and Jacksonville. Elizabethtown averages 26 degrees cooler than Malaga. This is a greater difference than that between Bar Harbor, Maine, and Jacksonville, Florida. Within the limits of New Mexico one can bask in the shade in January, or sit by a fire in July: it depends only on where he happens to be.

Everywhere within the state the nights are cooler and the days warmer than in eastern districts having the same average temperature. Nowhere in New Mexico will one find warm summer nights or oppressive summer days. He will find the winter days open and sunny as a rule, but even in the warmer districts he will find the winter nights chilly, and in the higher northern districts even a New Englander would call the winter nights downright cold. He will find that in midsummer he can work out-of-doors without risk of heat prostration, and that in four-fifths of the state he will need no overcoat or gloves on winter days.

Greater detail is hardly practicable within the limits of this article, because temperature conditions range from subtropical to sub-arctic. But a reading of zero or lower may be expected in winter over the colder two-thirds of the state, and 10 below zero in the northern mountains. All but a few southern districts have experienced zero or lower at some time or other. Ordinarily, the lowest for the winter will be about

20 degrees below the average daily lowest for that season. A temperature of 100 or higher has been recorded at some time or other in about three-fifths of the state, and of 90 or higher in all except a few of the higher districts of the north. The average daily highest in summer ranges between 72 and 96 degrees, depending upon the locality, and the average daily lowest in winter ranges between five and 33 degrees. In some southern areas, frost normally occurs only in two months of the year, while in some of the higher districts of the north only two months are free of frost.

The temperature is more variable in the plains area of the state (roughly, the eastern one-third) than elsewhere. That area lies within the western outskirts of the cold air masses that move southward over the plains states and produce the notorious "Texas Norther." The mountains bordering the plains on the west act as a sort of dam that holds off most of the cold air from two-thirds of this state.

Also, since New Mexico lies south of the normal "storm tracks," the typical blizzard of the northern and eastern states is unknown here. The state does have cold waves, but even in the more exposed eastern portion they are rather tame affairs compared to the howling blizzards of the Middle West.

Again, the debilitating hot spells produced in the eastern half of the country by "air stagnation" are unknown here, because the diversified topography of the state does not permit air stagnation.

The precipitation is more variable than the temperature. For the major portion of the state it averages between 14 and 18 inches per year, but it varies from less than 10 inches in the Rio Grande valley to over 30 inches in the higher mountains of the north.

Winter is the driest season. Over the state as a whole seven-tenths of the precipitation falls in the warmer six months (May to October, inclusive) and on an average four to six times as much precipitation occurs in July as in January. Winter precipitation is in the form of slow, general rains and snows—almost entirely rain in the warmest districts and entirely snow in the coldest—while summer rainfall takes the form of local thundershowers. Occasional heavy downpours occur in the summer.

But the precipitation is erratic. At practically all points in the state the wettest year of record shows four to six times the moisture of the driest year. Even greater variability applies to monthly amounts. This is most marked in the lower elevations.

The snowfall ranges from less than two inches in the lower Rio Grande valley to over 300 inches per year in parts of the Carson National Forest, in the north. In the warmer half, snow seldom lies on the ground more than 48 hours, but in the mountain districts it remains all winter and furnishes excellent skiing and other winter sports, as well as forming a reservoir of water for irrigation.

The number of days with precipitation varies from about 30 in the drier districts to 100 in the higher areas of the north, with an average of 50 to 60 over most of the state. For each of the winter months the average is two to four days; this rises to seven and eight days for each of the summer months and, in a few mountain districts, to about 15.

Then there is the matter of humidity. High atmospheric humidity has about the same effect upon the human system that a blanketed radiator has upon an automobile engine. In New Mexico a temperature of, say, 90, *feels* just as warm to the exposed skin as it does anywhere else. But the effect ends there; it goes no deeper. The summer heat does not engender lassitude as it does in more humid climates. Here a temperature of 80, right after a shower of rain, is more uncomfortable than is one of 90 degrees under the usual conditions of humidity.

The humidity is somewhat higher in the mountain districts than on the *mesas* and in the valleys, but it is low throughout the state. It ranges from an annual average of 45% in the southmost valleys to 60% in the mountains, with an average for the state of about 53%. An average between 50% and 60% is recognized by climatologists as the most desirable from the viewpoint of human comfort. For the country east of the Mississippi, the general average is about 75%. This difference of 20% to 25% may appear small, but it is big as measured by the result upon human efficiency.

Incidentally, in New Mexico the humidity normally is as low in winter as in summer. This is the only state of which that can be said. Damp air readily penetrates our clothing and renders it a poor heat-insulation, hence dry air is as desirable in winter as in summer.

He who comes to New Mexico must expect to see a good deal of the sun at all seasons of the year. No part of the state receives less than 70% of the possible amount of sunshine, and from that up to 80%. The percentage of sunshine is as high in winter as in summer; in some districts, even higher. This can be said of no other state in the Union, although it is true of extreme western Texas, which climatically is allied to New Mexico. Of the seven so-called "sunshine" states, embracing practically the southwestern quarter of the United States, New Mexico ranks first in winter sunshine and last in summer sunshine, and for the year as a whole takes rank only below Arizona. More than half the area of the United States receives more summer sunshine than does New Mexico. This is worth remembering, for sunshine is more desirable in winter than in summer.

Spring is the sunniest season and fall the cloudiest, as a rule, but there is considerable variation. Fall sometimes is very sunny and spring relatively cloudy.

Finally, we must notice the wind. My experience is that most eastern people believe New Mexico to be a wind-swept tract of utter desolation.

The truth is that most of the United States experiences higher winds than does New Mexico. If we cut off the eastern plains section, then only southern Arizona can boast of lighter winter winds than can this state. The average hourly velocity here ranges from 10 miles an hour in the northeastern plains area to seven miles for most of the state and to six miles for some of the mountain valleys. For spring the general average is nine miles, summer, seven miles, fall, six miles and winter, seven miles. The winter is no windier than the summer, and in fact daytime winds are lighter in January than in July. The highest winds are those local outsweepings that everywhere attend thunderstorms, but even these rarely are damaging. The climatic factors that I have thus briefly presented are of such quality, degree or distribution as to encourage life in the open. It perhaps is because of this that the New Mexico climate has for four centuries been remarked upon for its healthfulness. It invites people to get out of doors, summer and winter: the abundant sunshine and the dry, invigorating air do the rest.

Average daily highest and lowest winter temperatures are shown for 35 communities:

Summer temperature data for representative points:

	Temperature Average Daily Highest	Average Daily Lowest		Temperature Average Daily Highest	Average Daily Lowest
Alamogordo	57	30	Alamogordo	94	63
Albuquerque	49	24	Albuquerque	88	61
Artesia	60	26	Artesia	95	62
Bernalillo	49	22	Bernalillo	90	58
Bloomfield	44	16	Bloomfiield	89	54
Carlsbad	61	28	Carlsbad	95	64
Carrizozo	53	26	Carrizozo	89	60
Cloudcroft	40	21	Cloudcroft	70	47
Clovis	52	23	Clovis	91	62
Columbus	57	33	Columbus	93	68
Corona	47	23	Corona	82	54
Dulce	39	5	Dulce	84	43
Elizabethtown	36	5	Elizabethtown	73	39
Estancia	47	15	Estancia	86	50
Fort Stanton	51	21	Fort Stanton	84	52
Fort Sumner	56	23	Fort Sumner	92	61
Haynes	42	8	Haynes	84	48
Hobbs	55	27	Hobbs	93	64
Las Cruces	59	27	Las Cruces	93	59
Las Vegas	48	18	Las Vegas	82	52
Lordsburg	59	28	Lordsburg	94	62
Lovington	59	26	Lovington	92	62
Malaga	63	30	Malaga	96	66
Mountainair	47	20	Mountainair	85	52
Nogal	46	23	Nogal	77	47
Raton	56	15	Raton	84	49
Roswell	56	25	Roswell	91	63
Ruidoso	45	21	Ruidoso	76	60
Santa Fe	41	21	Santa Fe	79	55
Silver City	48	25	Silver City	84	57
Socorro	54	24	Socorro	92	59
Springer	47	14	Springer	87	52
Taos	41	14	Taos	83	48
Truchas	39	16	Truchas	74	48
Tucumcari	54	24	Tucumcari	91	63

FROM SAGEBRUSH TO SPRUCE
Ross Calvin

DR. ROSS CALVIN came to New Mexico for his health after some years as a college teacher followed by ordination in the Episcopal Church. After his recovery, he went on again with the sacred ministry, this time at Silver City and later at Clovis. He is pastor emeritus of the Pueblo Church of St. James in Clovis and is now living in Albuquerque. He has written numerous magazine articles and books, best-known of which is SKY DETERMINES. He has a Ph.D. from Harvard and an honorary degree of Doctor of Laws from the University of New Mexico.

The traveler who has viewed the southwestern panorama of nature from its sagebrush to its spruce trees has indeed seen most of it. The spruce tree, growing only well up on the higher mountains, is familiar to everybody because it has become a favorite in formal planting everywhere. But the sages—who knows them? To the newcomer almost any gray-looking plant is "sage." To my friends the cowmen, sage commonly means saltbush. To my friends the foresters, sage means an artemisia. But there are others who insist the romantic "purple sage" is Apache plume, a relative of the wild rose.

Something should be done about it! And about the cacti, too. There is more misinformation abroad concerning cacti than anything that grows, or runs or creeps—except rattlesnakes. The clever people who design travel folders and pictorial maps almost always put *sahuaros* in New Mexico. *Sahuaros* do not grow in New Mexico. That's final! And the yucca is not a cactus. That also is final. Nor yet the *ocotillo*, defiant, scarlet, splendid denizen of the desert, which botanically is rather close to the violet! The question that comes up at once in writing of our plant life is this, "Who wants to know?" The picnicker wants to know the names— and nothing much besides—of the wild flowers. My friend the cowman already has the names. If I chance to mention blue grama grass, he gently corrects me, "Black grama." If I chance to mention black grama, he says, "No, white grama." But at least he is concerned about something more vital than non-scientific names, and wants to know whether the thin old cows will eat it, and whether it stays green in winter, or whether it will hold the soil in place.

The tourist who pilots car and passengers some five or six hundred miles between breakfast and bedtime sometimes inquires what he was looking at. He, too, often asks for some predigested information. But nothing much can be done about it. The rest of us who get around enough to gain a comprehensive view of the panorama from north to south, or make an occasional trip to the West Coast, and who go into the mountains often enough to be impressed by the layer-cake succession of plants on their slopes—we can, with the aid of a little reading, amass a store of knowledge where others amass only mileage. On a tour it's mileage or knowledge. The choice has to be made.

From sagebrush to spruces may be thought of as an apt way of indicating the ascent from desert to mountain top, but in New Mexico our desert is not dominated by sage. That honor is held by the creosote bush *(Covillea glutinosa)* called by some of the old-timers "greasewood."

You will recognize it by the odor, for the creosote odor is responsible for the name. It is a thin-looking, spreading shrub three to six feet high whose small varnished evergreen leaves give it an olive-green tint both in winter and summer. It is characteristic of the creosote bush that it does not occur isolated, but in wide, uniform plantations sometimes miles in extent. In such areas the shrubs stand almost uniform in size and spacing with little or no invasion of grass or weeds. Since no livestock will eat it, the ground it occupies is therefore useless for grazing; and because of general aridity and stoniness, equally useless for agriculture. The shrub displays almost an intelligence in avoiding soil capable of irrigation, mounting always to the porous, light-colored soils of the table lands (benches) or the arid plains. The species is a vegetable coyote where survival is concerned.

By nature it is a dweller in the waste lands. The hottest driest, toughest habitat in the entire Southwest it claims for its own.

The traveler, then, descending from Taos to Santa Fe need not look for it. But about Socorro, as he comes southward, he will encounter it. Lieutenant Emory as he rode with the Army of the West in 1846 found it there. And in the same year Wislizenus, who first collected the type specimen of barrel cactus and ocotillo, collected a specimen of creosote along the Rio Grande in the same locality and sent it back to the famous Dr. Engelmann of St. Louis, who two years later published a description of it for the botanists of the world.

Plantations of it extend eastward far out on the Texas plains along Highway 80, and westward through southern New Mexico and Arizona on into California. In this vast range it varies not at all except in size. Snap off a little branch. If it is as brittle as broomstraw and smells like creosote, then you have the *Covillea.*

In the same broken, stony, arid country, you will find an abundance of cacti. These plants are supposed to be the most tenacious competitors of all tenacious growing things. But this is hardly true, for incredible as it may seem, there are whole regions where drouth is too prolonged for cacti. But since that is in southwestern Arizona and the neighboring parts of California, the statement may as well stand unchallenged for our State. Certainly none show such amazing adaptations to arid environment. Everybody, of course, has noted the grotesque shape of the plants—globes, cylinders, etc.—but not everybody has detected the working of a not-so-dumb nature behind it. A globe exposes less surface (that is, vulnerable area for evaporation) than any other solid of an equal volume. And another thing—cacti, being succulents, are filled with a watery sap or juice; but wound a plant and see how quickly the sap coagulates to mucilage and closes up the wound.

Cacti of more than sixty species occur within New Mexico, but more than nine-tenths of the plants seen along the highway—unless in a collection brought together for a garden—can be grouped into the one genus, *Opuntia*. The family likeness is shown not by the shape, or general appearance, but by the fact that all are jointed. Both the cane cactus (also called cholla and elkhorn) and the pan-caked prickly pear, unlike the great barrel cactus and the numerous small species which resemble it in shape, have joints and therefore may rightly be called opuntias. The "pancakes," incidentally, are not leaves, but divisions of the stem. A cactus gets along without leaves. A good rough-and-ready test is this: if it has leaves, it's not a cactus—which eliminates agave, ocotillo, yucca, etc.

The barrel cactus you will be sure to see growing in front of filling stations in the southern part of the state. Its name as well as its size identifies it. Note well the flowers and the large, lemon-colored fruits. If they do not occur on the south side of the plant, the evidence is plain that the plant has been transplanted, *and turned*. The test is as certain as the presence of moss on the north side of a tree in the forest.

Creosote, opuntias, barrel cacti, along with mesquite and ocotillo have a way of growing together in what is called a plant society. They are the markers of the bottom layer of the cake—the lower Sonoran zone. It is well exhibited along the Rio Grande *mesas* as one nears El Paso.

The layer next above it comprises the foothill country or the Upper Sonoran zone, which includes most of the state of New Mexico. Some of its commoner markers are juniper, piñon, mountain mahogany, live oak, lemita *(Schmaltzia)*, mescal and blue grama grass. It is exhibited all along the Continental Divide but perhaps nowhere quite so well as in the Fort Bayard Military Reservation. There, a tract, long protected from wood cutting, fires, and intensive grazing offers a large scale picture of the lovely land that was once New Mexico. There the character and amount of vegetation astounds the traveler who is familiar only with the close-picked, parched aspect of the country which generally borders the main highways. When seen from a slowly-cruising airplane, the very color of the grass-mantled earth is different from that of the bare ranges a few miles to the south.

The foothills are dotted—not covered—with juniper and piñon, while the ground between is occupied (or once was) by the famous blue grama grass *(Bouteloua gracilis)*. The dwarfed, rounded little junipers—properly enough called cedars—which the traveler generally observes, leave him unprepared to believe that they will ever become respectable forest trees. Yet in the Burro Mountains, the alligator-bark juniper, finest of them all, reaches a diameter of five feet and an age of approximately a thousand years. The largest specimen of this tree in existence is growing a few miles north of Fort Bayard.

The wood has an extraordinary fragrance; and when split into kindling, it tells the neighbors for blocks around that you are building your fire. Another notable thing is its resistance to decay in the earth. I have removed pieces of this juniper wood from subterranean ruins of the Mimbres culture, which according to the best archaeological opinion are some eight hundred years old.

The yuccas deserve a story by themselves. One small and rather unimpressive species greets the traveler from the meadows at the foot of Raton Pass; others have to be searched out on high limestone ridges where the foothills are deciding to become mountains. But the one chosen for our state flower is the *Yucca elata,* a superb species that is seen at its best along the Continetal Divide near Silver City. The genus reaches its greatest size in the grotesque Joshua tree which never fails to attract the eye on the Mohave Desert as one nears Los Angeles.

The tree yucca reaches far up into the Upper Sonoran zone from beneath, but the century plant reaches only half way down from the top. But let's be sure we mean the same thing. By century plant I mean the mescal. But besides these two names, it is called also maguey, and no doubt also Spanish dagger, along with various other spine-tipped plants. All of which clinches the argument for a scientific name which to all users is a certain designation for one object, and only one. It's not just because botanists like to appear learned that they call the plant *Agave parryi*. That title is as descriptive as middle C for one key on the piano, and, in the same way, international.

What is a century plant's life expectancy? An insurance man might make an inference from the name. The plant is a big compact cluster or rosette of rigid, upward-pointing, spade-like leaves, each five inches or so in width and each tipped with a vicious, heavy thorn. Year after year after year it just sits there. I question whether anything alive has a better life expectancy. So far as my observations go, it hasn't any diseases. It is invincible by drouth. Freezing doesn't harm it, and fire can't burn it—though a yucca, even when green will flame up like a torch. No hungry old cow can crop it, and no rodent gnaws it—at least, not enough to do harm. And since the Indians have gone, no human uses it. So it stays put.

In fact nothing less than a caterpillar can leave a dent on it—not, of course, the caterpillar that eats young tomato plants, but the caterpillar that pulls heavy road machinery. The plant just doesn't die before maturity, it would seem. A remarkable organism, indeed! But after many, many years —depending largely on the amount of water received—it makes up its mind to flower. In one tremendous effort it shoots up a ten-foot flower stock at the rate of several inches a day. The blossoming is a final, dramatic, beautiful gesture. By the time the flowers are withered and dry, the great, tenacious plant is dead!

Above the foothills, where the last yuccas, the mountain mahoganies, the century plants, the piñons, and the other plants of the association leave off, the yellow pines come in to mark off what is called the Transition zone. But the pines need no description, no printed promotion. The traveler—any traveler—can appreciate them even though he might not be stirred to the slightest interest by the lovely yuccas. Since the beginning of time, the pines, fragrant, cheerful, companionable, have been man's friend. Among the southwestern pines takes place most of the hunting, most of the camping, much of the picnicking.

There is no danger that the tourist will overlook the pine belt and the pines, for they are probably the most numerous tree in New Mexico. They occupy the next to the highest of the horizontal bands marked off on the mountain elevations by gradations of moisture and heat. The one above it, the Canadian, is but a vestige. Only in a few places on the map —and most of them north of Santa Fe—are there island peaks and ridges which tower up into the atmosphere far enough to tempt spruces. Yet such areas occur as far south as the Mogollon mountains, and thus bring Canadian scenes almost to the Mexican border.

The Englemann spruce forest can easily be fixed in mind by associating it with the 10,000 foot level. There the towering somber trees stand rank on rank, casting shade so dense as to discourage any under-story of shrubs and annual weeds. There summer nights call for heavy jackets and big fires. August is the month of chill rains, and the coolness is never interrupted by heat waves, nor the humidity by drouth.

The blue spruce is so similar in appearance to the Engelmann that only pretty good observers can tell them apart. Both are tall, very pointed, very slender trees, and both are likely to show a good deal of blue quality on their young twigs. But the blue spruce comes in at somewhat lower elevations, and its habit of growth is different. If the Engelmann makes a dense forest, interrupted only by scattering firs or a compact thicket of aspens, the blue spruce is more cheerful, less austere. It loves the water, and is the natural companion of the chill, cascading trout streams. Though it is fond of the shadows, it seems to grow equally well where the narrow little canyons widen out and admit the sunshine upon their tiny meadows of lush grass, cranesbill, velvety red cinquefoils, lupines, yellow columbines. And when one of the miniature openings is fringed with arrowy spruces whose pointed tips rise sharp upon the curtain of azure and cumulus cloud—then you have the loveliest vista in the mountains.

THE MAGIC OF WATER
Wilfred McCormick

WILFRED MCCORMICK has written more than 500 short stories, articles and serials for a score of national magazines. Besides his writing, he has lectured extensively to clubs and schools throughout the Southwest. After Pearl Harbor, he entered the army and rose from lieutenant to lieutenant colonel in a variety of assignments from public relations to recruiting. He is the author of the popular Bronc Burnett series of books for boys. During winter months he conducts a Community College class in writing for the University of New Mexico, Albuquerque.

John Chisum was a piker. Oh, I know he was the first great cattle baron to settle in the Pecos Valley—that his wide-flung herds from Horsehead Crossing up to the Bosque Grande once numbered 80,000—that he was a pivotal figure in glamorous frontier history. But compared to another man of that same region who is seldom mentioned in fact or fiction, John Chisum's personal role drops back into a poor second.

The man who really *made* the Pecos Valley was J. J. Hagerman.

Mr. Hagerman originally came from the east, a man of considerable culture and background. He was somewhere in his late forties when the lower Pecos Valley first got to know him about 1890. He was flush, then, from the gold fields of Colorado where the famed "Molly Gibson" mine and others had smiled on him to the extent of some five million dollars.

Maybe he was looking for a safe place to invest this money, or maybe it just burned his pockets—I don't know. But for some reason he gambled the entire fortune on the Pecos Valley. Yes, gambled—and lost. But that's getting ahead of my story!

The Pecos Valley at that time was a dry, cropless desert. As the cowboys would say, "it looked like hell with most all the people moved out"! There were few trees, fewer farms, and absolutely no good roads. Carlsbad and Roswell were only "wide places" in the cattle trail that paralleled the sandy, sluggish Pecos river, north and south. There was no town between these two, a distance of eighty miles.

Hagerman began to do some mental addition. He knew that an unlimited water supply underlay the grassy surface, and that the Hondo and Spring rivers flowed generously across the northern end of it. He knew, also, that the region had a matchless climate—ideal for growing crops, and unbeatable for health. The situation, then, added up to two major problems: Some means of distributing the water over the land, and some means of market transportation.

He pitched into both problems with every resource of his mind and pocketbook.

He built and equipped a railroad from Carlsbad up to Roswell. Likewise, with his own funds, he constructed a huge canal system from the rivers in the north down through the projected farm lands some thirty miles to the south. These enterprises, even with modern and high power machinery of today, would be considered stupendous. But Hagerman put them over. What he had lacked in tools, he more than matched with energy. Both jobs were finished in 1894. Now to attract people!

However, that proved easy. With only a little advertising in the East, they came in droves. He worked day and night to have the region ready for them.

Twenty-three miles southeast of Roswell, he fenced off a tract in the very heart of his finest lands. He named the place "Hagerman," after himself. From the start, it became his special pet. He laid the embryonic town off in streets and alleys, built a depot and switch yard, planted over a hundred sturdy cottonwoods, and provided irrigation leads from his canal to make them grow. Overnight, almost, he had a bustling little community, supported by thousands of acres of productive farm land. Outlying the farms, were homesteads and ranches—hangovers from the stirring days of the range and cattle wars.

I talked last week with Harry Cowan, an old-timer there, who mentions having seen antelope jump in and out of the fenced enclosure when Hagerman first built it. The region was still that wild! But one year later, when the Mrs. Cowan-to-be started a school there, eighty-five pupils attended. This, itself, bears testimony to the number of settlers who flocked to that part of the valley to make their homes.

From the very beginning, those early settlers raised bumper crops. The irrigation system furnished them plenty of fertile, muddy water, and the matchless climate did the rest. But they couldn't make any money! The markets were still too far away, and they couldn't live entirely off one another. Outside money had to be brought in.

They took the matter to their godfather, J. J. Hagerman. His railroad, they told him, was all right, except that it went the wrong way! They wanted a connection to the north— one that would give them an outlet on the main lines, which went through Amarillo.

Hagerman weighed the possibilities. The distance was more than two hundred miles, a desperate undertaking because the right-of-way would have to cross sand, desert, plains, and treacherous rivers. It would cost him millions. Still, if he didn't spend them, he stood to lose the investment he had already made because folks weren't going to stay.

It was a momentous decision, but the settlers won. Hagerman built them a railroad. The venture broke him, but it made the Pecos Valley for all time to come.

The village he created under his own name has grown into a city of which the old fellow today might well be proud. A boom town no longer, Hagerman has settled into an orderly, gradual stride that insures against any slump in the future. The cottonwoods he planted are still there—great, bulky giants, now, of majestic beauty and worth. The streets are just as he laid them, except that now they are paved; a modern sewerage system underlays them. The entire community—farms and all—has access to cheap-rate gas, electricity and water. The place has one of the strongest banking houses in the Southwest, good schools, churches, a newspaper, and up-to-the-minute city government. The old bugbear, transportation, has long since taken the count, with fast motor truck service over paved highways to supplement Mr. Hagerman's original railway which is now a branch of the Santa Fe.

These Pecos Valley folk, as a lot, are the happiest I have ever seen. They know that if they *work,* they have a cinch on security. Seeds planted in that soil simply have to come up. Drouths are of little concern. They don't depend a great deal on rain, anyhow, because the old Hagerman canal is still in operation. It supplies them with the world's cheapest irrigation water—to be technical, thirty inches of water each year to the acre, at a cost of only $1.25. More than ten thousand acres of valley land are supplied by this historic canal; and the many farms outside the "water right" district have flowing wells or pumping plants of their own.

The first week in October, each year, has come to be almost an institution of play. It is the period when Pecos Valley folks take time out to stage a mammoth four-day Fair at Roswell.

Opening with a burst of pageantry, gaudy bands, and colorful floats that move through a long avenue of tanned but eager faces, the celebration then gets underway back at the giant exposition halls. Valley products are there for a candid world to see. Nothing is lacking, because they've got everything right at home—a livestock show that ranks with the best, diversified farm produce that would draw blue ribbons anywhere, and a noisy good time for everybody from Junior to Grandpap.

But back of the whole gala celebration—back of the thriving Pecos Valley itself—looms the mind and millions of J. J. Hagerman, the man who made all these things possible. And it isn't unlikely that if the old fellow could return for a day, that he would be glad for having gambled on the Valley, even though, personally, he lost.

He was that sort of a man.

A-D-O-B-E SPELLS CONTENTMENT
Dorothy L. Pillsbury

DOROTHY L. PILLSBURY came to Santa Fe on a visit and found that the country so fascinated her, she could not return to Los Angeles and her social work. She settled down to writing, for which she had no training, but unknowingly located in the midst of a large group of Spanish speaking people and she began writing about them for the *Christian Science Monitor*. Through the interest of the *Monitor* editor, she was persuaded to submit a collection of published stories to the University of New Mexico Press which has published three volumes of them. She has lived in Santa Fe since 1942 in the little *adobe* house which still spells contentment for her.

Tomes have been written about the *adobe* houses of Santa Fe and vicinity. They go expertly into brick making, floor plans, *vigas, canales, portales, patios,* and corner fireplaces. They delve back into history and jump to modern architectural approval. But the cult of *adobe* lovers knows it is all surface stuff. It is like describing a lovely and beguiling woman by giving her physical measurements and naming her brand of cosmetics.

The cult knows that in all the world there is nothing so heart-and-eye satisfying as a little *adobe* house. They think of peach and apple blossoms stenciled pinkly against thick brown walls, of summer hollyhocks, crimson, yellow and cream, reaching for flat roof-tops. They think something should be said about the silver bubbles of piñon smoke that float from squat chimneys against autumn skies and fill the still air with that fragrance which will be forever Santa Fe. Especially they want mentioned little golden cubes of houses scattered like children's blocks over the bleak whiteness of a winter's night.

The most ardent of the *adobe* cult are converts with all the convert's zeal and fire. The natives, Indian and Spanish, take *adobe* all in their stride as they take the russet-hued soil and the rhythm of the seasons. It is the Anglo convert to *adobe* who has made of *adobe*-living a philosophy and a song.

All Anglos who live in *adobe* houses are not members of the cult. Some live in them as they would live in any other kind of house and curse the drafts that filter in under poorly hung doors and around out-of-plumb window frames. They shake their heads when one end of a room turns out to be eighteen inches shorter than the other.

Members of the cult drift to *adobe* living as naturally as a tumbleweed rolls to a fence corner. It is a mistake to think they are all artists and writers. Some are clerks, school teachers, business men, bankers, lawyers and plumbers. From time to time, some backslide, sell out and depart for what they call civilized living. Back they come wild-eyed and breathless to buy tottering walls and sagging roof in the hope of resurrecting the dear lost love.

Visitors passing briefly through the country often become converts. "I'll never be happy until I own one of these little *adobe* houses," they exclaim. Nobody knows how many school teachers, sales managers, stenographers and bank officials scattered through the length and breadth of the land are living with the memory of a little corner fireplace as a pillar of fire in the wilderness.

You can recognize cult members by the fact that they always refer to their *adobe* houses as to living personalities. Also at some time or another, they ask wistfully, "what is there about a little *adobe* house?" Voices trail off vaguely into space. The question is never answered.

Mary Austin, who was a member of the cult, knew. She says in her *Land of Journey's Ending* that one really knows an *adobe* house "only when the mud roofs are muffled in snow and the flames of cedar run up the walls of cornered fireplaces."

But, alas, what Mary knew she did not explain about her little mud house.

She, who loved this State with a passion, knew that the primal charm of an *adobe* house is its earthliness. It does not have to be coaxed to blend with the soil. It is the soil. Brown *adobe* walls are the strong warm arms of Earth-Mother around her children. *Adobe* lovers recognize this vaguely. "I feel so secure," they say.

Other house walls merely shut out wind and cold. *Adobe* walls, being often out of line around openings, do not shut out the elements as effectually as those of other construction. But— and this is the essence of *adobe*—they give the effect, not only of shutting out wind and cold, but the tumult of the world. That sense of security may well come down a long psychological ladder from those faraway days when pre-historic man found his first real shelter in a clay-walled cave.

Next to earthliness, the *adobe* house beguiles with simplicity. As life becomes more and more involved, snarled and confused, an *adobe* house becomes an island of sanity in a sea of jitters. There is something about its sun-burnished outer walls and its plain white inner spaces that says, "why complicate living?" That simplicity has the magic ability to absorb all electrical and mechanical gadgets of mundane living and to render them almost invisible. I have had people in my own *adobe,* equipped with electric refrigeration, instantaneous hot water, and theromstat-controlled heating, who have remarked kindly, "some day, dear, they will bring electricity out here and you can have some of the luxuries of life."

Perhaps this magic ability to absorb the mechanics of living is part and parcel of nature's protective coloring. In spite of thick walls, an *adobe* house has no sharply defined line between indoors and out. It is as if the landscape obligingly moves inside. Perhaps it is because those walls are only a little elevation of the soil outside. Perhaps it is because the *vigas*—those cinnamon-colored shafts of pine trees that hold up the low ceiling— carry the vistas of forest spaces down their lengths.

And then there is the *fogón,* that minute fireplace built across the corner of a room. It is whitely kalsomined like the walls and its opening is beehive-shaped. Indented shelves where blue candles burn in tin candle sticks make it a kind of earthy altar where a stand of scarlet *chiles* and five ears of Indian corn pay tribute to the earth.

To sit around that tiny fireplace is to know that it is like no other fireplace that man has devised, be they red brick, white marble or imported tile. If you watch piñon logs fluttering sequined butterfly wings up its sooty sides, you will know why this fire of logs, stood on end without benefit of andirons, is different from all others. It will dawn on you after months and years of chuckling companionship. That fire in a corner of your shadow-filled room is man's old friend, the camp fire. Around it have sat, from time's beginning, all of life's wanderers.

When the scent of piñon smoke fills the room, when the white walls turn geranium pink and the *vigas* mellowed amber, when shadows from candle flame and blooming plant sway along the plain white surfaces, look behind you in the darkening room. It may be that you will see a chipmunk scampering along a *viga* or a spotted fawn peering limpid eyed from the dim corner by the bookcase.

Such houses are not acquired merely by consultation with architects and contractors, nor by the signing of a check. The *adobe* houses of cult members evolve much as a sea shell adds a new cell from time to time or the wild plum tree sends a lace-draped branch toward the sun.

The cult of *adobe* lovers thinks someone, in the midst of brick counting and plumbing specifications, should mention the deep accord that exists between their little mud houses and the natural universe around them. Moonlight gilds their walls at night, stars stare primly over the edges of flat roofs. From the first froth of the wild plum blossom to the time of snows when black piñon tufts tie white hillsides together, little *adobe* houses hum with a deep contentment. It is a simple, humble little song, the merest thread of a melody caught from a deeper rhythm. But the person who lives in such a little house finds his own heart singing with it.

FORMULA FOR FUN & GRACIOUS LIVING
George Fitzpatrick

GEORGE FITZPATRICK, editor of this volume, has been editor of *New Mexico Magazine* for 27 years. He has written extensively on New Mexico subjects and also edited *Pictorial New Mexico*—an anthology of pictures from the pages of *New Mexico Magazine*—*New Mexico Home Plan Book, Poems of New Mexico,* and the Betty Woods travel guide, *101 Trips in the Land of Enchantment.*

Greer Garson was born in County Down, Ireland, and has lived in London, New York, Dallas, Hollywood, besides all the many other places where stage and motion picture commitments took her. But for the past several years, New Mexico has meant "home" to Greer Garson. Here in New Mexico, at Forked Lightning Ranch on the Pecos River, is where her heart is. Even though she can be only a part-time resident, her enthusiasm for New Mexico is full-time. From New York, where she had gone to fulfill a TV assignment, she wrote just the other day: "I have been talking about New Mexico, the land and the people so much during my New York press interviews, the press must think I am secretly retained by the Chamber of Commerce or the Tourist Bureau."

Greer Garson became a New Mexican by marriage, but she was soon a full-fledged New Mexican in her own right—and a goodwill ambassador for New Mexico when traveling elsewhere. When she married E. E. Buddy Fogelson, Texas oil man, he already owned Forked Lightning Ranch, and they came to the ranch for a brief stay. The ranch's marvelous setting:

Ranch house on a piñon-covered hilltop overlooking the river, fifteen miles of stream meandering through 20,000 acres, marvelous sunsets that held her spellbound, horses to ride, vast hills and forests to explore, spectacular scenery to enjoy on every hand—all these touched her with their magic spell to make her a New Mexican. And as his wife became more enthused, Buddy Fogelson's own business interests became more firmly tied to New Mexico.

"It used to be that we had no business interests in New Mexico," Fogelson explained. "Now most of our operations are in New Mexico." He has drilled several wells in the Four Corners area and maintains an office at the ranch to keep in contact by teletype and telephone with his Dallas headquarters and his field office. The ranch office is so well equipped, even with geologic maps, that he can operate entirely from there whenever he desires. One room of the office is given over to his collection of autographed photographs and his Colonel's commissions. He has received several such commissions from Governors of New Mexico.

Listening to Greer and Buddy Fogelson talk about the ranch, it is difficult to tell who is the most enthusiastic about New Mexico. They both have steeped themselves in the lore and historic background of the area. Prehistoric, too, for archaeological investigation has shown that the ranch area was populated hundreds of years ago by Indians. The ruins at Pecos Pueblo, now a State Monument, once were located within the boundaries of Forked Lightning Ranch. Near here the most important Civil War battle west of the Mississippi River was fought. And even more recent history of the ranch is interesting, too, for in the twenties it was owned by Tex Austin, the great rodeo performer and promoter.

The Fogelsons are attempting to write a new chapter in the history of the ranch. They have established here a foundation herd of Santa Gertrudis cattle, the first in New Mexico and the first at this altitude of 7,000 feet.

The Santa Gertrudis breed was developed in Texas for semitropical and tropical climate. Fogelson believes the breed may well be adapted to the mountain country of New Mexico.

Though the Santa Gertrudis herd is new to Forked Lightning, the Fogelsons are not amateurs when it comes to raising cattle. Fogelson has run Herefords on a commercial basis on the ranch for years, and for a number of years Greer Garson owned a herd of registered white Shorthorns, which she had imported from Scotland. The Fogelsons made a profitable deal on these last year and sold them.

Ownership of the white Shorthorns accorded Greer a highly personal satisfaction. She had wanted to own such cattle from the time of girlhood visits to her grandfather's farm in northern Ireland. She had a deep affection for the blooded Shorthorns, which were bought while on a visit to Scotland, and even today, though she no longer owns any, she still speaks of them with tender affection, describing individual beasts as "charming" and "gentle."

She has great admiration—though not quite the same personal feeling—for the Santa Gertrudis animals, splendid, deep-bodied cattle that are magnificent specimens of the new breed that was developed by the King Ranch of Texas by an infusion of Brahman blood on a Shorthorn base. When she talks of the herd, it is with an appreciative enthusiasm for these big—and expensive—animals.

But then, she is an enthusiastic person generally, and whatever the subject, whether it's cattle, the ranch, New Mexico, the movies, or T.V., she exudes enthusiasm, and her vivacious charm captures visitors in a *tete-a-tete* visit perhaps more quickly even than she captures an audience on stage.

She has the faculty of putting visitors completely at ease, and visitors to the ranch—strangers yesterday—are within minutes chatting gaily and acting like old friends.

Harvey Caplin and I—Harvey is one of the country's outstanding color photographers—spent a day at Forked Lightning Ranch to get pictures and gather material on Greer and Buddy Fogelson.

Harvey had been tentatively trying out the sound of "Mrs. Fogelson" and "Miss Garson" in talking with the actress, and finally asked forthrightly, "What can I call you?"

"Greer, of course," she answered, and her millionaire oilman husband was just as definite in making it "Buddy" instead of Mr. Fogelson.

So Greer and Buddy it was from then on, though Buddy himself often called his wife, Rusty, his own personal nickname for her. Greer explained that she had had other nicknames and that as a youngster her nickname had been Ginger but that when she went to Hollywood she could not use the name because Ginger Rogers was already so well known.

For both Greer and Buddy it must have been a long and trying day, for Harvey was relentless with his photographer's war cry of "just one more." And to get an over-all picture of her day's activities we had suggested several changes in costume, in addition to the day's variety of horseback riding, skeet shooting, bread baking, interviewing, etc.

Along toward the end of the day, Greer admitted that it was an even harder day of picture-shooting than the usual busy day at the studios. But throughout it all she remained charming and cooperative, even when it seemed to me that her patience must long ago have run out.

On this same day, a Minneapolis newspaper (Minneapolis being a flour-milling town) had assigned a reporter to Forked Lightning Ranch for an interview-story and pictures of the actress' bread baking in an outdoor oven. So there were dozens of questions to be answered for the Minneapolis paper and pictures to be shot of the dough mixing and bread baking.

And, incidentally, Greer actually did mix the dough and bake the bread—in an outdoor oven. It was not a gag.

Part of the staff at the ranch is a Spanish-American family, and they, like many other country families of New Mexico still prefer bread baked in an outdoor *horno,* even when the most modern facilities like the well-equipped Forked Lightning Ranch kitchen are available. Greer had become intrigued by the outdoor oven's products and was experimenting on her own with white and whole wheat bread recipes.

We had arrived that morning to find Greer—dressed in blue jeans and black shirt—standing at the kitchen work table mixing dough for a batch of bread that was baked later in the outdoor oven. We had some of the bread that evening—and it was easy to understand why the outdoor *horno* is still used so extensively. Travelers going through New Mexico by train see these outdoor ovens as they flash by—and they undoubtedly feel a momentary stab of pity for people who have only such primitive equipment. How little they realize what they themselves are missing!

Beginning with the kitchen where we came upon Greer at her dough mixing, we had a tour of the rambling ranch house that is built around a pleasant patio filled with flowers and greenery. It is a place for entertaining as well as for relaxing and enjoyment of living. All guest rooms have their own entrances from the patio, private baths, and colorful southwestern decor. Greer has been filling the house with New Mexico paintings, too, and some by Bernique Longley and Helmuth Naumer were prominently displayed. And on the fireplace mantel in the big living room is an old *santo,* of which both Greer and Buddy are particularly fond. It is San Ysidro, patron saint of farmers, long cherished by Spanish-speaking New Mexicans.

Greer and Buddy have their own formula for enjoying New Mexico. They both like to ride, and there are 20,000 acres to ride in without leaving their own property—and thousands of acres of forest land nearby. They both like to shoot, but neither cares about hunting, so they confine their shooting to the trap range—an elaborate set up that includes an electrically operated machine to throw out the clay pigeons. Greer has her own personal Jeep, and the ranch also has an English Land Rover to reach the more difficult isolated sections of the ranch. They live simply, yet comfortably. Their ranch house is ideal for entertaining and they seem to enjoy having their friends around. The rambling ranch house and its beautiful patio invite relaxing, but there are so many things to do, they can always keep busy if they get bored with just resting. All in all, it adds up to lots of fun and full measure of gracious living.

As we roamed the ranch house and grounds, Buddy would be called away frequently to his office to handle long distance calls or messages coming in on the teletype. He was working on a couple "deals" that kept him in a series of phone conferences. But finally he turned off the teletype, got into riding boots and took us out to see the cattle, his pride and joy. As we came down off the porch of the big house, we could see the herd below us in the distance, beginning to ford the river as Ranch Manager Jay Kirkpatrick moved them to another pasture. Here was a picture that would have delighted the sensitive soul of the most critical Western fan—the sunlight glistening on the rippling water, the herd moving slowly, stepping cautiously for good footing, a cowboy splashing to the opposite river bank to head the leaders in the right direction. With fluffy clouds against a deep blue sky, the sparkling reflections on the tree-lined river winding into the distance, and the herd moving across the water, it was a memorable scene. But it was a picture that could be etched only in memory, for though Harvey with camera at the ready, raced on ahead, almost jumped a fence and hardly paused for footing as he side-slipped down the hill, by the time he arrived at picture-taking distance, it was too late. The herd was across and headed for the uphill pasture.

There were other memorable pictures of the afternoon: A magnificent view of distant Pecos Baldy from the trap shooting range; Greer's personal Jeep with its gay "Auntie Mame" painted on the side, a rustic fishing bridge across the river that would have made interesting background for pictures (if we'd had more time) ; a flat pasture along the river, viewed from above, a pasture that archaeologists believe was once an irrigated field used by prehistoric Indians; a scene with Pasco and Pinkie, Greer's toy poodles, having a dog argument over who was getting the most attention, and Pinkie (or was it Pasco?) finally walking away in disdain, with nothing more to say, because actually he really had been getting more attention!

The pleasant and most lasting impression of the day was that here was gracious living by people who know how to work and how to enjoy life. They put on no airs, bragged about nothing except the country itself, and though both could be only part-time New Mexicans from the necessities of vocation, they had adopted New Mexico and its ways completely and thoroughly.

They had found their own personal Shangri-la on a piñon-covered stretch of New Mexico high country, along the Pecos River.

NEW MEXICO WAS OUR FATE
Conrad Richter

CONRAD RICHTER and his small family moved in 1928 from Pennsylvania to New Mexico where, he has said, his heart and mind were soon captured by the Southwest. From his arrival in the State, he has devoted himself to the writing of fiction. One of the earliest of his books, *The Sea of Grass,* was awarded the Gold Medal of the Society of Libraries of New York University. Another book, *The Trees,* also received the Gold Medal of the Society in 1942. *The Town* received the Pulitzer Prize in 1951, and *The Waters of Kronos* won the 1960 National Book Award for fiction. His other novels include, *A Light in the Forest,* 1953; *The Lady* (a tale of New Mexico), in 1957, and *A Simple Honorable Man,* published in 1962. Mr. Richter is again making his home in Pennsylvania, but still visits New Mexico.

It seemed inevitable that we should come to New Mexico. The first intimation, although it wasn't fully recognized then, came when I was five or six years old. A slightly older cousin and I resolved to run off West and fight the Indians. We thoughtfully accumulated food, blankets, tobacco, firearms and cartridges. These we hid in the cellar. My cousin had foolishly confided in his sister. The last night she burst into tears and gave us away. It's likely that the whipping I got wasn't so much for wanting to run away as for our cache of supplies, most of which in a spirit of joint family ownership we had set aside from the general store in which my father at that time was a partner.

The second sign, this time fairly accurate of the specific region in which we would later make our home, was while courting my future wife. Her neighbors played a certain record over and over on the phonograph. It became our theme song. The name I have forgotten but not the Spanish music. It was a Mexican song, and how it got to our Pennsylvania Dutch countryside I will never know. Blindly but surely events conspired a few years later to make us sell our Eastern farm-home, burn our bridges behind us and cast our lot on New Mexican soil.

It was perhaps the most significant move we ever made. Not for anything would we have wanted to miss the incomparably rich experience of the Southwest. From the very first we grew aware of phenomenon in sensation. We found that simple quiet scenes such as a green lombardy against an *adobe* house aroused in us a vitality of feeling not to be found elsewhere. We could sit and look at it by the hour or at an old craggy cottonwood with leaves stirring lazily in the sun. We were told that this was the spirit of *mañana,* but that far from explained it. Near the end of my book, *The Mountain on The Desert,* there is speculation on the secret of this Southwestern magic known locally as enchantment.

New Mexico became our second home. We acquired a fiercer love for it than for the state in which we had been born. Coming back to it, we shouted our delight the moment our car crossed its border. The New Mexican air, we thought, tasted finer, headier. Of course, there were early difficulties. One was a constant thirst for the sight of water. I recall once stopping the car on the dirt road, now Rio Grande Boulevard, to gaze for a long time at a large pond of rainwater caught in a nearby field.

At first we also lived under a strong sense of exile, despite our finding more interesting people to the square kilometer in New Mexico than any place we had known. For example, the first house we occupied as a family had as immediate neighbors: a geologist who knew the history of the mines of the State and his wife who knew the history of the mine people; a retired rancher from the mystical Ladron country; and a charming Spanish family, both adult members of which had been born in Mexico, the wife the daughter of a Mazatlan ship building family and a Scotch sea captain.

The Ladron rancher, also of Spanish blood, came over to see me one day when I was in the yard.

"You have some business?" he wondered after we had talked a while.

"I write," I told him. "You know, books and magazines."

He stared at me incredulously, then shook his head.

"The things some people have to do for a living!" he commiserated.

He told me with pride about his own work on the wide Ladron range, and his hunger for jerky since he had lived in town. He gave me my first native flavor of New Mexico. Indeed when I look back on it now, I can see what a rich bonanza of people and country that we as a writer's family had unwittingly been thrown into. When I went to the Cattle Sanitary Board to ask for the name of a man who might give me authentic material for a Western story I had in mind, they directed me to a house only a block or two down my own street. Here in a hall as wide as a room and hung with longhorns and oldtime photographs, I had the good fortune to meet a couple who had lived through many of the days of the Territory and who could tell me about them. Their names were Herbert and Lou Hardy, and very patiently they answered all my inept questions.

I did not always have such good fortune. We had come to New Mexico at a time when hundreds of men and women who had lived through the days before the railroad were still alive. I talked to many of them, and they told me what they knew. But in the case of a few, knowing something wasn't the same as being able to express it. I remember one man who had been friend and companion to a famous early character.

"Tell me about him," I said eagerly. "What was he like."

He thought hard.

"Well, he about five feet eight, dark complected and weighed around a hundred and sixty pounds." That was the most I could get out of him about an exciting human being.

Now the Hardys were different, articulate. That they had originally been Southerners undoubtedly helped. They could tell me what their friends and neighbors were like. Human incidents about them rose easily to their lips. When H. W. Hardy went with me to Socorro, Magdalena and other places, men crowded around to trade badinage and humor. His stories were priceless, and at this late date I want to pay tribute to his friendship and memory. It was unfortunate that Hardy's Socorro friend, whom he believed from confidences given to have been Frank Jackson of Sam Bass fame, was dead. You know the old song, *"And Jackson in the bushes a trying to get away."* But in the Hardy house I learned to know other old timers including Bob Lewis, the fabled marshal of Magdalena.

In New Mexico two regions had the strongest influence on me. One of these was the pinal. I mean the pine belt that, as all New Mexicans know, starts below seven thousand feet elevation although much of the ponderosa at this lower altitude had long since been cut down. Our second summer in New Mexico we took a cabin in the big pines on the eastern slope of the Sandia Mountains. We found the climate at 7200 feet that first June well nigh flawless. We loved it, stayed until Christmas and came back the following spring.

Now love is a very strange and powerful thing. It seems silly to suppose that such an inanimate object as a place or region can respond to this mysterious emotion and return it. And yet, curiously enough, that is exactly what came to pass. We were in the trough of the great depression. We had lost everything and were very poor. A member of my family was not yet completely well, and a living from my pen seemed most precarious. Nevertheless the pinal took care of us. The owner of our cabin and of the nearby store, Dayton Dalbey, showed us every kindness, and the driver of the mountain laundry truck that stopped at our door urged me to come and talk to his mother who, he said, knew Billy the Kid.

Now Billy the Kid happened to be my gauge of the veracity and authenticity of early New Mexicans. If someone claimed he had known the outlaw, I found it discreet to be skeptical of many things he said. On the other hand, if he said frankly he had never seen the Kid, I listened to him with respect and confidence. So I felt reluctant to talk to this unknown mother who had known Billy the Kid. But you don't willingly rebuff the only laundryman who comes within twenty-five miles of your house. When at last I called, there sat talking quietly to me from her chair a most authentic white-haired woman whose father had kept an early stage station at Antelope Springs when the Estancia Valley was a wilderness, and whose husband later on had run a general store at Ruidoso. Here, she told me, Billy the Kid had often hidden from the law, a friend of the family who took her small boy for rides on his horse.

Her stories about Billy the Kid, while interesting, still left me cold, although not so cold as he had left many who had incurred his displeasure. On the other hand, what she told me of her life as a girl during the sixties in her father's dot of habitation on this wild and lonely land moved me deeply. Her father couldn't leave the station, and she and her brother, neither of them more than children, used to drive the wagon to Santa Fe for supplies. It was then a trip of several days. They would camp far from the trail at night, not daring to light a fire for fear of the Apaches.

She gave me such a picture of herself and her brother that they made their way into my next story. Under the name of *Early Marriage* it took me into the *Post,* the first of a New Mexican series. The name of the laundryman who knocked on my door with such good fortune was Alfred Dow. It seems peculiarly American that a boy whose family had sheltered Billy the Kid from officers of the law should later become an officer himself and a member of the New Mexico State Police. (Alfred M. Dow is a veteran member of the New Mexico State Police. His pioneer mother, Isabel McAttee Dow was born Jan. 4, 1861, died Oct. 8, 1948 at the age of 87.)

If this were all that the New Mexican pinal had done for me, I would have reason enough to be grateful. But W. T. Boyd, a neighbor at Sandia Park, brought over two books for me to read. They were old and somewhat tattered, revealing none of the ultimate richness of the gesture. The books were Henry Howe's monumental historical collection of early Ohio first published in 1840. I read them by gasoline lantern light to the sound of wind in the pines. A new world of life in the deep forests of the early Midwest was opened to me. Out of it came my Ohio trilogy, first conceived and planned at 7200 feet in the big timber of the Sandias which, I think helped me to understand the big timber of a life 150 years and 1500 miles away.

The other region of New Mexico that returned my love was the grass lands. They had made a strong impression on me from the moment I had looked out of the Santa Fe car window and seen the great green meadows around Las Vegas and, a few hours later, the Glorieta country like a vast park planned on a monumental scale and planted with ornamental evergreens. Later on at Albuquerque we used to drive the many wheel tracks that threaded the then lonely and uninhabited outer *mesa*. Another favorite spot was a trail from Corrales up over the sand hills where the grass of those luxuriant summers of the early thirties ran on and on with no sign of life but grazing cattle and horses.

More and more the beauty, mystery and immensity of the grass lands got into my blood. The Hardys and others had told me about the San Augustine Plains, and I had explored them myself. But it was while driving to Quay County one day to see a man named Griggs, who told me many wonderful things from his long experience with western horses, that the impulse to put it into a long story came to me. It had been a rainy summer. Beyond Vaughn I found a green paradise of grass land, rolling, pitching, dipping, rising, fresh and fertile, studded with small ponds and flowing with milk and honey. That was where *The Sea of Grass* first took hold of my mind.

New Mexico has given me so much and there is so little space to tell it, but this testament of love can't be closed without mention of my gratitude to some others of its people, Agnes Morley Cleaveland, Judge C. M. Botts, Will Keleher, Ruth Laughlin Alexander, Thomas Matthew Pierce, Erna Fergusson, S. Omar Barker, to name only a few of the many who encouraged me and who have left the warm glow of New Mexico on the heart.

THE UNFORGETTABLE PAST

PARTY FOR A LADY
Myrtle Andrews

MYRTLE ANDREWS (GERE) grew up in Santa Fe before the turn of the century and has vivid recollections of the frontier period in New Mexico history. The story, "Party for a Lady," is a chapter out of her own life—a life filled with excitement and colorful incident. She has written as a hobby for many years and has published two books, but reports that when one gets to be a great-grandmother there are times when one feels there is little time for writing.

The brakeman scooped more coal into the stove in the corner of the passenger coach as the old E. P. & N. E. train bumped along over the rough road bed.

That was in 1903, and traveling was not so pleasant. Outside it was bitter cold and the wind whipped huge piles of tumbleweed over the desolate plains near Torrance, New Mexico. It would not be long before Easter, and I wondered what Easter in this country would be like without trees or flowers, with nothing but miles and miles of barren plains.

The conductor, taking my ticket, asked, "Say, lady, you ain't going to live in Torrance?"

"Yes," I answered, then hastened to ask "Why?"

"Well, maybe I ought not to tell you, but since the section boss's little two-year-old girl died there from a rattlesnake bite, the women folks moved away. It's a God-forsaken place all right," he mused as he looked out of the window.

With this bit of information, he left me to ponder how I would like living in a place infested with rattlers—where I would be the only woman in camp.

Opening the big paper sack and peeping inside to reassure myself my new hat was still there, then peering cautiously about at the few passengers and finding they were sleeping or reading, I arranged my hat on my big pompadour, using the window for a mirror. The low crown of the hat, trimmed with great bows of wired blue taffeta and two long orange-colored bird wings which flared out on the left side, did not fit down over my hair, but was perched on top of my head. The wide stiff brim of blue silk looked like a cart wheel.

I jabbed the hatpin through the gros grain ribbon band, the shiny head of the pin resembling one of the buttons of my shoes. I felt deep pride in my improved appearance and thought how delighted my husband would be when he viewed me in this new Easter creation. Then remorse smote me. I wished for my three dollars and ninety-five cents back. Torrance as I now knew it must be could not possibly justify my extravagance.

As the coaches jolted over the rails, they seemed to sing "Snakes-snakes-rattlesnakes," on and on.

When the conductor came through the car again, I asked, "What time do we arrive in Torrance?"

As he answered, he turned back to ask, "Somebody going to meet you?"

"Oh, yes, my husband; he is manager of the Pennsylvania Development Company store there," I told him.

"Well there's no place to go. If he knows you are coming, that's all right."

"I know he'll be there, for I sent him a wire from El Paso," I said reassuringly.

"We don't stop long in Torrance; only a minute to let passengers off or on the train," he replied.

"Will you call me in time to dress the baby?" I asked.

"Oh yes," he assured me.

It seemed I listened all night for the whistle for Torrance. Three o'clock was a beastly hour to get off a train.

I was startled by someone shaking my shoulder. "Torrance," the voice said.

With the shriek of a long, drawn-out whistle, the train groaned to a stop. The brakeman came for our baggage.

"Well, here we are," he said cheerfully, despite the hour.

I was helped off the train in the pitchy blackness of the night. I looked around. There was not a human in sight. I was alone—all alone on the plains. I stood in the midst of a strange country, my baby clasped tightly in my arms. I watched the fast disappearing train as it sped down the long, straight track, the near lights growing smaller and smaller.

I looked around the prairie trying to penetrate the darkness. Surely someone lived near. There must be an agent who met the trains. Just at that moment I saw a light from a lantern. I called frantically but there was no answer and the light disappeared. I ran in that direction and found a box car with a door in the end of it. I kicked and called. In answer a man came to the door carrying a lantern. He held it near my face, peering at me.

"What's the matter, and who are you?" he asked curiously.

"Do you know the manager of the company store here?" I asked eagerly.

"Yes," he drawled, looking me over.

"Will you take me to him?" I nervously asked.

"Yes. Just a minute."

We gathered up my baggage alongside the track in the cinders and started over a hill that obscured the small two-room house from the station. In a few minutes we were hammering on the door of my future home.

"Who's there? What do you want?"

"Open the door. Let me in," I said.

"That door won't open; go around to the other side of the house," he told me. In a long-tailed nightshirt, with a lamp in his hand, he met me. Hardly had he closed the door before he greeted me with, "Where the hell did you get that hat?"

"What I'd like to know first is why you didn't meet the train," I demanded.

Two days later the telegram was delivered to my husband.

The news leaked out we were to be given a surprise housewarming by the "boys" in the camp, there being no women there. I baked two big cakes, and everything was in readiness for the surprise party that evening.

The first guest to arrive introduced himself as Bill Moore,

saying he wanted to see my husband and would "sit a bit," which he did.

"You-all new to this country?" he asked me.

"Yes; I came from Santa Fé."

"Well, most of the families hereabouts come from a Bain or Studebaker wagon—they're rivals," he continued. "I tell you there ain't no better families brung up than them that comes out of a Bain wagon," he confided as he turned his hat round and round in his hands, refusing to give it to me.

The well-driller was next to arrive, splattered with mud from the top of his five-gallon Stetson to the high heels of his cowboy boots. His hat stuck to his head as tightly as the mud to his clothing. I asked how the well was progressing.

"I reckon we ain't a-goin' to get water! Guess it's another dry hole."

I knew this would be quite a disappointment to the company, as they had drilled several dry holes at a great outlay of money.

After a time that seemed ages—we had discussed wells and families from all angles—there was another knock at the door. I ushered in the dandy of the camp. He was the saloon keeper and was dressed for the party—red vest, with a big, heavy gold watch chain that crossed its entire front, striped trousers and a dark coat. He was a tinhorn gambler and a lady-killer of the first water.

I was getting anxious for my husband to come from the store. I didn't know that the wagons had arrived to get provisions and had caused his delay. This store carried the supply stock for all stores along the proposed new railroad.

With the advent of the saloon man, I had another topic to discuss of which I knew nothing—saloons and gambling. I was glad to be interrupted by the arrival of "Joe the Cook." He was the knockout of the evening. He was wearing a boiled shirt—too bad he hadn't waited until the party was over to chew tobacco—and he had no collar on his shirt, the neck band being fastened with a small white china collar button. A swallow-tail coat and a pair of greasy pants completed his "full dress."

With the arrival of each guest, I was more and more alarmed at my husband's delay. I was on the verge of asking someone to go after him when the door opened and he entered. He was duly surprised and told the boys to make themselves at home, which they were already doing. The well-driller kept his hat on, and the others removed their coats. They moved the table to the center of the room.

"Now gents, lay off your firin' arms; this is a party fer a lady."

Out of their pockets came bottles: they were well supplied. They had a drink around. A lamp had been placed on each end of the table. I didn't like the way Bill Moore fingered his gun as he placed it on the table to his right; lovingly his fingers slid along the notched handle of the gun. I recalled what notches stood for—a man for each notch—and I wondered how many men he had killed, or if he had fudged a little and carved a few extra.

As they were ready to start their game of poker Frank produced a bright colored pencil. "This pencil will write any color you want. Who wants to name a color?" he asked.

The men watched him with interest as Bill Moore excitedly asked "You mean any color?" Taking the pencil, he examined it.

"Yep, any color."

"Well, let's see 'er spit out a little green," he said.

"G-R-E-E-N," my husband wrote midst roars of the boys.

Bill reached for his gun, but as he put his hand out they all began to razz him. "Can't you take a joke—'Little Green'?" And so the matter was settled without bloodshed, amid an uproar of laughter.

The game continued. At twelve o'clock I was ready to serve the food, only to be told it was too early. The first grey light of another day was creeping through the small windows when I placed the cake and warmed-over coffee before them. I assured the boys it had been a wonderful party—though I was nearly dead for sleep, I was grateful to the oil driller for having removed the guns from trigger fingers during the game and arguments which ensued.

Poor Joe, this was his last party, for two weeks later he decided suddenly to leave town.

He was awakened by a voice that even in his sleep he recognized as his old time enemy. Too well he remembered the night he had left Texas with another man's wife—and had been dodging him ever since. This fateful morning when he opened his eyes, it was to look at a butcher knife held in the hands of his enemy. With a shriek that brought his helper from a nearby cot, Joe was out of the window, stopping for nothing.

The last Torrance ever saw of him he was running down the railroad track in his red flannel underwear!

Everyone in camp regretted Joe's departure; he was a good camp cook, and the big Easter dinner was not far off. Joe Saint, dictator over all food supplies for the camp, had promised turkey, perhaps because they were as cheap as beef, and the men were becoming very much dissatisfied with the camp. Bill, the new camp cook, arrived dirty and unshaven the day before Easter.

The next morning was ushered in with a terrific wind storm that swept everything on the plains before it. I was awakened by the celebration of the boys, and they were not singing Easter carols either.

It had been bedlam in camp all day. Nightfall I stood at my small sliding window. Shot after shot came from the cookhouse. I saw men running from it, shooting as they came, hatless, and some coatless. From the store shouting and swearing was brought to me by the howling winds.

With trembling fingers I fastened the window and locked the door, then taking my baby in my arms, I rocked her in the little wicker rocker. Hour after hour I sat there in the darkness afraid to move. Hours before my husband had sent word to put out the light as the boys were hell-bent and swore to shoot every light in camp out.

The wind had died down and only occasionally was there a fresh outburst as sand and gravel hit my cabin walls. I could still hear the uproar, with now and then a shot.

Then I heard stealthy steps outside my window. I cringed

in fear. Then a man's screams, "Let me in; for God's sake, let me in! They're after me; they'll get me!"

Chills went down my back and I shook until I bumped my head crawling under the bed with the baby in my arms. I lay there listening to his threats and pleadings until I pulled the pillow over our faces, having grabbed it from the bed as we went under.

Then there was an unearthly scream that penetrated the one thickness of boards that made our walls. I could hear a man running, followed by someone not far behind him. I could even hear his labored breathing as he stopped against my wall, hiding perhaps from a man pursuing him.

Then a shot and a scream.

"They've killed him!" I cried aloud.

Then I heard my husband's voice as he, with others, came to the rescue. After the lamps were lighted, we discovered that the back of the wicker rocker where I had been sitting had a bullet hole through it. The man who had been begging for help was having delirium tremens; the boys were trying to take care of him, and he was doing the shooting.

The rattlers that were holed in for the winter are coming forth again. The Easter excitement is over. Grading for the railroad has begun and each day sees a Bain or a Studebaker wagon drop its cargo of human beings with a small flapping tent on the vast prairie. The plains are populated. And so ended my first and last Easter in Torrance.

143

LAMENT FOR LA BAJADA
Kyle Crichton

KYLE CRICHTON regained his health in Albuquerque and went into the advertising agency business there. He wrote short stories and articles on the side, and this led to his appointment to the staff of *Scribner's*. From *Scribner's* he went to *Collier's* and was a staff member for several years. He has written a number of books including, *Law and Order, Ltd.*, a biography of Elfego Baca; *The Proud People*, a novel about New Mexico, a book on the Marx Brothers and a book of reminiscences titled, *Total Recoil*. Crichton died in New York in 1962.

As an old codger who came across the Santa Fe Trail in an ox team and poled my way over Raton mountain, I have a theory about state highway departments which possibly doesn't belong in a state of New Mexico magazine.

Among other things I contend that the gentlemen who eliminated La Bajada hill should be subject to punishment and exile for undue excess of efficiency.

This is all based on the assumption that La Bajada hill *has* been eliminated. If not, ignore the matter. It was still there when I was asked to leave the State but runners have struggled through with the news that one may now drive from Albuquerque to Santa Fe in something like thirty-five minutes flat, though why has not been explained.

Nobody was going to Santa Fe in thirty-five minutes in my day. My first trip with the late Howard Gruehl was made in a trifle over four hours and with only three changes of tire. There was a stretch between Bernalillo and the foot of La Bajada which could only be discussed in terms of indignation but there was certainly no lack of adventure. If you reached Santa Fe, there was no certainty that you would ever get home again. A great portion of the difficulty was in the rocks that the highway department distributed on the highway in the belief that they were aiding transportation, but the rest could be blamed on La Bajada hill. If you had a big car, you practically went up the hill backwards, making the turns only by such maneuvering as would do credit to a coal truck discharging its load in an alley.

From this you might assume that I was not fond of La Bajada but you would be entirely wrong. There was a sense of triumph in either ascending the thing or coming down intact that could be attained in no other way.

There is the further occasion when I was being escorted to the Holy City at no cost by Miss Erna Fergusson, who was conducting the Koshare Tours in a Franklin touring car, which used no water and, according to the fond hopes of Miss Fergusson, no gasoline. At the last grade, the steep, long one just as you came to the top, Miss Fergusson's Franklin decided that past indignities could no longer be ignored. It came to an abrupt halt. Miss Fergusson was considerably annoyed but she had the presence of mind to step on the brake. The only hitch to this was that the brake was also in a bad mood from past neglect. It refused to work, and we and the Franklin staged a retreat which was only halted when the lady practically threw me out of the front seat and I began to pile rocks to the rear.

This seemed slightly less than hilarious at the time but we came later to regard it as one of our more humorous moments, and there is no topic of conversation better calculated to get off the merits of the current political controversy than the old days when tourists, upon returning to Indiana, bored the neighbors not with Los Angeles and the movie stars but with the time they navigated the death-defying curves of that mountain in New Mexico.

When you take that satisfaction away from a tourist of Indiana, you have practically ruined his tour. In their zeal to get from Santa Fe to Albuquerque, the engineers of the highway department have overlooked the cosmic import of their meddling. We may agree that nobody in his right mind would remain in Santa Fe when he might better be in Albuquerque—or vice versa—but this is surely no excuse for flouting the heavenly injunction that a mountain is something which must be climbed rather than avoided.

There is something mean and immoral about sneaking round a mountain.

When I used to speak with my friend Elfego Baca about La Bajada hill, he invariably assured me that the subject held no threat for him.

In those days he possessed a Buick roadster which distinctly had its points. Under Mr. Baca's guidance it went at a pace which could only be regarded as precipitous. With his usual direct method of action, Mr. Baca considered that the prime objective of a motor car was to carry him from one place to another with the briefest possible delay. He placed the car in high and proceeded to his destination, honking the horn at intervals to warn animals, children and traffic cops and waving his hand out of the window in admonition to all others to get safely out of the way.

His trips to Santa Fe always worried me. There was some chance that his method of disdaining the turns in the road by the mere process of going straight over the *mesa* would get him to his destination safely, but there was no certainty that he could employ the system with success on La Bajada hill. How he encompassed the feat was never clear to me and I never went along to find out, but it is historically true that nothing ever happened to him on the hill.

He came to his grief on the stretch north of Bernallilo which I previously referred to. In forgetting to turn the wheel to the left when he came to an abrupt turn to the left, Mr. Baca collided not only with a law of nature but with a portion of the *arroyo* which had crept to a resting place close by the road. The car made three complete turns in the air before alighting safely on its feet at the bottom of the declivity and Mr. Baca was unhurt, but he was so agitated by this treachery on the part of the machine age that he shortly thereafter gave up the car entirely.

These are extreme examples which may not have been taken into account by the highway engineers, but they might at least have considered the social problem of uniting Santa Fe and Albuquerque.

They have nothing in common and indeed belong in different centuries. But that is another subject. At the moment all I have time for are my views on **La Bajada**.

They are based completely on the supposition that the hill has been eliminated. If not you can return the article and institute suit for return of the check.

DOWN THE RIO . . . IN BOATS
Harvey Fergusson

HARVEY FERGUSSON was born in Albuquerque and first attracted nation-wide attention as a novelist in the early 20's with *Blood of the Conquerors*, a novel with a New Mexico setting. Since that time there has been a growing list of books which includes, *Rio Grande, In Those Days, Hot Saturday, Women and Wives, Wolf Song, Grant of Kingdom, Conquest of Don Pedro*. In 1961 *Grant of Kingdom* was reprinted in an anthology of Western fiction, titled *The Old West in Fiction*. Since 1942, Harvey Fergusson has lived in Berkeley, California.

I choose this subject because it is perhaps the only one upon which I can claim to be the highest living authority. I have spent in all seven days riding the current of the Rio Grande in boats, and have traveled by this means nearly two hundred miles, not counting the distance I swam, waded or walked, and pushed, pulled or carried the craft.

If anyone can claim a more extensive experience than this, let him come forward.

The proper approach to any subject is the historical. Upon this head it must be recorded that diligent research fails to reveal more than one or two pioneers who tried to go either up or down the Rio Grande in boats.

An early editor—before the days of the railroad—managed to freight his wife and his household furniture down the river from Albuquerque to Socorro. That was the year of high water, and a liquor dealer, with an eye to business, also took advantage of the flood stage to float a couple flat boats loaded with beer down the *rio*, thereby saving the railroad construction crews from dying of thirst.

The editor's feat is notable in that he kept up with the railroad construction train for nine miles, and the entire trip was made in two and one-half days. Type cases, which he did not trust to the boat, did not arrive until eleven days later— by ox team.

Research reveals, however, that the pioneers, for the most part, were willing to call it a day if they could get across the river.

It remained for certain descendants of the old timers really to exploit the *rio's* possibilities as a common carrier. Considered by most of their contemporaries to be all wet, the record shows that ultimately, if not initially, they were.

My own relation to what may be termed semi-arid navigation is much like that of the Wright Brothers to aviation.

While I am not the first man who had the idea or made the attempt, I am the first man who really got anywhere. If it be asked where I got, my answer is that once I got to Socorro and both times I got back, which is something. Upon both of my more important expeditions I was accompanied by my brother, Francis, but since he merely went along for the ride, and that in a somewhat derisive and skeptical humor, I feel that the credit, if any, belongs wholly to me.

Concerning attempts to navigate the Rio Grande above Albuquerque, previous to my own, little is known. One Richard Woodson, a citizen of Albuquerque, is said once to have traveled from Alameda to Albuquerque in a canoe during a flood stage of the river. Unfortunately, there seem to have been no witnesses of this feat, and it is generally regarded as a romantic legend rather than historical record.

I believe Harry Johnson is my authority for the statement that back in the horse-and-buggy era a party of Albuquerque duck hunters used to build a flat-boat every fall and float a few miles down the river in pursuit of sport. No one knows how far they went or how often they got stuck, and probably no reliable testimony could now be obtained on the subject. I remember hearing that this form of hunting was considered one of the few reliable methods of getting a goose, but here again no authentic particulars are available. It is not known whether the geese died of astonishment or thought the sportsmen were a washout.

Boat travel on the Rio Grande was inaugurated in a serious way in the summer of 1922. During June of that year my brother and I built a flat-boat approximately ten feet long and three feet wide, loaded it with bedding and canned goods, launched it near Barelas Bridge and traveled in three days to Socorro.

The trip was eminently successful and without untoward incident, but it was not, strictly speaking, a boat journey all the way. Where the water was deep one of us always swam in order to lighten the load, and where it was shallow both of us waded.

It was in the summer of 1929, however, that the most heroic and important event in the history of New Mexico shipping took place. That year I imported an Acme folding canvas boat and with it traversed the river from Otowi bridge to Bernalillo, including the entire length of White Rock Canyon, part of which, I believe, had never before been traversed except by a few suckers.

The boat used in this expedition, as it came from the factory, looked like a picture puzzle, and it required a high order of analytical intelligence merely to assemble it. Nevertheless, this and all other preliminary difficulties were overcome and the boat was launched early one morning in July, 1929, containing myself in the stern to propel and steer the boat, a camp outfit admidships, and my brother in the bow to hold down her nose, take soundings and offer more or less appropriate comment. As a navigator, it should be explained, my brother is a gifted critic.

We had not gone half a mile before we approached a rapid with a forty-five per cent grade, studded with large boulders and foaming like a seidel of tap beer. In fact, this rapid was only one degree removed from a cataract. Right there the question had to be decided whether this expedition was to be a boat ride or a walk. After some argument it was decided that it should be a boat ride for me but a walk for brother Francis. It seemed to me two men were one too many. It is fair to say that this decision was protested by my brother, but he was over-ruled by the owner of the boat and sat down on a rock to watch the proceedings.

There ensued one of the most rapid journeys I ever made in or on anything. What is more, I arrived at the lower end of the rapid right-side up and comparatively dry. But there must have been some technical flaw in the procedure because when I started I was looking downstream, but when I finished I was looking back upstream. I never knew at what point in the descent the boat had swapped ends. The effect was much as though I had met myself coming back.

My brother contended that had he been aboard, this reversal would have been avoided, and he insisted that we ride the next rapid double. It was not so steep as the first, but it ran in beautiful foam-capped waves about three feet high. The boat rode the first wave perfectly, it came down on the second with a heavy swat, and it nose-dived under the third. This made it necessary to wade and swim ashore and to spread out the entire outfit all over about an acre of sandbar to dry. No real damage was sustained except by the bread and the cigarettes. The cigarettes were a total loss; the bread was never itself again.

During the rest of the journey we travelled by boat where the going was smooth and walked and led the boat with a rope where it was rough. This prudent procedure was not dictated by timidity but by the fact that about fifty miles of river lay between us and the next smoke.

After we emerged from the canyon the trip was wholly enjoyable, with a good current and only minor riffles to provide a mild thrill. It not only afforded pleasure to the voyagers but also much innocent amusement to the natives, who gathered along the bank shouting with delight and amazement. We got as far as Bernalillo, and even there we abandoned the river with reluctance, chiefly because most of it had abandoned us by way of the *acequias*.

Since that classic journey, little or nothing has been done to promote navigation on the upper Rio Grande, much to my regret. I have sometimes thought that the Albuquerque Yacht

Club might justify its name by taking the matter up in a serious way, but so far the subject has not even been mentioned. This admirable organization never fails to generate a high wind. All it needs to sail is a boat and some water.

I have hopes, too, that the Federal Government may yet do something to promote this worthy cause. Perhaps when it gets done planting a row of trees from Canada to the Gulf, it will consider putting in a row of dams and locks from Albuquerque to El Paso. Such a project would provide all the inhabitants of the valley with unlimited employment for an indefinite period, thus solving a great economic problem. I myself would be glad to handle the publicity. While not a strictly self-liquidating project, it would effect an enormous saving in gas. Moreover, it would make it possible for the first time to go to El Paso without eating your own dust, and it would undoubtedly make of Albuquerque the foremost port city of the state.

Meanwhile, my own researches and experiments have been interrupted rather than abandoned. For several years I have been contemplating a trip through the gorges of the river north of Taos. Nothing has deterred me from making the trip except the lack of a suitable companion. Whenever I bring up the matter, friends show a tendency to move away or change the subject.

Although the fact is little appreciated, those upper reaches of the river are among the unexplored areas of North America. Moreover, there must be some trout in there about two feet long who never saw a fly and wouldn't know how to act if they were hooked.

My experience in White Rock Canyon convinces me that in the low-water stage of the river a boat trip through the upper gorges would be entirely feasible for any good walker who can swim. I would be glad to hear from any qualified adventurer who would like to undertake such an expedition.

ACCENT ON OUTDOORS

BOYHOOD BUCKS
S. Omar Barker

S. OMAR BARKER before becoming a professional writer, taught school
and served in the First World War, was forest ranger and a member of
the State Legislature. He has been a professional free lance writer since
1925, has published approximately 1500 short stories, 1000 fact articles
and 2500 poems in about 110 different periodicals. He has an honorary
Doctor of Literature degree from New Mexico Highlands University
and in 1961 won the Western Writers of America Special Award, the
Justin Golden Boot for distinguished writing on the Western scene.

Some of the most satisfying hunting of my experience dates
back to 'teen age days when a good many of us mountain
country kids tackled a deer season with no more than half a
dozen to a dozen loads, for the very simple reason that we
couldn't afford to buy more.

The oldtimers, furthermore, didn't seem to care about
shooting just to hear the bang. The function of a shot was
to kill. "One's all it takes if you hit him right" was their
motto. There is a story of a mountaineer doling out cartridges
from a very limited supply to his boy about to set out on a
hunt. The lad was going out for deer, but with some possibility of other game:

"Here's your cartridges, son: One for your buck, one for
a mercy shot if he ain't plumb dead when you git to him; one
for a coyote or a bobcat—you ain't li'ble to see both; you won't

git no shot at a lion, but you might come onto a bear, so here's one more; and one extry to be careful you don't shoot yourself with."

Maybe the story is tinged with exaggeration, but in my own memory one of the dollywhackin'est deer hunts I ever enjoyed was a brief trip with my brother Marion (gone now to the Last Great Hunting Ground), when our total fire power consisted of Charlie's .38/55 and about a dozen cartridges. The trip was our reward for working hard through September and October to help get the crops in, instead of going to town to school. To us it was, so to speak, a few precious days of grace between the potato patch and past participles.

Since the Porvenir Game Refuge was not then in existence we could have found good deer hunting within easy hiking distance of the house. But in us was a yearning for far woods and wilderness that any true woodsman would understand. Pa understood it, and let us go.

"But you'd best not take Old King," he advised, and we didn't have to ask him why. Half spaniel, half "mongrolian," as old man Teeter called it, King was a curly black dog-of-all-work, as fine a watch dog, stock dog, and with snow to trail in, cat and lion dog as ever barked treed. But in one respect he was an unreconstructed rebel. No matter how often or how hard he was whipped, he *would* chase deer.

Our camp outfit was nothing to brag about, consisting only of such "third best" comforts and blankets as we could tie on in cumbersome rolls behind two saddles, with part of our grub inside of them, the rest slung in gunny sacks from the saddle horns. It seems to me now that Ma had fried us a chicken and spared us one loaf of bread. For the rest, the larder was "sowbelly," flour, salt, sugar, baking powder, coffee and maybe a few home-grown spuds and apples. Even without venison, we wouldn't starve unless we lost our frying pan.

Our destination was some Shangri-La of the high country —some place we had never been before, probably somewhere amid the big black timber and big gray burns of what we always called the "Main Range," in the vertical wrinkles of whose brow are born the Sapello, Beaver and Hollenger

Creeks. Beyond lower Beaver Creek, in those days, there was
no trail. Even today parts of it are tough for steepness. The
burns, which then were a maze of snaggy logs and poles, made
horseback passage almost impossible; today they are easy
going, most of their remains of ancient forest fires flattened
by rich brown rot and the trampling of cattle.

Crossing the open stretch of Lone Tree Mesa, we chanced
to look back. Some two hundred yards behind us, his brownish
black head carried low in the bunch grass, trotted Old King.
Somehow he had given the folks at home the slip. We called
him to us, whipped him and headed him homeward again.
We didn't really expect it to do much good, and it didn't.

Halfway down to Beaver Creek some deer crossed the trail
ahead of us and one or two of them stopped beyond a steep
draw in the fir timber. Being older, Marion was carrying our
one rifle. With more excitement than grace, I somehow managed to get my leg over the hump of bedding behind the saddle
and "fell off my horse."

"Gimme the gun!" I whispered. "I see 'im! He's got
horns!"

Firmly Marion held on to the gun. I can still see his grin.

"You got too much buck fever," he said in a low tone. "You
couldn't hit an elephant!"

"Gimme the gun!" I begged.

"Besides, it's just a little 'un. I saw him when they crossed
the trail."

"He's a big 'un! Gimme the gun!"

"Besides, what you want to shoot a deer this close home for?
I thought you was the one that wanted to hunt somewheres
way off!"

"Gimme the gun!"

"All right," Marion shrugged. "Suit yourself, but don't shoot
away all our cartridges!"

As he pulled the Winchester from the scabbard and handed
it to me, suddenly the timber came alive with deer as the whole
bunch whirled and sped high-bouncing back into the aspen to
recross the trail a hundred yards below us. The first to cross
were does. Feverishly I tried to be ready for the buck—but

wasn't. The sleek gray four pointer (I count both sides) leaped the lane of open trail in one jump and bounced away into the aspens. My hasty shot in his general direction missed. Marion claimed he saw it cut an aspen limb twenty feet over the buck's cream-puff rump. "You had the right direction," he grinned. "But just a mite high." Later I was glad I'd missed. Right then I was humiliated to think how wildly I'd wasted a cartridge. I was young then, and had not yet learned the rare art of timing the trigger to miss trees and hit a buck running through the timber. I'm older now—and still haven't. But now I don't often waste cartridges trying unless I am sure I can hit him—even if I don't.

What had spooked the deer back across the trail was no mystery. After running them a couple of hundred yards, Old King came skulking down to us as we watered our ponies in Beaver Creek. His curly tail was down as if he expected another whipping, but in his big brown eyes was a look of hope—which proved justified. We switched him perfunctorily for running deer, but since it was no use trying again to send him home, he recovered his good spirits in a hurry. Secretly I wasn't sorry to have him along. After a dogless experience Marion and I had once gone through with a midnight bear that wanted our camp worse than we did, it seemed to me that a four-legged barker might be handy to have around.

We hadn't aimed to hunt on the way, but twice King suddenly quit his place at our heels to put up deer and run them past us. It was a peculiar knack he had. Whether accidentally or purposely, about three times out of five whenever hot deer scent on the wind would tempt him beyond resistance, he somehow managed to run at least one deer within sight.

One that he bounced past us that day was a swelluva big buck. It was Marion who wasted the cartridge this time.

"Buck fever—and a mite high," I remarked.

"Like fun!" said Marion, and proved it by leading me to half a hat full of hair his bullet had shaved off. I sometimes wish I'd carried a sack all these years and saved all the deer hair I've seen thus bullet-barbered—without blood. I'd have enough to insulate a bomb-shelter.

As we zigzagged a back-up-and-try-it-again course through the logs of the Big Burn, the whimper and whine of wind in the naked snags still standing was a wild and eerie sound. With darkness coming on, we made camp in a motte of spruces beside an ice cold spring on the first bench shouldering off from the burn toward the head of Beaver Creek. It was an old sheep camp, long unused, and not only was the grass knee-high, but we enjoyed the novelty of building our inner spring mattress of spruce bows exactly where a big buck had bedded not so long since.

"What'll we do if he comes back for his bed?" I asked.

"We'll let him have it!" said Marion, but I don't think he meant the bed.

Dry salt pork rolled in flour and fried brown, Texas butter (flour and water gravy made with the grease), pan-fried batter bread, ash-roasted spuds and coffee, plus a proper woodsgoing appetite made our supper a feast. Ma's bread and fried chicken we saved for midday lunches to carry with us hunting.

As we undressed for bed (by removing our shoes), a white light flashed somewhere far out beyond the foothills north of Vegas that we surmised to be the headlight of a train; but the stars overhead looked closer. The weight of Old King snuggled on our feet was considerable, but the added warmth was welcome. Twice in the night we were wakened by his sudden spasms of bristle-necked barking as the challenge of bear or coyote scent drifted down wind to his alert nostrils; and once by the snort of a deer, puzzled by the mingled odors of our camp as he topped the black timbered brink a few yards away.

"That ol' buck lookin' for his bed," I surmised.

"Just a doggone doe," Marion grunted and went back to snoring.

Probably he was right. In the *odocoileus hemionis macrotis* family the female of the species is as snorty as the he. Anyhow the philosophy that any buck you can't get a chance at "is just a doggone doe" is a pretty good one to go by.

Over a pre-dawn breakfast we had an argument.

"If we leave King in camp," I said, "we're liable to run

onto fresh lion sign and wish we had him."

"If we take him with us," Marion warned, "you'll shoot up all our shells missin' the bucks he chases."

"Me and who else?"

"All right," he agreed, when I persisted. "Let's toss for it. I'll throw King a piece of bread. If he catches it, we'll take him. If he misses, we'll tie him up in camp."

Without waiting to consult the dog about it, Marion tossed a pellet of pancake up onto a sagging spruce branch about six feet from the ground, where it lodged. But the old dog's eyes never left it, and when a moment later I shook the limb to dislodge the morsel, his quick jaws didn't miss.

"He gets to go!" I crowed.

"Yeah—on a rope," was the head-man's ultimatum. "And you got to lead him!"

The trouble with that was that just as Marion was dropping to his belly to crawl up behind a log for a shooting view of a buck we'd glimpsed feeding in the timber's edge just out of the Burn, Old King's sudden notion to "go git 'im," caught me loose fingered, and away he went, leash and all. Maybe, if the rope hadn't caught on a snag, King would have jumped the buck out into the open where Marion could have Natty-Bumpoed him. As it was, not only that buck but two more with him showed us one bouncing flash of rump and antler and vanished deeper into the timber.

Marion—and I don't blame him—was mad.

"I've a notion to make you take your darn dog and go back to camp!" he growled, but didn't do it.

Bucks, tracks indicated, were fairly plentiful, but somehow things didn't break right for us to get the shot we needed. Cartridges were too scarce to risk banging away at mere flashes through the timber though we each wasted one that way. Also the range of the old .38/55, good gun though it was, canceled our chances at two bucks we spied trotting across the Burn some three hundred yards away. So the first day's hunt netted us no venison.

But it did produce a thrilling prospect. On a rock-boney ridge between the twin heads of Beaver Creek, we found lion sign fresh enough for Old King to enthuse over. But, though the black mongrel was a whiz on a lion trail with snow to trail in and had many winter lions to his credit, he was no sure-nosed hound, and his best, that day, was not good enough to find the lion.

Next day there was no question whether to take him or not. Deer hunting was not forgotten, but the bare prospect of getting a lion certainly made it secondary. Circling high around canyon heads, toward noon we picked up the lion sign again—and fresher. For half a mile King followed it well. But in a country pocked with burns where it is actually easier for a cat to walk on logs than on the ground, our one-dog equipment proved inadequate. It was nearing sundown when we gave it up somewhere west of the range on the head of some canyon whose name we did not even know, and headed for camp.

Not five minutes after we had started back campward, King suddenly quit us. As usual, in a jiffy we heard the *clump-clump* of several running deer and a six-point buck flashed by in the timber, apparently not entirely certain which way to run.

Though the country was new to us, we had taken careful notice of it, and now, without need for consultation, we both ran as hard as we could, quartering the course of the now vanished buck. Leaping logfalls to emerge at timber's edge, yonder we spied our buck, quartering a bowl-like cove at right angles to us about 100 yards away, only a few snags of dead timber between us.

The speed with which Marion got the gun up and shot was, to me, amazing. The suddenness with which he busted out cussing and handed me the rifle, even more so.

"Dammit, I can't hit anything" he snorted. "You try it!"

Still winded from our run and seriously doubtful of my ability to hit anything on the run anyhow, I raised the rifle—and, wonder of wonders, the buck stopped and shook his head, just as my sights found him. No time for buck fever or anything else but to pull the trigger and see the buck go down.

We were glad that King, chasing one of the other jumped

deer, had run into some more fresh lion sign to delay him, and thus arrived too late to associate the kill with his own bad habit. My bullet had been, through sheer luck, well placed through the shoulders. But there was also a trickle of blood on the buck's head where Marion's running shot had clipped through the gristle of one ear. That, of course, was what had made him stop to shake his head.

"Team work," Marion grinned. "I stop 'em, you kill 'em!"

The next day he hunted alone, while I took King and tried again to work out the lion track. If King should tree him, I was to circle all the high cove rims yelling my head off. If he heard me, Marion would rush the artillery. Old King, we knew would stay quite awhile with a lion. Our plans proved over-optimistic. I not only lost the lion trail, but for a bad half hour, myself. Not really lost, perhaps, since I knew I was west of the Main Range and by crossing it could locate the far off familiar landmark of Hermit's Peak to go by. But anyhow I was glad to hear the shot around toward the head of the Hollenger which netted Marion a fine ten-pointer and me a guide back to camp.

It was a long old drag in home the next day, with a scolding probably waiting for us for overstaying our allotted time. But the parental reproof didn't materialize. I think Pa was as tickled over our two fat bucks as we were—and he would have been just the same even if they hadn't saved him the necessity of cutting into a beef he had butchered to market when he took us into Las Vegas the next day, two fuzzy-necked nimrods in search of an education.

COW PASTURE POLO
By Peter Hurd

PETER HURD is the internationally famous landscape artist. He was born in Roswell and educated at New Mexico Military Institute, West Point, Haverford College and Pennsylvania Academy of Fine Arts and also studied art under N. C. Wyeth, the famous painter. His paintings hang in many museums and public and private collections. Polo is his favorite sport and he writes entertainingly about polo as played at his home ranch in San Patricio, New Mexico.

Ask the average easterner what polo is, and the chances are he will tell you it is a strange and little-known sport conducted on horses by rich playboys. In the Southwest, in New Mexico and the adjoining states, we know that this description doesn't apply. For here, with nary a rich playboy to act as angel for a team, it has withstood the attrition of two wars and worst blow of all, the abolishment of horse cavalry and artillery. There is even strong evidence that it is again increasing across America, and with the growing interest in horses and horsemanship may return to pre-war popularity. Absent, of course, will be the military with its martial show and the panoply of smartly trained troops. We who remember those days will always think of them with nostalgic regret.

In this article I am referring only to traditional polo brought from India nearly a century ago: a game generally recognized to be without peer among all competitive sports. Recently a game called Palmetto Polo has been invented, which beyond the fact that it is played with a ball by horsemen, has no relation to real polo: in fact, to me it appears to relate more to girl's basketball, and the word polo seems to be a misnomer.

Polo very possibly is the oldest of all games played with a stick and ball, and its origins are lost in legend. Certainly it had its birth in the Far East but just where or when no one knows for sure. Many centuries ago the game was played in China and in Tibet where the word for ball is *Pulu* and is cognate with the Chinese word for willow from which some polo balls are still made. In Persia the game is called *chagun* which means mallet and it was there in the 17th Century that it became the game of princes. Fascinating Persian paintings of the game exist from this period and much symbolism is artfully employed by the painters who show the field of play dappled with flowers to denote the spots where the Shah's ponies stepped. Musicians earnestly playing their instruments often hover in the background, for it was considered that only through the symbol of music could the artist convey the exultation of the game.

Space here will not, of course, allow the full tracing of polo from the Orient to America. But in brief, it came from India to England via the British army in 1868. From there it was soon brought to America where sportsmen enthusiastically took it up and practically at once altered the rules so as to speed up the game. Horses were no longer limited in size and hitting was permitted from the left side instead of only the right as previously. The game was soon being played on Thoroughbred or part-Thoroughbred horses at a wide-open gallop, and became one in which quick-decision tactics and split-second timing are essential.

The rules of polo today are few and simple and consist for the most part of a set of traffic rules aimed at fair play and safety. In outdoor polo on a standard field of 300 x 200 yards four players are aligned on each side and play six periods of 7½ minutes each. These periods are called chukkers, and mounts are changed at the end of each one with a 10-minute rest at the half. In indoor polo and the newer "indoor-outdoor" or arena polo, essentially the same rules apply and the principal difference is that two teams of three instead of four players compete on a considerably smaller field.

Arena polo, while surrendering none of the excitement and physical competitiveness of outdoor polo has the spectator advantage of being more easily visible from the side lines. The player advantage is that being on a smaller field one can get by with fewer horses per player. Problems of transporting horses of course are also proportionately reduced.

We at San Patricio are amused at the rich playboy definition. Polo here actually began one day in 1935 when a young captain of cavalry paid a visit to our ranch. He was returning to New Mexico Military Institute from a polo match at Fort Bliss and our conversation on that afternoon turned to polo as we sipped long tequila drinks. From the patio where we sat we could see the four wiry little saddle horses that had come with my newly acquired ranch. Suddenly the captain asked, "Why don't you guys up here start playing cow pasture polo?"

Staying here with me at the time were the late Eric Knight and a horse-minded youngster from the East known as Chico. Eric had been drudging as a writer in a movie studio and had fled Hollywood to be with me a couple of months and help get the ranch operation started. It was Knight who jumped up and said, "Why not? Pete has one of the few flat pieces of uncultivated land in the whole valley!" Within minutes we drove to the spot Eric had spoken of, a nearly flat though gently rolling piece of land 700 by 400 feet.

Centuries ago a pre-Columbian village had stood there and shards of pottery and occasional stone implements still littered its grassy surface. There was some cactus—tall cholla and prickly pear—and reasoning that these might prove detrimental to our game we yanked them out with a log chain tied to the rear of a pickup. Then Chico and the captain penned the ponies and saddled them while Eric and I hauled four bales of hay up to the field for goal posts. Using the captain's mallets and some old polo balls he had in his car we entered into an impromptu scrimmage. The captain taught us rules and coached us as we played. Even that little taste of the game was tremendously exciting; the polo virus had definitely been planted and fever was building up!

We were all for more of this wonderful sport and though the captain had cited the similarity between our set up and that of other ranch teams he had failed to mention one difference: that was the important missing ingredient—money. We were all broke. Eric Knight and I were living somewhat precariously from writing and painting, respectively, and the amiable Chico had a year of freedom with a small monthly allotment from his parents prior to entering college. These were the dark days of the Depression and though money was scarce there was no stopping us now. We shamelessly scrounged used polo balls after games at NMMI. When soaked overnight in water, dried and repainted these did very well. Mallets were a little harder to get. In those days a new Meurisse mallet cost $3.50 or about a day's cost of living for the three of us. But we learned of a janitor at the Military Institute who had a hoard of 23 used sticks—collected, he said, from cadets' quarters after they left for vacation. A pint of whiskey was discreetly shown him and the sticks were at once ours. This gifted janitor proved a ready source of mallets for several years and prudently we never inquired into the matter of his apparently endless supply. After our initial barter deal, price was set at 25¢ for a mallet with a fair head: for one with a good head, 50¢.

Although short on cash we were long on enthusiasm and practiced daily in the cool late afternoons of summer in the mountain country. On weekends we had games with neighboring horsemen who sometimes rode in to see what was causing the dust cloud on the flat above the ranch house. We all had helmets, for on a trip to New York I had bought out (for a dollar apiece) a collection of these in off sizes which I found gathering dust on the shelves of a saddle shop. Mostly small and all of the East Indian tropical topee type and bearing the trade mark of an elegant British firm, they were a perfect fit for the skulls of our more Indian players. We learned to mend the malacca canes when broken, with string and glue. Chico, an able craftsman, experimented with local varieties of wood to replace broken mallet heads. After quickly shattering a number of his new heads, each beautifully carved of pear, apple or live oak, we found that the seasoned wood of the native soapberry tree—*Sapindus Drummondi*—was excellent, its tough interlacing fibers withstood the double attrition of balls and a stony field. For pony boots we used pieces of sheepskin to which we fastened billets. Saddles were a hodge-podge of ancient stock saddles, a couple of fox hunting ones, and a steeple chaser; patched, re-patched, riveted and in places wired together.

The ponies we used in those days were literally ponies in that they were seldom over 14 hands, two inches in height. They were tough and compact like the cow ponies in drawings by Will James. Once I made a swap for a pony named Pecos, a short-coupled sorrel with neat legs and good head. After the bill of sale had been executed the former owner looked musingly at my new possession: "You know," he said, "that's bound to be a hell of a good pony. Look at the number of brands he's got arned out. Ever' time they arned a brand it means somebody stole him."

Once in those early days at San Patricio word came that Eric Knight had sold the publication rights in Denmark for one of his books. A check for thirty-five dollars was enclosed in the letter from his agent and when Knight disappeared for a few hours we all knew where he had gone. On a neighboring ranch there was a trim little sorrel filly whose owner wanted just $35 for her. As we anticipated, when Eric returned he was leading the filly. Her name, he said, would be "Danish Rights." The name didn't stick, probably because the *Mexicanitos* who made up the majority of our team found it difficult and unintelligible. Instead they called her "La Bamba" for her saucy, dancing trot, like the Mexican dance of that name.

In that time there lived not far from us a family named Herrera. There were five brothers, four of them in their twenties. All were enthusiastic and dedicated horsemen. They worked variously as cow hands and horse-breakers and were always flamboyantly conspicuous performers at local rodeos and *fiestas*. The oldest of the brothers was José, nicknamed *Pino* for a Navajo grandfather. Like myself he was just past thirty years old. Next was Antonio, called *El Gordo,* then Manuelito, and after him Aristeo, called *El Cadillo* for his ability to cling like a cocklebur to the mane of a wild pitching *mesteño.* The youngest was Frutuoso known as *El Huero* for the habit he had of bleaching his black Indian hair to a startling yellow.

The Herreras were obviously perfectly endowed for our purpose and it wasn't long before they were all enthusiastic *polistas.* Anglo American cowboys from surrounding ranches also joined us but they were always less spectacular, had less showmanship than the Herreras. Occasionally cavalry officer friends dropped in to watch or even participate in our rustic sport. From one cavalryman came a widely circulated rumor about polo as played at San Patricio in those days. The ground rules according to the story were basic and four in number:

Rule 1. Number of players—no more than 15 on the field at one time.

Rule 2. Equipment—no guns or knives allowed. Carrying of catch ropes is frowned upon.

Rule 3. Unseemly menacing of an opponent—if a player should become unseated it is considered unsportsmanlike to club him while on the ground.

Rule 4. Boundaries—as formal lines on the field are nonexistent, when and if the ball goes out of Lincoln County a rider will be sent up to the top of Cerro Centinela to fire a gun and light a signal fire to rally the players to the ranch house for a round of tequila *copitas.*

The story obviously has no basis in fact as anyone should know, for Lincoln County stretches 100 miles in one direction and ninety in the other. Another fable is that we once applied to Washington to have the W.P.A. make a relief project of our polo team. This is untrue, but it is a fact that at one time three of the Herrera boys were full-time W.P.A. workers which limited our games to Saturdays and Sundays.

So it was that polo became an established institution at San Patricio and though no one had any money for new or fancy gear, there was no lack of willingness to match games with all comers. Our opponents were widely varied and consisted of teams from Roswell, El Paso, Ft. Bliss, and Juarez. When they played us we lent them mounts and as there were not enough to go around at two or three horses to the player, we would rest between chukkers. When we played on their fields our opponents provided the horses and we were assigned three each and allowed a 10 minute rest only at the half.

One time in the late '30s we were preparing for a big game: General Jaime Jesus Quiñones of the Mexican army was bringing a team from Juárez and we had arranged a barbecue. A publican friend in Roswell contributed beer for the occasion—64 cases of it—which I'm afraid resulted in a sort of equestrian bacchanalia. Local kids had been recruited with the promise of all the soda pop they could drink to pick the stones off the field. A roller made of poured concrete was dragged behind a pickup truck and, although the field after this bore little resemblance even to the usual polo field, it was, for us, like Meadowbrook. But on the Friday preceding the Sunday of the game, disaster threatened: two of the Herreras, including the star, and another played named Juan Baca came to me and sadly announced they were leaving for South Texas early the next day. A labor procurement agent had lured them with high wages to go and pick cotton. They departed ruefully, toasting our success in swigs of *tinto*.

Our place at San Patricio was little more than a camp in the '30s. The two old *adobe* houses on the property were barely habitable, so much of this time my wife and children were in Pennsylvania. With the polo infection racing in my veins, I found myself selecting my cook always with less interest in his cooking than in whether or not he could ride like hell and was willing to risk his neck on our polo field. Spills were commonplace and there were occasionally broken bones, but nothing worse.

As time went along and our team became locally known, polo-playing friends would make us presents of gear they no longer needed. In this way we collected a big assortment of mallets, balls, helmets, bridles, polo boots, riding breeches, six horses, four saddles and one pair of magnificent Peel boots, made in London. These boots we all tried on but we finally had to agree that they fit Pino best. They became his. One day, soon after this transaction, we played a game in Roswell. Following the game, the cavalry colonel who had been our referee invited the players to his quarters for drinks. I had noted our host, a newcomer in Roswell, earnestly conversing with Pino in border Spanish. Later he came up to one of our other players and asked:

"Don José, that is Señor Pino—is he a big rancher?"

"No sir, I don't think so."

"Has he some mining interests in Lincoln County?"

"No, sir."

"Just what does he do?"

"Ever since I've known him, he's been working as a hand on Pete Hurd's ranch. Why?"

"Well," said the colonel, "if that isn't a pair of Peel boots he's got on I'll eat a bale of barley hay!"

One day in 1941 my old and close friend, Paul Horgan, then an officer at NMMI, sent me word that the father of a cadet wanted to give his son a Thoroughbred polo mare. Moreover, the father had asked that I select her. Touched by this confidence in me, I spent a day at the stud farm in Roswell, inspecting all eligible mares. When, at last, I had made my choice, Paul asked:

"Are you sure this is the one?"

"Yes."

"Then load her in your pickup. She's *yours*—a present from Eric Knight, who's just sold his novel, *This Above All* to the movies."

The mare I had selected was 5-year-old Cherry Stick by Fervor out of Cherry Blaze—a beautifully-made registered Thoroughbred with a fine disposition and an abundance of purple blood from the Eclipse line through her grandfather, Broomstick. With this generous gift of Eric's our horses began to improve, and her sons and daughters and even grandsons and granddaughters are now playing polo, while she, in queenly middle age, enjoys a life of leisure in our pasture.

With better horses, our game began to improve and, although we still play on the same field without benefit of sideboards and the game is still sometimes halted while the ball is retrieved from an *arroyo*, our game is now orthodox.

When I came from the war I was delighted to find that a new and enthusiastically horsey family had bought the property adjoining us on the north. They were Mr. & Mrs. Tom Babers and their young son, Bill. Tom who, like me, was born in New Mexico and in the same year, had cowboyed and rodeoed many years for a living. He was immediately a pushover for polo and, like many another I have taught, was soon outplaying me. When his son Bill was 14 we put him on old Pecos with a 48-inch mallet and it wasn't many months until he was playing regularly. In 1948 Bill entered NMMI—becoming the only cadet ever to make the first team his first year. After graduating and following his service with the Army, Bill was appointed polo coach at NMMI. That year his team won the Intercollegiate Indoor Polo Championship in New York by defeating Yale and Cornell.

The war years marked a change in polo at San Patricio. For one thing, we lost three fine friends and hard-riding players in Sergeant Burciaga, Lieutenant Jenkins and Major Eric Knight —all killed in action. Eric's spurs and mallet we have hung over our tack room door. It is he, I keep thinking, who should be writing this story—he with his humor and his feeling for the extravagant and fantastic in life. This plus the fact that he was himself a participant in much of it.

Of those of us who began polo at San Patricio, only Pino and I are still playing. Pino, who has been my foreman for 22 years, has eleven children, all but one of them born on the ranch. One son, Félix now married and working on our ranch is a regular player and has the same dashing horsemanship as his father and uncles. My younger son Michael, now sixteen, is at an eastern Prep school but summer afternoons see him smacking polo balls along with the rest of us. Pino's younger sons and their cousins are the "hot walkers" whose duty is to keep the sweating ponies walking between chukkers and after the game until cooled. A principal activity of theirs is playing furious games of foot polo with sawed off mallets. Judging from this there seems to be no want of enthusiasm in the junior (and certainly not in the senior) division. So one can assume polo is due to continue here for some time more.

As Tom Babers says: "Anyone who comes along with the idea of getting up a little polo game will find us ready, willing and waiting. Pete and Pino and Bill and I have played success-ful polo in every kind of weather there is here except one. One day a hailstorm came up while we were playing; hailstones big as polo balls commenced falling and we couldn't tell which was which. Had to give up and go to the house!"

ROADSIDE GEOLOGY
E. R. Harrington

E. R. HARRINGTON lives in Albuquerque and has been a school teacher, principal, school superintendent and is presently Director of Secondary Education in the Albuquerque Public Schools. He has written more than 250 magazine articles and five textbooks. In addition he holds a card as a journeyman machinist which is kept up to date so he can fall back on this source of revenue whenever he wishes to do so. He has found it useful in paying his way through frequent summer school courses and to date he has formal college credits in excess of 600 semester hours, with degrees in civil engineering, geology, secondary education, and a Ph.D. in physical chemistry.

The mountain men who once made history in New Mexico were expert observers because their lives depended upon it. They read stories in tracks and broken twigs, and they retained their hair because they could read signs that others could not. The mountain men are gone, and we now ride safely across the State; but there are still "signs" along the roads which very few people read. The geologist is the modern mountain man who reads these stories in stone, and if you had ever taken a trip with Nevin Fenneman, Stuart Northrop, or the late R. W. Ellis, you too would become one of these modern scouts. Under the hands of these masters the country lives and takes on a new beauty while a history of a billion years unfolds before you! New Mexico is the natural setting for such a vision. It is a wonderful laboratory for the geologist. Here we have rocks from the oldest clear down to the youngest. We have beautiful displays of folding, faulting, volcanic activity, erosion by frost, water, wind, and ice. Geological formations are not obscured with vegetation, and our climate is such that field trips may be taken almost any day in the year.

The geologic factor has determined the course of our State, and all other states for that matter. It determines where we shall live and by what means. It determines our food, our culture, our recreation, and perhaps even our politics. A study of our culture without some little knowledge of geology is like taking a trip through ancient Rome without a knowledge of history.

One need not be an expert geologist to travel profitably across New Mexico. The amateur may make the study a hobby and it will pay dividends in satisfaction as he travels across the country. A few interesting and comparatively simple books on the subject will give him some insight into the problems of rock formation, erosion, mountain building, volcanic activity, faulting, the different kinds of rocks, and the formation of minerals and ores. We might even list a few observations of such an amateur as he journeys across New Mexico on two of our transcontinental highways.

Before making an entry into our State it will be well to set the geologic clock back approximately one billion years into what is known as the pre-Cambrian Era. It is a time before the rise of well-developed life forms. Most of the rocks are volcanic, like the common granite, made up chiefly of the two minerals, quartz and feldspar. Most of New Mexico is dry land being dissected by streams very much as it is today. The quartz crystals in the granites are being broken down into sand while the feldspar crystals are forming clay. The central part of the United States is a great sea encroaching on our borders. Our rivers are washing gravels, sands, and muds into this sea and depositing them in layers according to their weights—the heavier gravels being next to the shore. The Paleozoic or "Old Life" Era has begun and will continue for half a billion years. During that time the gravel beds will be consolidated into conglomerates; sand layers will form sandstones when cemented by iron oxide, and the layers of clay and silt will form shales.

Lower forms of life will flourish in the Paleozoic seas and by evolutionary process the life forms will become progressively higher until finally the amphibian will forsake the sea to take up his home upon the land. Land plants will flourish in the generally warm climate of the Paleozoic time until in the latter part of the Era vegetation becomes so luxuriant that huge swamp deposits are formed, later to be covered by sands or muds and compacted into great beds of coal. A half billion years of time will take in various fluctuations of the inland sea covering the United States to the east. The sea encroaches on our eastern boundaries and by the middle of the Era has completely covered our State. The dry land is to the south and west, chiefly, and in our shallow sea great deposits of limestone are being built up from the shells of billions of shellfish. Finally even the Zuñi Mountain section of our State is submerged and sediments deposited over the top of the old granite core that for so many years raised its head from the sea. The Paleozoic Era comes to a close with a general retreat of the seas in our area. The uplift of the great western block is accompanied by a severe change of climate marked by aridity and a fall in temperature. Many life types, both on land and sea, pass out of existence. Shallow arms of the sea are cut off and dry up, the soluble materials in the water are precipitating and forming deposits of gypsum, salt, and potash.

The Paleozoic Era closes with what is known as the Appalachian Revolution. Some of the beds deposited beneath the sea are raised and folded. In some cases the strain of the folding is enough to break the layers and push one side up above the other forming what is known as a fault. The Appalachian Mountains start their formation and we have a further rise of the Ozarks.

Most of New Mexico is still beneath the sea but land has risen to the north and east. We have entered the Mesozoic or "middle-life" Era which will continue for some two hundred million years. During that time we will have a renewal of evolution in plants and animals. In isolated, shallow basins vegetation will be deposited to form our State's great coal fields. Land life will flourish and be dominated by reptiles whose size has never been equaled. These reptiles lived in the sea, in fresh water, and on the land, while some even could fly. Again the generally mild climate changes. The great dinosaurs unable to change to meet it become extinct, and the early mammals are left as the rulers of the earth. Again a great mountain building time, called the Laramide Revolution, is at hand and the Cenozoic, or "recent-life" Era has begun.

New Mexico is now mostly land. The Paleozoic and Mesozoic sediments have been upturned and are being eroded— their debris being deposited as sediments in many lake beds. This is the era of the mammals during which time we had large ground sloths, sabre-tooth tigers, mastodons, camels, horses, and other animals that became extinct at the close of the Era as far as America was concerned. Many other types of life survived the changes that brought on the Ice Age, possibly a million years ago. During that time an ice sheet starting in Canada moved south upon the United States as far south as the Ohio River. New Mexico was not reached by this ice sheet, but Mount Wheeler, Truchas Peak, and other mountain heights maintained such snowfields that their glaciers moved far down into the valleys gouging them out as they went. It is during this period of glaciation that man makes his first appearance and we have a beginning of history written in artifacts, pottery, pictures.

With such a sketchy history as a background let us enter New Mexico from the west on U. S. 66. We pass along a fine display of massive sandstone reaching from under the Painted Desert over to the Rio Puerco. The sandstone layers are horizontal, or nearly so except near Gallup where we note some of the upper layers dipping steeply to the west. Here the sediments have been broken, or faulted, and the west side raised above the east and almost set vertically. This is the "hogback" which marks the eastern side of the Gallup coal basin. South of Manuelito we note further evidences of faulting in the sandstone.

East of Gallup the horizontal sandstone, known as the Wingate Sandstone, has been carved by erosion into huge bastions, sharp spires, and fantastic castles. These great sandstone layers were being deposited grain at a time beneath the sea two hundred million years ago while dinosaurs were playing on the sea beach up in what is now southern Wyoming. To the south we see the Zuñi uplift and judge that these sandstone layers once extended clear over it. Now the top beds have been eroded away and we see the old granite core in the center with the sediments dipping away from it in all directions. This Wingate Sandstone, and a closely related upper member known as the Navajo Sandstone extend far to the east and south and make up such landmarks as Acoma and El Morro.

We pass close along the south side of Mount Taylor, an old volcano that built itself up on top of the horizontal sedimentary beds. At one time this volcano extended its lava beds as far east as the Rio Puerco and as far west as Grants. As we ride along we can see a fine section showing the softer sediments capped with the more resistant black lava (basalt). Here again crustal movements can be noticed on the north side where two sedimentary beds fail to meet properly. We see that some strain has been put upon the formerly continuous bed and it has broken, and one side has been lifted up above the other; a typical normal fault. Farther on near Laguna we find examples of differential erosion; sandstone *mesas,* some with lava cap rocks. Some of the fantastic forms are due to erosion by running water. Others are due to the sand-blast action of wind, heavily laden with abrasive sand grains. A long lava flow has filled the San José River channel and we cross it several times.

We cross the Rio Puerco valley noting various remnants of the harder sedimentary rock. In some places the sand stones have been cemented together with more iron oxide than at other places. These sandstones have been better able to resist erosion of wind and water and have "weathered out" as ironstone concretions. Some of these concretions several feet in diameter are seen just west of the river bridge. We cross the narrow divide between the Rio Grande and the Rio Puerco, suspecting that we are crossing a fault line. We look down into the great alluvum-filled Rio Grande Valley and see the Sandia-Manzano fault rising as a back drop to the east.

Across the Sandia Mountains we go, making a perfect section through Tijeras Canyon. A huge mountain block has been raised across our path. The fault block has been raised at least two miles. The limestone cap rock, now ten thousand feet above sea level, was laid down in the ocean during the Carboniferous period, during which the coal beds of Pennsylvania were formed. The mountain's granite core shows fine examples of erosion by water, wind, and frost. The limestone cap-rock, and other sediments resting on the limestone dip steeply to the east, flattening more and more until they are again practically horizontal under Estancia Valley. Tijeras Canyon cuts clear across the uplift from east to west showing that this creek had the same position before the great uplift started. It is evident that the uplift and faulting was a slow process as the stream was never turned from its path, showing that its rate of down-cutting was as great as the rate of mountain rise across its course.

Going on to the east we note that the sedimentary rocks have flattened out and are practically horizontal once again. We note the presence of shallow sink holes as we near Santa Rosa. During the latter part of the Paleozoic Era we remember that considerable gypsum and salt were formed by cutting off some shallow seas. These materials are somewhat soluble in water. As these beds have been dissolved out by the ground water, great caves have been formed and the overlying sandstones and shales have collapsed forming these sinks. We note that near Santa Rosa there are some "bottomless" lakes occupying similar and larger sink holes. We note also that fish planted in one of these lakes soon show up in adjacent lakes so we suspect underground connections formed by caverns which have not collapsed as yet.

We cross the Pecos River at Santa Rosa and continue on east, noting as we go that we are getting farther and farther beneath the sandstone cap-rocks over which we rode in Estancia Valley. Erosion has left various remnants of the capping in such localities as Tucumcari Mountain. We find that the cap rock here is the Dakota Sandstone, laid down in the sea some one hundred million years ago, during which time most of the State's coal was being formed into the coal basins near Gallup, Cerrillos, and Raton. Farther on to the east near the Texas line we see that we have reached the plain and that remnants of the once overlying beds are now fewer and fewer. We suspect that there are similar underlying sediments dipping gently off to the east and we prove this to our satisfaction in the few outcrops we see before we get to Amarillo.

Now let us suppose we are re-entering the State from the north and are taking U. S. 85 across the State. South of Trinidad, Colorado, we find ourselves in a country of horizontal sedimentary beds against which the Rocky Mountain core rises to the west. Going south we note a black shale. Evidently the mud originally deposited here must have contained a large amount of organic matter to give this rock such a pronounced color. Soon after, this presence of organic matter is proved when we enter the coal mining country at Morley. Over Raton Pass now! What a view for anyone, specially a geologist. From the top we see the horizontal sediments stretching on the south. And in some places the horizontal layers are capped with black lava (basalt) like that we crossed at Grants. We see more black shale as we go down the Pass and again we note some evidences of faulting in certain continuous beds, now distorted. We cross some coal seams in our last pitch down into the town of Raton.

On to the south we go, noting the sedimentary rocks capped with lava. Some of the cones are beautifully symmetrical with black *mal pais* capes around their bases. The *arroyos* have cut down into a black shale again, and we keep noting this as far south as Las Vegas where some of it has been used in making brick. At Colmor the lava-capped sediments close in on us and we readily see what protection the hard caps have been to the underlying rocks. We note some lava plugs, one of which is the famous "Wagon Mound." As we go south of Wagon Mound the lava capped buttes become scarcer and farther away and we are soon riding over a level plain which we suspect is resting upon horizontal sedimentary rock.

We find this is the case as we cross the Mora River at Watrous and note the outcrops through which the river has cut. We near Las Vegas with the mountains crowding in on us from the west. Just south of Las Vegas we note that the sedimentary rocks are dipping rather steeply to the east and in the next few miles we cross the great Sangre de Cristo anticlinal arch and cut through a series of sediments dipping to the west. Farther on we skirt the northern escarpment of Glorieta *Mesa*. Here horizontal sediments have been cut through to a depth of more than a thousand feet, in some places leaving such remnants as Starvation Peak. The Pecos River cuts through the northern end of Glorieta *Mesa* and here we see what geology has to do with the location of a river valley and what effect this has had upon the location of a railroad and a highway and also why it was that soldiers should choose this place to make a stand.

We hit granite again a few miles east of Santa Fé and follow this through the town until shortly afterwards we are again out over sandstones and shales. Half way between Santa Fé and Albuquerque we drop down two thousand feet across lava capped sediments, cross-bedded sandstones, shales, gravels, and a layer of volcanic ash. Down through the Rio Grande Valley we go, noting the lava-capped *mesas* to the west of the river. Near Algodones we see an almost perfect volcanic plug which has been bisected by the river. Near Bernalillo we pick up the giant Sandia-Manzano Fault. We follow along this escarpment for almost a hundred miles or until it ends in a fantastic and extravagant display of cross faulting east of the river near Socorro.

From Lemitar south to San Antonio our attention is divided between the faulted area east of the river and the faulted sediments with their volcanic cappings which make up the steep mountains to the west. The valley widens below San Antonio and we ride along a gravel bench until we get to Elephant Butte where the river makes a good section cutting across the north end of the Caballo Mountains. From here south to Rincon we fellow the fault escarpment which resembles, in some particulars, the Sandia-Manzano escarpment to the north.

Near old Fort Selden we cut across the rhyolite ridge and come in sight of the great porphyry spires that rise in jagged magnificence east of Las Cruces. On down the river we go until the Franklin Mountain block rises near Anthony. We follow this mountain block until the river valley narrows near El Paso.

Some of the above remarks are observations made only on Highways 66 and 85, our two transcontinental roads. No mention has been made of other sections of New Mexico which can be reached by other good roads: the mining districts of Silver City, Santa Rita, Hillsboro, and Mogollon; the rhyolite section from Datil to Silver City, the volcanic section on U. S. 380 near Carrizozo.

In the Tularosa Valley we have one of the world's grandest displays of block faulting with the San Andres and Sacramento blocks on each side and the valley floor making a "graben" between. Not even Death Valley can compare with it in geologic magnificence! In the western part of the State we have the Zuñi Uplift, the Mount Taylor lava country, and to the north the eruptive section of Jemez and Valle Grande. The sedimentary section between Abiquiu and El Vado would delight any geologist, amateur or professional, and one scarcely needs mention Ute Park, Elizabethtown, or the Red River country.

We have not touched on the unusual geological phenomena of Bandelier National Monument, the White Sands, Carlsbad Caverns, Shiprock, Bottomless Lakes, Playa Lake, Chaco Canyon, the Ice Caves, Capulin Mountain, and other localities. Everyone enjoys seeing these places, whether he knows anything about their geology or not, and to a person with even a slight knowledge of the subject, they bring added joy. In New Mexico we can see more geology in a trip of fifty miles than the citizens of most states can see in a trip of a thousand miles. By becoming "roadside geologists" we learn to appreciate our state.

ART & ARCHITECTURE

ART IN NEW MEXICO
Ina Sizer Cassidy

INA SIZER CASSIDY has been contributing to *New Mexico Magazine* for over 30 years. An authority on art subjects, she has been interested in art not only as a spectator but also as an artist; for she has worked in ceramics, hand crafts, water colors and oil. She served as chairman of the Old Santa Fe Association from 1946 to 1956, when she became honorary chairman and a member of the Board of Directors. She is a member of the New Mexico Women's Press Club and the National Women's Press Club, and year after year was the recipient of awards for her art columns in *New Mexico Magazine*. In 1956 she was named the outstanding woman writer of New Mexico and given the annual Zia Award by the New Mexico Women's Press Association.

It is generally thought that the beginning of New Mexico as an art center dates from the settlement in Taos of the Taos group in 1898, but this is a mistake. The beginning really dates back to the early Spanish colonization, as is shown in old wills among the archives in which are listed paintings and sculptures. These were, of course, religious works of art, for in the sixteenth and seventeenth centuries art was the handmaiden of religion. It naturally follows that where the church led art followed.

The colonization of New Spain, which included New Mexico, being as much a work of the church as of state, art was brought along for adornment of churches as well as of homes. No mission church was complete without its painted and carved reredos, and its stations of the cross, its crucifix and its saints. These were all a part of the things necessary for establishment of a church. So we have here in the state very old paintings of the Spanish and Italian schools, some in private collections and some still in the churches. The "St. Joseph" of Acoma Church is one of the best known, perhaps because of the unique lawsuit over its possession instituted by the Acoma pueblo against Laguna pueblo in 1858. Another old master is claimed by the church at Isleta, while San Miguel possesses a canvas claimed to be from the brush of Cimabue. There are others also in other churches besides those in the hands of private collectors. These, so far as known, have never been authenticated. But that they are old and of the quality of the period there is no doubt. New Mexico would be a rich and interesting field for the art expert.

Old records tell of visits of itinerant wood carvers who came up into New Mexico from Mexico City to carve *bultos,* others who came to paint *santos* for church and home. In those early days every home of importance had its chapel in which was to be found sacred paintings and *bultos* about its altar, and every home, no matter how humble, had its own patron saint. It is not unusual to find in a remote pueblo room, or in an isolated sheep herder's hut, a valuable old *bulto* or a *santo* in the mellowed colors age alone gives. Many have already passed into the hands of collectors who, knowing their real value as art objects, have used the ruse of ridicule to induce the owner to part with them in exchange for a glaringly new papiermaché or gaudily painted plaster image of the household saint.

In the will of Joseph Garcia, a tailor of Santa Fe, dated March 9, 1754, are listed three pictures, "one of the crucified Lord, one of Ecco Homo and one of our Lord in the Wilderness." Another in Santa Fe, that of José Antonio Griego, "soldier of the garrison," declares he leaves "nine house images to be divided between his 15 children." How the division was made has not been discovered.

The will of Miguel Lucero, resident of Tomé, dated January 20, 1766, lists "one wooden statute of St. Joseph having two reliquaries as ornaments, appraised and valued at 30 *pesos;* two oil paintings *on linen* appraised at 12 *pesos;* one small wooden statue of Christ appraised at four *pesos.*" The will of Monte Vigil, of Taos, dated Oct. 13, 1780, lists "24 pictures on canvas at two *pesos* each," together with "two Canton mirrors." The first mention of pictures in glass is in the will of Francisco Antonio Torres, retired soldier of Santa Fe, in which he lists five pictures, "including one of Maestro Señor Esquipolo in glass."

If all the old Spanish wills could be examined there is no doubt that many more works of art could be listed.

But the really outstanding work of art and one whose history is recorded beyond any doubt is the stone carved reredos of the old Military chapel, the Castrense in Santa Fe dedicated in the spring of 1761, now housed in El Cristo Rey Church in Santa Fe.

Art critics say that this reredos is "the most extraordinary piece of ecclesiastical art that has been preserved within the boundaries of the United States from Spanish Colonial times .... Captivating in its quiet and serene beauty and fascinating through its intricate but harmonious blending of Spanish and Indian motives of decorations."

Carved as it was by pious Spanish and Indian hands in the best period of Spanish-Mexican baroque style this carved stone reredos is said to be a "unique expression of the amalgamation of the two cultures" and Santa Fe, as well as all of New Mexico is most fortunate in possessing it.

The reredos, entirely of stone, stands thirty-nine feet high and eighteen feet wide, carved from native New Mexico white stone, and tinted in beautiful old fresco colors. All its sections are intact except the original panel containing the relief of our Lady of Light, *(Nuestra Señora de la Luz)*, which for some reason was replaced by a wooden panel of San Juan Capistrano, although the Lady of Light is not lost, as it was preserved also.

The reredos was the gift to the Military Chapel by the then Governor, Francisco Antonio Marín del Valle and his wife, Doña Maria Martinez de Ugarte. Bishop Pedro Tamaron of Durango, in his journal of 1760 tells of his visit to Santa Fe and of the Castrense and its beautiful reredos. The Castrense is said to have been the second church in Santa Fe, the first having been located in the now destroyed southeast tower of the old Palace.

If this ancient reredos were found in Europe modern experts say that its frame-work would be credited to the 16th century, but if in Mexico it would be the 17th century. Made in Santa Fé in the 18th century, it is the style of the previous centuries. The carving has been compared to that of the Cathedral of Zacetas, and as it is known that Del Valle visited Zacetas in 1759-60 it is reasonable to suppose that he brought back with him stone carvers from there to carve his reredos. One of the interesting things about this old reredos is that it is made from native New Mexico stone, a "vein of white stone" having been discovered within 80 leagues of the capitol, as is recorded in one of the old documents.

The Castrense was abandoned as time went on, and when Bishop Lamy came he found it was being used as a court room by the United States courts and at once sought its return to its proper owners, the Church. This he accomplished, and moved the reredos to a place in the new church—the present Cathedral—where it was placed in one of the chapels.

(In 1940, it was moved to the new El Cristo Rey Church.)

What state in the Union is more actively art conscious than our own New Mexico? With the State Art Museum leading in point of age, with its comprehensive Annual *Fiesta* exhibit held each summer, the State Fair Fine Arts Exhibit, displaying paintings and sculpture from New Mexico's leading artists, and the rotating exhibits of the Art Museum, New Mexico is definitely art conscious.

What other state as a part of its service to the people is as art conscious and doing as much for its art and artists—with the exception of the purchase of works of art for its public buildings and parks, as many of our states have done? New Mexico is rich in undeveloped resources but short on revenue as compared with other states, so it is not able to do as the French Government, for instance, used to do—buy art for its museums, public buildings and parks. These, after purchase, were collected in the Luxemburg Gallery and from there sent out on exhibition to the branch museums throughout the nation. The art works could not, however, be retained permanently but had to be sent back to the Luxemburg, at Paris. But it did give the more remote towns an opportunity to enjoy the nation's art.

Our State Museum is in a manner, doing the same thing for our people with this difference: The State does not own the paintings exhibited, but arranges one-man shows of our leading artists and gives the local art lovers and patrons an opportunity to see, to enjoy, and in many cases to purchase for their own collections any of the paintings exhibited. It gives the people the opportunity also to see, before they are shown anywhere else, paintings which later capture coveted prizes in National shows.

With nationally recognized names our New Mexico artists cannot be termed local or provincial. And behind this wealth of creative talent there banks our own great contributions to American art, the art of the Indian painters whose work has met with praise wherever exhibited. With all this why should not our State be art conscious?

THE MIRACULOUS STAIRCASE
C. Chavez Lowe

C. CHAVEZ LOWE is a native New Mexican of Spanish descent. Her grand-parents owned the San Joaquin Rancho near Socorro, which was famous in its time for its hospitality and for the staircase, which was patterned from one in the old Socorro County Courthouse, razed many years ago. For a number of years she has collected little stories about pioneer days in New Mexico and is doing a book that will incorporate some of this material.

Growing in interest as a mecca for visitors to Santa Fe is the "Miraculous Staircase" in the chapel of Our Lady of Light, the chapel of the Loretto Nuns in Santa Fe.

The legend is, that after the structure was completed in 1878 it was found that the stairs to the high choir loft had not been built. The funds for the building had long been over-drawn, and the height to the choir loft made it necessary to give more space to the staircase than could be spared. The architect who had designed the Chapel was the same who had come from France at the request of Bishop Lamy to design and build his beloved Cathedral. The architect was also an expert stone mason and had become 'stone blind' while building the Cathedral.

The Nuns despaired of their beautiful chapel being finished. They offered prayers and novenas and implored the aid of "Our Lady of Light" the Patron Saint of the chapel.

One morning an old man with a long white beard, carrying a box of carpenter tools, knocked at the convent gate. He asked to see the Mother Superior. Being taken before Mother Mary Magdalen he said he had come to finish the stairs to the choir loft of the chapel. The Mother explained to him that they had neither funds or material for its erection. The old man said he would build the stairway and the reward for his labor could be made later. He took his tools into the chapel and closed the doors. Neither sound of hammer nor saw was heard as the work progressed. In a very short time the workman had completed his task, a circular staircase thirty inches wide, in five spiral turns, containing thirty-three steps. Perfect in its mechanical balance, the stairway is a masterpiece of the craftsman's art. It is constructed throughout of a dark highly polished wood. The balustrade on each side is waist high and the handrail flows in an unbroken sweep from the protecting rail of the choir loft. The tradition is that it is built without brace or nails. When the stairs were completed the old craftsman gathered up his tools to depart. As he was leaving Mother Mary Magdalen asked for his name that they might, at some later date, reimburse him for his labor. His answer was *"Soy el Carpintero,"* and legend has it that this beautiful staircase was built by the Holy Carpenter, Saint Joseph.

"El Carpintero" had never been seen in the town before he appeared and offered to build the staircase. He left as mysteriously as he came, the Nuns never saw or heard from him again.

TEACUPS TO TIMBERLINE

COOKING SECRETS OF MESILLA

Miguel Hambriento

MIGUEL HAMBRIENTO is a *nom de plume,* and belongs to MARGARET PAGE HOOD of Las Cruces. She has written six novels, the first *Tequila,* had a Southwestern background, the other five, *Silent Women, The Scarlet Thread, In the Dark Night, The Bell* and *Drowned Wind* all have a Maine background. In addition to English editions and several paperback editions of her books, one television show was based on a novel.

Señores y Señoras, in a recent issue of this magazine the Honorable Thomas Dabney told you a tale of *sopaipillas* and *comidas sabrosas de Nuevo Mexico. Ay! ay! ay!, mis amigos,* it was as if a learned astronomer set out to tell you the story of the heavens and mentioned only *Canícula,* the Dog-Star. For what are *sopaipillas* but a mere dot of brightness in the star-glow sky of New Mexico cooking. You may pass by old Santa Fe, stumble with blind eyes through the Carlsbad Caverns, forget the Indian pueblos, but, according to Honorable Dabney, if you eat of *sopaipillas* you know New Mexico. *Otra vez, ay! ay! ay!,* again alas, *mis amigos,* he has misled you. What are *sopaipillas* but wisps of *tortilla* dough with wind on the *estómago.*

Oigan, mis amigos! It is true that Coronado was munching on a stale *sopaipilla* as he traveled through New Mexico. *Conquistadóres* were men of iron! It is indeed true that the early Spaniards knew *sopaipillas,* for listen, I myself picked up a fragment of petrified *sopaipilla* at the foot of Inscription Rock. "A bit of sharp quartz with which our ancestors carved their names for eternity," said the learned professor who accompanied me. But I know better, *mis amigos;* it was petrified *sopaipilla* upon which one of our illustrious forefathers chipped a front tooth.

But what of *buñelos!* How the learned have erred. It were better to call bread "bread" because it is oval in shape, and cake "cake" because it is round than to say *buñelos* only differ from *sopaipillas* in shape. *Una señora muy simpática* who for years feasts all her friends at Christmas eve on *buñelos, La Señora Amador de Las Cruces,* tells me of assurance a *sopaipilla* is merely a common *tortilla* inflated in hot fat and turned into a fancy shape, while "for *buñelos* I use the finest ingredients," she says, "pastry flour, sugar, choice spice, eggs."

A *buñelo* is a bit of honey on the tongue. Its fragrance is of a kiss dreamed in the night, but poof! gone before it is fully savored. And historical! *Maria santissima!* What history the *buñelo* has made. In the town of La Mesilla where I live it turned the tide of battle. You may read in Twitchell's *History of New Mexico* how the slack-sided Major Lynde of Vermont, in command of the troops of the Union Army at Fort Fillmore, was routed in ignominious flight by the brave General Baylor of the South. But listen, *mis amigos,* to the inside story. The troops of Major Lynde had fraternized to a degree *deliciosa* with the maidens of the Mesilla Valley. So when these beautiful *morenas* learned their lovers were to march away across the Organ Mountains they baked a prodigious baking of *buñelos* and borrowed several casks of their *padre's* best *vino.*

With these luscious products of Mesilla they filled their lovers' haversacks and canteens. *Ay! ay!* what a sweet fate. As the Union soldiers fled across the burning sands of the *mesa* they hungered and thirsted, so they sat down in the shade of the mesquite and ate and drank heartily. Replete and drowsy with good eating and drinking, they stumbled blindly up the mountain pass—*borrachitos* and fell easy prey to the sober Baylor. And if you don't believe this story, I can prove it to you if you come to my valley, for there high up in the Organs is Baylor's Pass as plain as the tail on a hound.

Sopaipillas—pfui! *Mi amigo,* have you ever eaten a *biscocho? Biscochos* are not biscuits, and the blood of a good New

Mexican boils when he hears the *gringos* order *"biscoches calientes"* when they want hot biscuits. *Biscochos* are heaven's own little cakes blended delicately of sugar and spice, flour and wine and other secret ingredients, shaped by the swift fingers of the *linda señora* into small diamonds and baked until they are the delicate brown of the maiden's cheek kissed by the New Mexico sun. *Biscochos* go with *vino* like an egg on an *enchilada.* And the best *biscocho*-maker in New Mexico, I declare on my honor as Miguel Hambriento, is a lovely widow of Mesilla. Round and plump with eyes of a mourning dove, *la bonita Minda* makes and sells at Christmas time such *biscochos* that the good saints in heaven might bend down for a nibble. In fact, while *la gente* of Mesilla fully believe that the holy hermit who lived in the *cueva* in the Organs traveled the long path across the stony *mesa* to Mesilla once a month merely to bless their community and sing *ave marias* at sunset, if the truth were known he was tolled hither by the thought of the *biscochos* of Minda's grandmother. This hermit from Italy lived to a great age and attributed his health to *biscochos y vino,* and for all I know might have been living yet if he hadn't been murdered one dark night at the mouth of his *Cueva.*

But that story is small change compared to the part *biscochos* played in the history of Mesilla. You may read of the famous battle of the *republicanos y demócratas* which was waged to a bloody and murderous finish on the *plaza* of Mesilla with dead men sprawled in blood and dust. But have you read the true reason for this combat? *Mis amigos,* that is a secret I now reveal to you. The *republicanos y demócratas,* hungry as all good politicians are, were hurrying to reach the little *puerta* of Doña Isabella which she had set up in one corner of the *plaza* to sell *biscochos y vino* to the parading *políticos.* And the whole fight started because in their parade about the *plaza* neither side would give ground, fearing the other would reach Doña Isabella's *puerta* first and eat up all the *biscochos.*

Of stuff is history made. And *verdaderamente,* do you know why the defeated *republicanos* who fled to Ascension in Mexico finally decided to forget and forgive and return to Mesilla? Because they were big-hearted men and wanted to make friends with their brothers, the *demócratas?* No! Because in Ascension they could not buy the fine white flour for their wives to make *biscochos.*

Did *El Señor* Dabney mention *empanadas? Desgraciadamente* for him, he apparently is not familiar with these delights. *Empanadas,* little ovals of pastry stuffed as tight as a Strasbourg goose. Sometimes with one thing and sometimes with another, but most deliciously with mince meat, a dust of cinnamon, a few cardamon seeds, *piñones,* with a drop of *vino* to moisten, and pinched with the mark of *la cocinera's* dainty thumb, then baked or fried and rolled in sugar. Who could even attempt a nodding acquaintance with New Mexico until an *empanada* has melted on his tongue.

I weep for those who never tasted an *empanada,* and I sigh for Billy the Kid who did. Perhaps you thought Billy the Kid escaped from the *juzgado* in La Mesilla through sheer brute strength alone. Oh no, *señores y señoras,* Billy the Kid had a *dulce corazón* in Mesilla, a lovely creature with eyes shining like stars behind a hedge, and she could bake *empanadas perfectamente!* So Billy asked her to bake him up a batch, which she did and delivered to the *juzgado* piping hot and crisping with sugar. It was noontime and the jailer, *pobrecito,* a married man with a wife who cooked only *sopaipillas,* was pecking at his unappetizing lunch. "Hist!" says Billy, "come into my cell and I'll share my *empanadas* with you." And he waves the tidbit under the jailer's nose until the scent is enough to tempt a saint. So the jailer goes into Billy's cell and is eating an *empanada* when Billy overpowers him. Such is the marvellous influence of a properly baked *empanada.*

En efecto, I will no longer be cruel to you. I will tell you how, *mis amigos,* you can taste of all these delights. Come to Mesilla and knock at my door—a blue door well faded in a tumbling *'dobe* wall. The latch is of iron wrought by my grandfather and the leather thong is from the hide of my grandmother's pet cow long deceased. A bell green with age hangs over the door. Once it called to vesper in the old *capilla* at Doña Ana. But now if you ring it *con amistad y gusto* it calls me. But if I don't appear, knock at any door in Mesilla, for there is a good cook in every house and hospitality is always at home. As we drink *vino,* made from the offspring of the vines brought to town by the private winemaker of *El Señor* Bermudez, first collector of customs for the territory, we have a special toast for La Mesilla *"Salud y comidas sabrosas y el tiempo para gozarlas."*

SOUTHWEST CRUSADER

Dudley C. Gordon

DUDLEY C. GORDON is associate professor in English at Los Angeles City College and a member of Mayor Yordy's Committee for the Preservation of Los Angeles History. He is president of the Lummis Memorial Association and has researched and written extensively on Charles Fletcher Lummis, the southwestern crusader about whom he writes in this volume. He has served as president of *Las Fiestas de las Americas* and has lectured frequently on our southern neighbors. His home is in Los Angeles.

Along about Thanksgiving, back in 1884, a weather-beaten foot-traveler and his dog reached the outskirts of Santa Fé on the Taos Road. Night had fallen. They were tired, hungry and thirsty, especially thirsty, for a misdirection on the way from San Ildefonso stretched their hike for that day to forty-two miles.

After doing their best to drink dry the first well they met, the traveler asked the way to Fischer's Drug Store. Soon he was in the hospitable clutches of A. C. Ireland and other friends.

This was the introduction of the multi-talented Charles F. Lummis to the town and State which were to know him and his phenomenal works so intimately. For nearly a half-century thereafter this unique human dynamo; this linguist, poet, author, editor, archaeologist, ethnologist, museum builder, photographer, friend of the First American, and advocate of the Southwest was to be found pursuing his many interests along the highways and in the byways of this area. Once seen, the green or brown corduroy suit; (material made in Spain) the bandanna or Stetson-covered head; the Indian-made, white, drawn-work shirt; the turkey-red undershirt; the red scarf belt and the perennial cigar of Charlie Lummis were remembered ever-afterward.

Following his appearance in Santa Fe the daily *New Mexican* ran a story announcing his arrival and describing him as follows: He was small of stature, spare of figure, with light hair, blue eyes, and a dainty mustache. He had close-cropped hair and a high forehead, and was wearing knickerbockers, red hose and low shoes. At first sight he looks all forehead and feet. As a souvenir he left a copy of his Birch Bark Poems. (Today that souvenir is a collector's item.)

In this costume Lummis had set out from Ohio in September for a transcontinental hike to Los Angeles where he was to become the first city editor and, later, part owner of the Los Angeles *Times*. He reached his destination on February 1, 1885, having covered 3,507 miles in 143 days, including the enlightening week his Santa Fe friends induced him to spend with them.

While on this continental trek Lummis experienced a host of hazardous adventures. In general his route paralleled that of the Santa Fe Railroad which was then being built, but sight-seeing and the pursuit of food often took him far from signs of civilization. It was these times when his life was endangered in turn by rattlesnake, wildcat, and cougar, or by two-legged "rats."

Once, when he was on the trail of a deer which had run up a draw near Billings, Arizona, he sought to head off the animal by climbing the fifty-foot face of a *mesa*. On the way to the top a piece of shale broke, and down he went to the bottom of the draw. When he came to, his arm was broken. There was no help within miles. How he set the arm and proceeded over fifty-two torturous miles to Winslow, together with a thrilling account of his other adventures is told in the characteristic Lummis manner in his book, *A Tramp Across the Continent*.

Whatever misfortunes Lummis experienced in his human

contacts on the trip must be charged to Anglos. The Spaniards and Indians he found to be altogether agreeable. The friendliness of Martin Valles, Amado Chaves, the Abeitas and the poorest peons won his heart. He thereafter became the staunch friend and advocate of the First American and the sons of the *conquistadores*. And what a hard-hitting, uncompromising crusader he was when he rolled up his sleeves in their defense.

A man with the vitality and vitriolic pen of a Lummis was bound to make enemies, and those he made were peculiarly vicious. Few 'armchair historians,' misguided Indian agents, thieving whites and other fakirs could withstand his blistering exposures of their shams and frauds without retaliating in some way. Since he was irresistible because he was supported by fact and disinterest, he could be discredited only by the circulation of scandalous stories at the expense of this colorful figure who was their superior in every way. Needless to say, these stories evaporated when this writer sought verification of them from competent authorities.

Prominent among the malicious stories created to undermine the character of the man who has done more to make New Mexico known to the world than has any other individual living or dead, were those that he had taken a squaw wife at Isleta, that if any Indian woman brought a baby to him he would admit his paternity, and that the scars on his face were the result of a shooting scrape over the honor of a woman.

When questioned about the authenticity of these stories the late Pablo Abeita said, "Yes, I have heard those yarns, and more, too. They are a pack of lies. A more honorable man I have never known." Of Lummis Dr. Edgar L. Hewitt remarked, "Charlie Lummis was one of the cleanest men I have known, morally and spiritually. He had a remarkable mind and was a splendid character."

As to the scars which marred Lummis' face and neck Senator Amado Chaves explained, "Few persons have borne as depressing a lot of gossip as that passed about C. F. Lummis and the scars which were quite noticeable on his weatherbeaten face. It is a pleasure to be able to clear up the mystery relating to these scars. Mr. Lummis was at my home during Holy Week in 1885 and we heard that the Penitentes were to have a crucifixion of one of their fanatics on Good Friday. He was anxious to witness the ceremony and to secure photographs. The ceremony was to take place in San Mateo canyon near our ranch, and my brother Ireneo, conducted him to the place. When the Penitentes saw them approaching they attempted to stop them but my brother drew a gun and insisted upon being permitted to witness the ceremony. Mr. Lummis secured a number of negatives which so angered them that they solemnly swore they would kill him. Lummis afterward went to the Pueblo Isleta, where he lived for several months.

"One evening, after he had been writing until after midnight, he stepped to the door for a breath of air, when he received a charge of buckshot that was fired at him by a Penitente."

The would be assassin not only missed taking his life, but, by a queer turn of fate, he brought romance into it. When Lummis was found in a collapsed condition the Isletans enlisted the services of the pueblo school teacher, Eva Douglas, to act as nurse.

When the patient regained consciousness Miss Douglas learned that his estranged wife, Dorothea, was a medical doctor living in Los Angeles. Dr. Dorothea was informed of the shooting and she came posthaste to the bedside of the victim. Together, as doctor and nurse, they brought Lummis back to health. Meanwhile, they developed a devotion for one another of such intensity that Dr. Dorothea, who was a genius in her own right, agreed to a divorce so Miss Douglas could marry her patient whom she had come to love.

Characteristically, Lummis dedicated his next book, *The Land of Poco Tiempo,* 'To Eve and Dorothea.' And later, when his first son was born, the boy was named Amado Bandelier for two noble men who also played important parts in the development of New Mexico.

An assignment to cover the War Department's campaign against Geronimo and his Apaches brought Lummis back to Arizona and New Mexico in 1886. At this time he began his long acquaintance with Generals Crook, Miles and Leonard Wood. Also, he came to appreciate the personality and military skill of Geronimo whose praises he sings in a poem dedicated to that intrepid leader of a handful of braves who eluded the army for years.

After two years of strenuous work on the Los Angeles *Times,* Lummis suffered a paralytic stroke which left his injured arm useless. It remained so for several years. To assure his convalescence he went to the Amado Chaves ranch at San Mateo. During the next four years his headquarters were here and at Isleta where he found the Tewa people to be "The best neighbors I have ever had."

While recovering his health and enjoying the companionship of Pablo and Antonio Abeita, who were to become lifelong friends, Lummis began writing the voluminous notes which were to be the substance of his many books on the life and customs of the people in the Southwest, and the natural and man-made wonders he found there.

It was while pursuing his archaeological and ethnological studies that he came to know the foremost pioneer scientist in the field, a man whose champion and disciple he was to be for a quarter of a century, Adolf F. Bandelier.

Lummis describes their meeting in the following excerpts in his preface to the second edition of Bandelier's great novel of the pre-Columbian people of Rito de los Frijoles, *The Delight Makers:*

One day in August, 1888, in the teeth of a New Mexico sandstorm that whipped pebbles the size of a bean straight to your face, a ruddy, bronzed, middle-aged man, dusty but unweary with his sixty mile tramp from Zuñi, walked into my solitary camp at Los Alamitos. Within the afternoon I knew that here was the most extraordinary mind I had met. There and then began the uncommon friendship which lasted till his death; and a love and admiration which will be one of my dearest memories so long as I shall live.—Aside from keen mutual interests and ethnologic study, we came to know one another humanly by the hard proof of the Frontier.

Thousands of miles of wilderness and desert we trudged side by side— camped, starved, shivered, learned, and were glad together.—I have known many scholars and some heroes—but they seldom come in the same original package, as they did in Bandelier.—Among my dearest memories of our trampings together is that of the Rito, the Tuonyi. It had never in any way been pictured before. He had discovered it, and was writing, *The Delight Makers.* What days those were. The weather was no friend of ours, nor of the camera's. We were wet and half-fed, and cold by night, even in the ancient tiny.caves. But the unforgettable glory of it all!

Upon the death of Bandelier in March, 1914, Lummis wrote his obituary as reported in *El Palacio* for April of that year. In it he says, in part:

It is seldom that the death of one scholar makes so little noise in the press yet so serious a vacancy in the ranks of the world's science as the passing of Ad. F. Bandelier.—It is not too much to say that he was the greatest genius of those who have in the New World devoted themselves to the study of Spanish-America.

Lummis knew Bandelier as few men could for in addition to his contacts with him in the Southwest he had accompanied him upon an expedition into Peru and Bolivia in 1892 where they shared the joys and hardships of an archaeological camp for nearly two years.

Upon his return from this trip into South America Lummis again became a human dynamo. Lecturing, writing and publishing books, and entertaining celebrities as only he could entertain them consumed much time and energy. Not content with one full-sized job at a time, he simultaneously accepted the post of editor of the regional magazine, *The Land of Sunshine* and began construction of El Alisal, his stone house in the Arroyo Seco near Los Angeles. Both tasks occupied him for more than a dozen years. In the former he produced some of the best material ever written on the Southwest, together with many fiery editorials and exceptionally pointed book reviews. In the building of his home he had the assistance of a series of Pueblo boys who are now full grown men and recall their experience with him as being among the richest in their lives.

Meanwhile, to preserve the California missions which were being allowed to crumble, he founded the Landmarks Club. This club is directly responsible for the saving of the missions at San Fernando, Pala, San Juan Capistrano and San Diego.

Later he founded the Sequoya League which sought "To make better Indians by treating them better." This league took up the cause of the Indians who had been evicted from the land they had held from time immemorial at Warner's Ranch by an unjust decision by the Supreme Court. The victims were poorly represented and the court ignored or was uninformed upon the Spanish practice for nearly two centuries of permitting Indians to retain the land upon which they had been born.

When Lummis informed his Harvard friend, President Theodore Roosevelt, of the plight of the Warner's Ranch Indians the President appointed him chairman of a commission to seek and transfer them to another reservation (without pay). This was accomplished and for the first time on record a tribe of Indians "was transferred from one reservation to a better one."

In 1903 Lummis founded the Southwest Society of the Archaeological Institute of America which soon sent several expeditions into this region upon extremely important explorations. A typical project of the Society was the recording of more than 600 Indian and Spanish folksongs of the Southwest, most of which were done by Lummis himself. He called the task "catching archaeology alive" because the songs were known only by old timers.

As head of this society he founded the now famous Southwest Museum. This, his monument, has since become the leading repository for archaeological and ethnological evidences of early civilization in this region. Its library is especially rich in books dealing with Arizona, California and New Mexico.

In 1906 Lummis took on the additional duties of Librarian for the City of Los Angeles. To do this he had to relinquish his post as editor of the magazine, *The Land of Sunshine,* which had changed its name to *Out West.* During his administration of six years he transformed the library from "An old ladies reading club" to one of the great libraries of the country.

About this time he began his herculean task of compiling, with the help of experts in various fields, what he considered his chief work—a concordance-dictionary-encyclopedia of

Spanish America from 1492-1850. This project, which was never completed because subsidy was lacking, would have reduced to a universal index every title, author, place, prominent figures and words of historical, biographical, geographical, ethnological, etc., interest from their original sources.

Lummis envisioned this invaluable work as being larger than the Encyclopedia Brittanica. Had it been completed through the help of enlightened capital or through a 'writers project' it would now be returning enormous dividends in understanding and cooperation, instead of discovering us to be almost ignorant of the culture, industrial needs and national characteristics of our neighbors to the South. It is tragic to realize that this great work failed for the lack of the money spent on a senatorial goodwill tour.

Meanwhile, despite his multiplicity of interests in California, this crusader for the Southwest was not forgetting New Mexico. That would be impossible for the man who created the slogan 'See America First' and who had informed the world about Acoma, the Enchanted Mesa, and El Morro. The Sunshine State was his principal literary mining claim and it was not likely that he would abandon it.

During these years he aided Theodore Roosevelt in the writing of "Winning of the West." On becoming the President of the United States, Mr. Roosevelt summoned Lummis to Washington to advise him upon western affairs in general, and upon Indian affairs in particular. New Mexico's affairs were presented by an informed advocate. In addition, his Southwest Society was instrumental in the establishing of the New Mexican Archaeological Society. He was a member of the Executive Committee which brought this splendid institution and the School of American Archaeology into being. He also became Regent of the State Museum. About this time St. Mary's and Harvard did honor to themselves by conferring degrees upon him, and the King of Spain knighted him as *"Comendador de la Real Orden de Isabel la Catolica"* with the Grand Cross, and the Royal Spanish Academy of History elected him to membership. Similar recognition came from the Casa de Espana de Puerto Rico.

MEDICINE WATER
Betty Woods

BETTY WOODS probably knows New Mexico more thoroughly and intimately than any other writer in the State. For thirty years, she and her
writer-husband, Clee Woods, have traveled over New Mexico reaching
every remote spot that has any current or historical interest. Mrs. Woods'
fact articles have been widely used in libraries by researchers of the New
Mexico scene. She won a number of awards in fiction and factual writing. Her book, *101 Trips in The Land of Enchantment,* made up of her
Trip of the Month feature in *New Mexico Magazine* is now in its fourth
printing.

Up through the hot wet earth slender wisps of steam curl
and hiss and disappear. Pools of thick yellow-gray mud bubble and gurgle. Hot springs heavily shrouded with sulphur
fumes and humidity boil out of the rocks, adding speculation
and wonder to this bit of Jemez mountain country, seventy-
three miles north of Albuquerque. The resort of Sulphur
Springs occupies several barren acres at the head of an otherwise beautifully wooded canyon. The eruptions of steam and
mud geysers have killed vegetation that might have lined this
strange, geological pocket.

For generations Navajos, Pueblos and Apaches have come
here to bathe in the mud and to drink the curative waters, but
Sulphur Springs became known to white men only fifty-five
years ago. Before the turn of the century Mariano Otero arrived at the springs, not because of ill health but to mine sulphur. For weeks his lumbering freight wagons crawled over

the mountains from Española hauling machinery with which the mine was to be operated.

But nature refused to let the miners bore within the earth's crust; workmen could not endure the 143 degrees of heat they encountered in the tunnels. Today the abandoned machinery lies rusted on top of the dug-up soil and visitors are always inquisitive about the reason for its presence here. Besides the old overturned hopper lies ore so heavily laden with sulphur that it will burn like pure sulphur itself, although the ore has the appearance of soft rock.

So Sulphur Springs was left to become again a health resort as it has been for hundreds of years, only now cabins and a hotel, managed by W. E. Culler, replace the brush shelters and buckskin tepees. The springs are yet in only a pioneer stage of development. Nevertheless both red men and white journey up through the piney mountains to drink the healing waters and to bathe in the curative springs.

It has long been claimed that the numerous springs have properties to heal a great many human infirmities, and to each spring is attributed specific medicinal qualities. The seltzer water spring is for stomach and kidney troubles; the alum springs are helpful for eye, ear and nose ailments and it is said that this water is so fine a mouth wash that tooth paste is unnecessary with it. The queer "electric water" spring is for skin diseases. The Indians say the hot lemonade spring, which actually tastes like lemonade, is a sure cure for backache. Steam rolls out from the rocks at this curious spa and the yellow earth is hot and smells of sulphur. Near here is a mud geyser, in the steaming mixture of which people soak off their corns! The thick yellow-gray liquid bubbles constantly and it is so strong with acid content that one drop on a piece of cloth will burn a hole. Foot-soakers sit on papers so as to avoid leaving a part of their clothing on the edge of the pool.

The hot sulphur mud baths are the most frequented of the curative waters at the resort. They are of thick substance, strong in mineral content and muddy-gray in color. Signs over the grounds warn visitors against carrying off the sulphur mud, but one may buy all he wishes priced at $2.50 per pound! Flowing past the hotel is a small clear sulphur creek which spills over rocks and disappears around a forested bend. There are no fish in this stream, but plenty of trout flash through the cool waters of the Jemez river only a short distance away.

About ten miles below Sulphur Springs on the Jemez, other mineral springs have built a dam entirely across the canyon by leaving deposits of their heavy mineral content. This Soda Dam has forced the river to the extreme east side of the gorge. Here the river water pours through a comparatively small hole which the flow has been able to keep open. The springs are still building actively, their warm waters bubbling up through sizeable cones along the crest of the dam. Several springs come out in the river itself and somehow, in spite of the river water, are building up their cones. At these fantastic formations where springs bubble out of the rocks and even out of the river itself the Jemez Indians come to worship every ten years according to ancestral traditions. On the brown and red sandstone cliffs above the river, the Indians have painted a scarlet snake which guards the place from evil. However, at night very few of the older Indians will pass the dam with its shallow caves and strange ghostly coloring.

Each year the healing waters of the area attract more and more people, but the country itself is an even greater attraction and new thousands discover it each year.

That region of the Jemez country surrounding the sulphur springs offers a variety of magnificent scenic beauty and abounds in a variety of interest. In this area are cliff dwellings and ancient ruins to interest the archaeologist, unique and unusual geological history to interest the geologist; streams that abound with trout to interest the fisherman, and game of all kinds to interest the hunter. Yet, in many ways the Jemez country is still a primitive area where Nature is still seen in the original. And Nature has been lavish!

ROUNDUP OF THE WATERS
Lawrence Clark Powell

LAWRENCE CLARK POWELL attended Occidental College where he received his A.B. degree. He received a Ph.D. from the University of Dijon, France in 1932. From 1944 to 1961 he was University Librarian at U.C.L.A., and since 1960 has been Dean of the School of Library Services there. Occidental College awarded him an honorary Doctor of Literature degree in 1955 and Carnegie Institute an L.H.D. in 1961. He has nearly a dozen books to his credit. He is a regular contributor to *Westways Magazine* and a frequent contributor to *Arizona Highways* and *New Mexico Magazine*. Among the most popular of his writings are *A Passion for Books,* published in 1958 and *Books in My Baggage,* published in 1960.

Though born on the banks of the Potomac, I am really a son of the Southwest, having come over the Santa Fe Trail in the winter of 1906, at the age of four months. Mine was an orange-grove boyhood, before Southern California was subdivided and the water-level lowered halfway to China. Well-water made up the deficiency of rainfall. I loved to see an orange grove under irrigation. Then we took to the trees and lived in the branches, in that dry season between valencias and navels, when the hard green fruit was good only for ammunition in the wars of boyhood.

Unless one is my age or older, he can't have known the land, for it is gone now, the trees snaked out by the roots, the earth moved to make room for pre-fabs. Inexorably the Angel City proliferates, engulfing all in a sea of stucco, beautiful only from the air when visibility permits: sea of pastel roofs and cars by day, pool of jewels by night.

He who sickens of smoggy city escapes not to the West, for there is virtually nothing but water clear to Asia. To the south San Diego bloats toward Los Angeles. In the north San Francisco loses her hilly charm, as the peninsulas on both sides of the Golden Gate are bulldozed to look like L. A. The Decline of the West, forsooth.

Beyond the Tehachapi Mountains, the southern end of the San Joaquin Valley, fast being Bakersfielded, recalls boyhood summers spent in the weed patch as a laborer, cutting and tying grapes, irrigating melons, working as water-boy, and worshipping the concrete standpipes which brought water to the surface, fountains in the sand.

I know about water and its ways, having been taught never to waste it, and I believe that every town in the Southwest should have a fountain dedicated to the water gods, such as the great one by Milles in St. Louis, at the meeting of Missouri and Mississippi. Now resident of the Malibu where water comes from wells, I can circulate conscience-free in the Owens Valley and Arizona, not being a water thief as Angelenos are.

In latter years I have turned away to escape the pressure under which I live, and found haven in New Mexico. Westbound from Kansas City by plane, having taken off in cool rain one night last summer, I slept during the three-and-a-half hour flight to Albuquerque, awakened once by the brilliance of an electrical storm around which the plane detoured.

The next morning I rose to a cloudless day of 100° heat and the good fortune of an early bookstore encounter with Paul Horgan. We adjourned to the Franciscan Hotel for coffee, and talked about books and writing, about libraries and people, about water and the lack of it, and the contrast between the Missouri, on whose eastern bank I had been for a week, and the Rio Grande, up which I was bound on my annual field-trip. When there is as much water as the Missouri bears, then it is meaningless. A son of the Middle Border would find the Great River at Albuquerque a contemptible stream, for like most Americans, he has been taught to value size above all else. At no point in its course is the Rio Grande a great river in volume of flow, and yet in its importance to the cultures it nourishes, it is a supreme natural resource.

From the crude suspension bridge between Santa Fe and Taos at Glen-Woody, I saw more water than I had ever known in the Rio Grande, the run-off from the winter's record snowfall. Coolness of air and water, smell of artemesia, sight of swallows, and the knowledge that once again I was northbound up river away from the heat of lower lands, renewed my sense of well-being lost all year in the city.

"Go all the way," said the inner voice, "see where the river rises. Your papers are in order to enter Colorado. With your rented New Mexican car, no one will know that you are a Californian."

So I continued north, bearing landscape and history in the form of remembered reading, of Escalante, Pike, Gregg, the Fergussons, and Horgan, seeing the land with multiple vision through the printed page and the lenses of Laura Gilpin and Ernest Knee. Alice and Haniel Long and Frieda Lawrence had died since I came last to New Mexico, so I tarried not in Santa Fe or Taos. Landscape consoled me. All that I saw on the high road to Questa was therapeutic, flanked by Wheeler, Pueblo, and Lobo peaks, and the engorged river. Ahead was the blackness of storm clouds tiger-striped with lightning, as I followed the wet road and the smell of rain.

The Arroyo Hondo arrested me. All sense of urgency vanished when I looked down on that deep valley, the fields alfalfa-green, whitened with sheep, a few natives going slowly about their affairs. They all knew where the post office was, but the streets were confused, and it took me a while to thread them to the *adobe* whereon flew the Stars and Stripes. In the gloom of her wicketed cubicle, the postmistress' teeth gleamed like pearls as she smilingly sold me one 2-cent stamp and gave me directions to the hot springs. Years ago I had read in D. H. Lawrence's letters of his bathing in springs beyond Taos, and also the exciting opening of Harvey Fergusson's *Grant of Kingdom*, describing another spring nearby, all of which led me to inquire as to the springs' whereabouts.

Directions took me along the mesa bank of the *arroyo* to a fork in the road near the Rio Grande, thence a mile on a rutted road through sagebrush to where it ended in a grasy turn-around, scattered with beer cans. An old wagon road staggered down to the river bottom, and it was along this that I was due to find the springs. A strong animal smell chilled me. There in a sandy ledge above the road were the tracks and droppings of predators. I could not suppress the primitive dread that rose in me, a poor librarian, armed only with a book. I abandoned my quest, remembering the postmistress' directions to another springs on the west bank of the river, and made my way back to the *mesa* road which dropped into the Hondo, then followed it to its confluence with the Rio.

That was a good sight. Submerged was the riverbank mud into which I had plopped stones two years before, in an effort to summon the river gods. Now the water was running high and muddy, convoyed by swallows. Plunging toward union came the clear water of the Hondo, straight from the melting shoulders of Wheeler, and fierce though the little stream's flow, no direct entry could it force in the larger water course. Sharply rejected and turned aside, all the clear water could do was to sidle along the bank and finally be swallowed by the devouring stream. Metamorphosis of *agua fria,* into *agua caliente, agua colorada.*

Across the bridge I switchbacked up to the *mesa* which wandered off toward Tres Piedras. Nothing but sage and rabbit brush, magpies, heat, and the prospect of three stones. Back down the road at the lowest switchback, I parked the car, and followed a narrow rock-trail down river, scolded by blue jays exploding out of the junipers. Where the hot springs should be was only a timbered dry cavern. A bay of the river offered warm swimming, but I feared the swift current, which coaxed every bank-side thing to join the rush to the Gulf. Once in that flow, the next stop might well be Boca del Rio.

Besides I recalled the grassy bank of the Hondo above the junction, sought it, stretched out and ate fig bars, and noted the lush growth of watercress and a bluebird who lit to drink. No summer in New Mexico without the twin omens of bluebird and rainbow. *Esta bueno, siempre bueno.* I considered crossing to the greener bank on the other side, but the stream boiled, pools were deep, footing unsure, and the water was numbing cold, even though the sun was hot and all the lower lands were sweltering.

Farther upstream I saw unused *acequia* water pouring off the *mesa* in a high fall. I made my way up to the edge, crossed the cascade by grasping juniper branches, and peered back down onto the truly named Arroyo Hondo, to where cattle were browsing on cress. Directly across, on the other high bank, a house of *adobe* and a rock corral were nearly indistinguishable from the earth—a natural architecture to shame the professionals.

The road from Questa follows Cabresto Creek up through the life zones—Upper Sonoran and Transition to the Canadian at 10,000 feet, where the dark Engelmanns surround the brimful lake. Nearly dry during the years of drouth, the basin was filled with water from the winter's snow melt. At Questa I had learned that when the Forest Service men sought to open the flood gate to relieve pressure on the earthen dam, they found it silted shut. Then the dam began to leak, spurting water at a hundred points, threatening to give way and loose a fatal torrent down creek. At the moment when all seemed lost, their desperation forced the gate and eased the pressure. I could see and hear the runoff falling in a series of cataracts. *Canto hondo.*

High, remote, peaceful, deserted by humans, Cabresto Lake was a true aquamarine color in the afternoon light. In the shade of the western shore I sensed the cold that would mark even a summer night, once the sun had set.

From Questa I took the road to the Colorado border, twenty miles away, through ruinous Costilla to Fort Garland, thence west across the San Luis Valley, guarded on the north by Blanca Peak, outermost sentinel of the Sangre de Cristos, the dunes of sand shining at its base. Far away in the west my goal was mountains that might have been clouds—the San Juans wherein rises the Rio Grande. First I had to regain the river, and did so at Alamosa, finding it wide and tranquil where the people had slowed it with a weir. It was bazaar day, and the shopkeepers had moved their goods onto sidewalk stands and were doing a lively business.

Not with me. My way lay west across the fertile valley, through Monte Vista and Del Norte, following the Rio Grande to where it entered the mountains, flowing wide and fast, the road climbing, climbing, through Wagon Wheel Gap and up to Creed, a mining town of doubtful prosperity. From there it was another sixty miles to the headwaters, just short of Stony Pass and Silverton and the road I had once followed south from Ouray.

I chose instead to descend to the South Fork and take Wolf Creek Pass over the Continental Divide and down the San Juan to Pagosa Springs and lodge there for the night. Up and up through groves of glistening aspens I followed white water until, at the 10,850-foot summit, I was surrounded by snowbanks. Here was the roundup of the waters—*el rodeo de las aguas*—as melting snow fed a thousand brooklets, some flowing east to the Atlantic, others west to the Pacific; and I poised there a moment on the backbone of the North American earth, before joining the flow that fed the San Juan and the Colorado, and eventually the Gulf of California—Oñate's *mar del sur*.

From the snowpack under the dark trees and from drifts on the rocky faces of timberless peaks, water was pouring from every ravine and gully, sheeting over cliffs, falling in smoking streams, obeying Newton's Law, seeking to unite in a single body, and finally succeeding, in the river called the San Juan.

By the time I had dropped a few thousand feet into a great meadow, the river was wide and handsome and very high, a different stream from the San Juan I had once followed west from Farmington and its junction with the Animas to Shiprock, where I turned south to Gallup.

I coasted into Pagosa Springs and liked it not. There was a rodeo going on, and the street was filled with the dregs who couldn't make it to the stadium.

The road signs offered good choices—west a hundred miles to Durango and the Mesa Verde, east forty to Chama. *Chama.* There was a name! I chose the east-running road, following the narrow-gauge D.& R.G., glad to be back in New Mexico, the countryside cleanly deserted, everyone gone to the rodeo. Yet there was nowhere to sleep, nor was there in Tierra Amarilla fifteen miles beyond; and so I tightened my belt and began the seventy-two mile descent of the Rio Chama to its junction with the Rio Grande at Española. A lovely drive it was, mostly in the Upper Sonoran zone of piñon and juniper, funneling through colored canyons, past Echo Amphitheater, along the Escalante trail in reverse, a route unchanged by the two centuries save for a strip of pavement to smooth the way for motor vehicles. Storm clouds conditioned the air to coolness and dramatized the sky one sees only in New Mexico. It was good to be driving away from the sun, for my eyes were dazzled by the glitter of many waters.

In Española I harbored as darkness fell, crossing the bridge over the Rio Grande, 360 miles from where I had taken off at Questa; and after a meal of home-cooked food (steak, salad, freshly boiled potatoes), I fell asleep feeling like a native son.

In Los Alamos, signs are reasonable, even solictious: *Drive Carefully—Children at Play.* I recalled Dexter Masters' novel *The Accident.* It was Saturday morning and the "mountain men" had knocked off for the week end. It was like a movie set. I drove along unchallenged, ready to exhibit my UCLA parking permit, gained the Jemez road with its cool sign "Impassable in Winter."

Now in summer I climbed through aspen glades and alpine meadows, up and up, under the big sky now darkening, now molten with light, finally gaining the Valle Grande, pastured with fat cattle and sleek horses, and watched over by Redondo Mountain.

The roundup of Jemez waters was less spectacular than that of the San Juans. In fact the Jemez River, which I gained near its headwaters and began to descend, was only a muddy creek. Down past Soda Dam and the novitiates of the Paraclete and Handmaids of the Sacred Blood, I followed the true source of life to within sight of Jemez Pueblo, where I stopped and tested the colored water with my bare feet. Lukewarm. No snowwater this. Tender young cottonwoods greened the bank. I lunched again off fig bars and soda pop, launched a boat or two, and remembered childhood delight in begging my mother to recite the poems of R.L.S.

> *Dark brown is the river,*
> *Golden is the sand.*
> *It flows along forever,*
> *With trees on either hand.*

Golden indeed was Jemez Pueblo in the late sunlight, one of the most shining of the Seven Cities of Cíbola. Later, Zia and Santa Ana were shadowy in the gathering darkness.

Once again river junction at day's end, homing with the Jemez to union with the Great River, streams and travelers, sedans and pick-ups, all rounded up and bedded down for the night by the hither and thithering waters at Bernalillo, town of journey's ending. *Buenas noches.*

WORLD'S GREATEST WONDER
Keen Rafferty

KEEN RAFFERTY has been in New Mexico since 1938. Most of that time as a college professor. He is professor of journalism and chairman of the department at the University of New Mexico. Born in Robinson, Illinois, he was a newspaperman in Terre Haute and Evansville, Indiana and then for ten years head of the copy desk of the *Baltimore Evening Sun*. He has written for many publications including the *Saturday Review, Journalism Quarterly, New Mexico Magazine, Newman Reports, New Mexico Quarterly* and *Southwestern Review*. In 1961, he was president of the American Association of Schools and Departments of Journalism.

When Bob Ripley, who has been everywhere and seen everything, broadcast his "Believe It or Not" program recently from the depths of Carlsbad Caverns he told his listeners that the Caverns are the world's greatest wonder.

About ten million visitors will agree with him, and probably another million right now are looking forward to finding out whether he's right.

Like Bob Ripley and most everybody else who has seen the Cavern, visitors can't find the words to describe it. It's a more difficult job for them to sum it up in a few words than it was for the little boy who said of the Grand Canyon, "Golly, what a gully!"

Visitors get a variety of impressions. Like the little man I met in a Roumanian restaurant in Baltimore. "Dey got elewaters," he said.

Yes, they've got 'elewaters.' They've got trails too, and steps, and little mountains and canyons down in this place that looks like those fanciful pictures of the land where the Moonmen live. They've got a restaurant under 750 feet of solid rock, with rest rooms and running water; hot coffee and post cards. They've got electricity, too—indirect flood-lighting that turns the underworld into a fairyland of indescribable beauty. They've got *everything*.

The Caverns are situated in the foothills of the Guadalupe Mountains in Southeastern New Mexico, twenty-seven miles from the city of Carlsbad. What happens is that you climb through a canyon and up these hills to their peaks, and then you go right back down, but *inside,* into the caves. It's as if Nature had laid out a monster plan of tunnels and rooms and then built up masonry and stone walls and domes, and laid the rock of the hill over the whole thing and decorated the outside. Decorated it with cactus, scrub evergreen, desert grass and sand. Not a tree lifts itself above the yucca on these slopes, but somehow there is an impression of luxurious growth, for here the United States government, in an enormous natural park, has preserved every kind of plant-life that grows in the area, almost every pebble.

Arrived on the hills, you are conducted to the natural entrance to the Caverns, a huge hole in one of the slopes, with a dome of rock at its top and the blackness of nothing dropping off below you at a 45-degree angle. Uncle Sam has arranged it so that you don't attempt to go straight down: you walk back and forth along smooth, protected trails, descending for two and one-half miles.

Let us follow your party. You come into New Mexico in your automobile, say at Clovis, drive down through the fertile irrigated artesian valley of Roswell and Artesia, and arrive at Carlsbad in the evening. You can stay at one of the excellent hotels or motor camps in Carlsbad at about average rates, or you can drive on out toward the hills and stop overnight in one of a score of fine tourist camps.

If you get into Carlsbad sometime after breakfast, it must be early if you want to take the full trip through. By 9:30 a.m. you are ready. If you are in your own car you start at once on the Cavern road; if you are traveling by train or bus, the Cavern bus stops at your hotel promptly at 9:30 and picks you up. You must arrive at the cavern entrance before 10:30.

If you are a woman you will want a coat of some kind over

your dress or slacks; if a man, an ordinary business suit—perhaps with the addition of a light sweater—is enough. Night and day, winter and summer, the temperature in the caverns is 56 degrees. Humidity is about 86. The air is in natural circulation from an unknown source and is always fresh.

At the entrance you buy your tickets to get in—it costs $1.50. The party forms on the slope and a dozen park rangers, including a very trim girl who is also a registered nurse, come down alongside you carrying five-pound flashlights, and in a minute you are off, winding down and down.

You pass the privately-owned branch where 3,000,000 bats live in the summer, arriving in about an hour at a relatively level floor.

It is now 11:30, and there are two things you can do. You have already seen the whale's mouth and the baby hippo and have a good idea of what this part of the caves is like. If you are a little creaky in the joints, or just getting over the flu or naturally lazy at 11:30 in the morning, you can drop off with a smiling ranger who leads you along a lighted trail that is a short cut to the lunchroom.

Nearly everybody elects to take the longer trail, but five or ten per cent drop out and wave good-bye to the others of the party, whom they will meet at lunch in an hour. Those who drop out reach the lunchroom in a few minutes and can eat at leisure. The rest arrive at 12:30, feeling superior about the extra things they have seen and describing the King's Chamber, Queen's Chamber, Papoose Chamber and the Green Lake Room.

Lunch is over. Cost is moderate, and it may consist of two sandwiches, an orange, a piece of cake, pickles. coffee or milk, and potato chips. If you want extras you can buy them, but the lunch is specifically designed for the day and the trip, and you will probably find it just right.

At one o'clock you enter the Big Room, and it knocks you down. The whole party—there will be 200 on an average winter day and 1400 on a summer day—slows up. Your breath leaves you and you just want to stop and look. Hidden lights play on millions of stalactites and stalagmites, on great pillars and domes and castles and poles and shrines and little lake-like formations in the stone. You have arrived.

This Big Room, 4000 feet long, is encircled by the two and one-half miles of trail that you are going to traverse in the next hour and one-half. No typewriter has yet been able to describe this room. You may have heard about it for years, read books and pamphlets and articles and fiction about it, but no flow of sentences can capture it.

The public sees five or six miles of cave; thirty-two miles have been explored. Below your 750 foot level lie two other caves, almost as extensive as the one you are going through. At one point you can see far down into the next cavern, where there is no electricity, where the formations still are growing, where through a hole big enough to admit your head you could see the room whose floor is covered with tens of thousands of loose stone marbles.

By presidential order there was added an additional 49,000 acres of Guadalupe territory to the park area, containing 100 more caves. Do these all connect? Are the caverns actually hundreds of miles in extent, instead of forty or fifty or sixty? Nobody knows. Exploration goes on all the time, but it is slow and dangerous. Sometime you may get to see these other places. Right now, dry and in perfect safety, you are going to be satisfied with what is already the world's greatest wonder.

Before three o'clock you are back in the lunchroom. Hidden in a pillar of solid rock are two elevators that rise in a 750-foot shaft, the second-longest single lift elevators in the world, to the surface. If you wish you may ascend in one of these elevators, eleven at a time. It takes 67 seconds.

Probably more than half the party chooses to walk out and up over the same trail traveresed that morning. This takes about 45 minutes. You are all back together on the hill-top by 3:30, ready for your bus or car.

Your trip is over, but you are going to do a lot of remembering.

OUR GOOD NEIGHBOR, TEXAS
S. Omar Barker

The Texas letter which appears below has been reprinted more times than anything else S. OMAR BARKER ever wrote. The letter was written originally to the *New York Herald-Tribune,* then appeared in *New Mexico Magazine* in June 1945. It has been reprinted elsewhere, read at dinners, quoted and misquoted, and has drawn many amusing, sometimes caustic, replies from state-proud Texans. For a biographical sketch of Barker, see the note preceding "Boyhood Bucks."

Despite a profound reverence for the self-confessed colossalitude of Texas, I feel that the Lone Star's tall shadow should not be permitted unduly to adumbrate the modest merits of her nearest neighbor to the west. I refer to New Mexico, 47th star in the flag, not to be confused (though it generally is) with Mexico, the good neighbor Republic which supplies, via the southwest wind, 50 percent of the Grade A sand in every Texan's craw. New Mexico, of course, supplies the rest.

Actually, of course, Texas is no bigger than New Mexico. It only appears so because it is spread out so much thinner. The mean average thickness of New Mexico from sunshine to sea level is 5,066 feet, and the higher you climb into the mountains the meaner it gets. Straight down from the snow-capped crest of Truchas Peaks, New Mexico is 13,300 feet thick, and a little over. Mashed down and rolled out to the same thickness as Texas, New Mexico would reach all the way from Yalta to the Atlantic Charter, with enough left over to flap in the well-known Texas wind. On the other hand, at the thickest point in Texas, an average New Mexico screw-billed angleworm could bore through to the bottom in one wiggle.

Compared to New Mexico, Texas is a newcomer. A million years before Tex Columbus discovered America, an early settler known as the Folsom Man was actually practicing point rationing in New Mexico, using arrowheads for red points—no points, no buffalo meat.

Fourscore years before the first Texas cowboy scuffed a high heeled boot on Plymouth Rock, a Mr. Coronado of Spain was eating corn off the cob in New Mexico and mailing home pictograph postcards of five storied Pueblo tourist courts marked "X—My Room—X. Come on over—the climb, it's fine!"

Speaking of climate, New Mexico is where Texans come every summer to cool off and brag about the Texas climate. New Mexico has plains so flat that the Highway Department has to put up signs to show the water which way to run when (if) it rains. Yet its mountains are so steep that the bears which inhabit them have all developed corkscrew tails so they can sit down once in a while without sliding off into Texas.

There is no place in New Mexico from which on a sunny day (which means any day) you cannot see a mountain, smell a pine tree or hear a Texan. Snow falls so deep in New Mexico's mountains that it takes 40,000 automobile loads of Texas hot air each summer to melt it. On that fabulous river, the Río Grande, New Mexico and Texas split 50-50; New Mexico furnishes the water and Texas the sand for it to sink away in.

New Mexico is game country, too. If all the deer horns in the state were clustered together into one giant hatrack, it would make a good place for Texans to hang their hats when not talking through them. Combine all the mountain lion tails in New Mexico into one brush and it could sweep all the heel flies out of Texas in one swish.

Whenever you hear a Texan bragging about Texas oil, just remember that oil you have to do in southeastern New Mexico to start a filling station is to stick a garden hose down a gopher hole and whistle for a Texas gas tank. Sometimes you don't even have to whistle.

New Mexico raises everything, including cotton, cattle, beans, buckaroos, wheat, sheep, atomic bombs and the hopes of all Texans who hanker for some place to go fishing for something besides mudcats. Numerous valiant New Mexicans also raised hell with the Japs on Bataan, thus saving Texas once again from invasion. The other time was when T. R.'s New Mexico Rough Riders charged up San Juan Hill in 1898—said to be the only time anybody ever went anywhere without finding a Texan talking.

There are more writers, artists, jackrabbits and politicians in New Mexico than there are Texas bureaucrats in Washington.

However, the charge that half the votes in any New Mexico election are sheep is erroneous. Buy and large, votes are no sheeper here than they are, for instance, in Jersey City, Chicago or any other outlying Texas precinct.

But the sunshine is, 365 days of the year and twice on Sundays. That's doubtless why so many Texas noses look sunburned.

GLORIETA BAPTIST ASSEMBLY
Olen C. Jeffries

OLEN C. JEFFRIES lives in Artesia where he is a junior high school librarian. When he attended the University of Oklahoma he came in contact with the late Walter S. Campbell, better known in the writing world as Stanley Vestal. He took some of his courses simply by ordering his books and doing the work at home without credit. He assembled material for his Glorieta article in this edition while he attended a writing workshop at Glorieta Baptist Assembly.

Clustered like jewels in a setting of unusual lustre are the ultamodern buildings of Glorieta Assembly. The Glorieta area, located nineteen miles east of the capital city of Santa Fe, comprises a 1300-acre portion of the southern extremity of the Sangre de Cristo Mountain Range.

Every summer more than 20,000 vacationers—most of them from the South and Southwest and very nearly all of them Southern Baptists—drive to these cool heights for a week of vacation and work for the causes of God.

The construction of Glorieta Assembly did not begin until 1952, but since then has grown to one of the country's outstanding summer conferences. Bounded by craggy sub-alpine peaks on the north, south, and west; and by the Spanish settlements of Pecos on the east and Glorieta on the south, the site for Glorieta Assembly is unique.

It is like a huge, gala-colored, flower-bedecked bowl, on which some master decorator has arranged models of striking buildings, then set this off with a background of piñon-studded peaks, towering far above.

Somewhere in the center of the bowl add a mirror lake and paint in above all of this an azure sky startlingly beautiful with suspended cotton-ball clouds, and you have something of the picture, but not all of the breath-taking charm that you would see in the original.

If you should approach Glorieta from Santa Fe, the perspective is one extraordinary beauty: to the south are the purple Sandia Mountains rising to an elevation of nearly 11,000 feet; close by, hazy and mysterious, sloping majestically into formidable summits, are those sentinels of the early snows, the Sangre de Cristo Mountains. Glorieta Baldy, northwest of the Assembly, looms 10,200 feet into the sky. One trail to the top of this sheer peak passes by the old Bradley gold mine built in 1881 by a relative of President Garfield. Remnants of the mine, which was operated for forty years, are still visible in the mine shaft, fallen timbers, rusted equipment, and two-story log house.

Always alluring and fascinating, the spiraling peaks point upward toward the Infinite, the Almighty Being to which man's soul aspires. The peaks seem to inspire one beyond one's self like church steeples pointing upward and ever upward. The very name of the range at Glorieta, being translated the Blood of Christ, is suggestive of affinity with the Creator.

About thirty-five percent of the trainees to Glorieta are sponsored by their home churches; others pay for their own lodging. Although chiefly Baptist, youth and adults from all denominations are invited to attend. Within the next ten years it is expected that eventually 40,000 trainees will attend Glorieta each summer, bringing with them a great boon to tourist trade and carrying home with them a wonderful amount of salesmanship for the State. Always the sojourners, enthusiastic over the bracing mountain air, the constant sunshine, the beauty of earth and sky, have one most-quoted comment: "New Mexico is wonderful!"

Once inside the gates of Glorieta the visitor will be charmed; you behold a rainbow of colorful flowers, spray upon spray, tier upon tier, in a romantically landscaped, rugged scenery. Cecil Pragnell, horticulturist and landscape architect, likes to relate that the Gardens of Glorieta were not planted for the purpose of becoming exotic show places, but rather to teach the lesson of the creative power of the Divine in all those who will look and understand.

During the summer thousands visit this setting of unusual landscaping and gardening. To give you some idea of the floral beauty of the gardens, the unusually exquisite color variations, it is significant to point out that an astounding 80,000 annuals and 30,000 perennials are raised and planted during the year.

One special terrace contains herbs used for medicinal purposes throughout the world. The numerous gardens have such names as Poet's Garden, Memory Garden, Spanish Garden, God's Garden, and Prayer Garden. God's Garden will consist of flowers, shrubs, and trees mentioned in the Bible which are adaptable to Glorieta's 7,500 feet altitude.

Contributing to the project, the New Mexico Iris Society sponsors twenty-four different plots of iris of different species and colors. Eventually this project will include 10,000 irises of a thousand varieties from all over the world. The sun-flecked blossoms manifest the bountiful nature of even the lofty altitudes when water is abundant.

Literally millions of dollars have been spent on erecting fine, large, architecturally outstanding buildings. Today the guests are domiciled in the enumerated halls: Oklahoma Hall; Texas Hall; Hall of States; Cedar, Pine and Spruce Lodges; two dormitories; Yucca Lodge for girl staff members; Cactus Lodge for boy staff members.

In addition, cottages were built by churches, colleges or individuals, ranging in price from $4,500 to more than $50,000 each. Further accommodations are provided by rustic cabins and a hook-up for trailer units located in a camp area opposite the Auditorium. Provided with light housekeeping facilities, these cabins accommodate two to six persons each.

Among other buildings, is New Mexico Hall, the summer administrative headquarters, and the first building erected on the site. Its massive lobby will hold 1500-2000 visitors at one time. Six fireplaces in the lobby with cast-iron grills are ideal for steak fries. A book store, gift shop, snack bar, postal counter, and registration desk occupy the remainder of the building. The atmosphere is one of friendliness, relaxation, and awe.

From the pillared western porch of New Mexico Hall burnished, iron-clad lamps swing freely in the wind. Standing in this spacious portico, the visitor may catch some of the exciting enchantment of the area leading to the Dining Hall. The walk, leading across an inevitable *arroyo*, is bordered to some depth with the most gorgeous flowers this side of heaven. Terrace upon terrace of flowers lead up to and surround the dining hall, which will seat 1500 at a meal. With spacious porches overlooking geometrical gardens, the building is replete with a loud speaker system for announcements. It is estimated that as many as 260,000 meals are served here in one summer. Much of the work is done by college boys and girls who work for their lodging.

The first unit of Holcomb Auditorium is large enough to seat 1,800 persons and is equipped with an audio-visual room as well as fifty class and conference rooms. The large unit, to be built in 1964, will seat 3,500.

Owned and operated by the Baptist Sunday School Board of the Southern Baptist Convention, Nashville, Tennessee, the Baptist Convention of New Mexico took the leading part in securing its establishment in New Mexico, contributing $150,-000 toward its progress.

On the drawing boards for the future, over two million dollars worth of construction is yet to be done for it is still a growing place. It is now about two-thirds completed but it does not have the look of an unfinished place.

E. A. Herron, Baptist lay leader and a New Mexican since the age of 11, has been the manager-director of the Assembly since its opening.

"You might say," Mr. Herron explains, "that people come here for a vacation plus. This is beautiful country and the weather is wonderful, but they come here for more than that. They come here to study church leadership."

The Assembly offers a series of week-long courses in various fields. There is a church training leadership course, a Sunday school course, a seminar on music and courses on libraries, public relations and radio and television activities. There are week-long conferences on foreign and home missions as well as for religious writers and recreation specialists, and one for college students. The growing curriculum attempts to cover every field of lay endeavor in Baptist churches.

The whole affair is, of course, nearly purely Baptist. People go to the Assembly because they learn about it at their home church, or because their preacher suggests that they join a particular group going there to study a specific subject. The place is open to all, however, and there are even fifty or so persons from other churches who come here every summer to attend one of the courses.

Glorieta is in the center of a most interesting area for the visitor to New Mexico. Nearby is Glorieta Pass where Sibley's Texas Brigade was defeated during a Civil War attempt to break the Union defenses of the West. The lushly green and beautiful little town of Pecos—a spot which receives perhaps less attention than it should from the visitor—is also nearby. It is quite normal that the tourist should drive by the Baptist Assembly and wonder if he might come to take a closer look. He should by all means and he would be welcome.

"We don't go out of our way to try to get them in," says Mr. Herron of the chance visitor, "but they are welcome and we are always glad to show them around."

And Glorieta is truly one of the show places of New Mexico.

INDIANS

PUEBLO POLITICS
Florence M. Hawley

FLORENCE HAWLEY ELLIS is a full professor at the University of New
Mexico. The past two years have been spent in directing the field school
students in excavating San Gabriel, the first capital of New Mexico and
the associated Yunque Pueblo. This was the site of Oñate's first colony
in New Mexico in 1598. Dr. Ellis has written and lectured extensively
on anthropological subjects.

The sun glinted on the shallow river as we crossed the splin-
tered floor on a narrow bridge at the foot of the pueblo. The
curved wall of a white *kiva* above, the golden brown of mud-
plastered houses—what a picture against the rich blue of a
New Mexico sky! But at the pueblo end of the bridge stood
a sign, "No photographs allowed." That sign had not been
there at my last visit, not for the years I had visited the pueblos
up and down the Río Grande. Who was responsible for this
apparent lack of friendliness to visitors?

We climbed the hill past the corrals, past the old mission
church, and where the stone foundations of older forgotten
dwellings marked the ground into squares we left the car to
the watchful surveillance of twenty brown children and walked
over to knock at the house of a friend. But no need to knock,
for the escort of children who trailed around us already were
signalling through the window that guests were at the door,

and a cheerful "Come een!" greeted us as the blue door was opened and weatherbeaten chairs were set forward for us.

We talked about the crops, about the last corn dance, about the new baby born two weeks before and comfortably asleep beneath closely protecting covers pulled down from the hood of the cradle-board onto which the little one was tied. Then I asked about the new sign at the entrance to the village. The answer was simple: the governor had it set up. One could still take pictures, yes, but only after a fee had been paid to the governor. Why? The governor had said that after the whites took pictures of the pueblo, they made those pictures into post cards and sold them. Thus the whites gained money while the Indians had none.

I demurred that very few whites were successful enough photographers ever to think of making their pictures a commercial proposition. Unconvinced, my hosts remained politely silent. I hazarded another question. "What does the governor do with the fee he collects?"

"He says he going to buy wire and staples to put the fences up around the fields."

Thus the governor collected his tariff and planned his state expenditures.

The governor is the man primarily responsible for seeing that you, as a tourist or as an old friend, do not take pictures of dances, that you do not pry into ceremonial rooms or *kivas,* that you do not introduce strange cults into his village. When the whites in charge of Indian affairs decide to sink a well or to repair the village windmill, they must consult with the governor. The white teacher of the day school and the visiting priest who officiates at the thick-walled *adobe* church deal with the governor as representative of his people. He is, as my friends explained to me, the chief "for the whites," the buffer between whites and Indians. If you should ask for the chief of the pueblo, you would be referred to the governor. But the governor is not "the chief for the Indians" and he is not "the big boss around here." The latter two officers are chief priest and director of Indian affairs, offices which have come down from the dim past of the legendary emergence of the Pueblo people into this world from a dark, slimy world below.

Pueblo religion, social organization, and government are so interwoven and so inter-dependent that every happening in the secular world is linked to events in the spiritual world, to the practises of a religion which pervades life. The irrigation ditches must be opened with ritual; a slain deer must be ritually rewarded for its life by gifts of corn meal; the new baby is protected by the perfect ear of corn laid beside it as a fetish, a "corn mother." The chief priest, or *cacique,* as he is often known at present, is literally the "big boss" because it is his responsibility to see that everything goes right in his village, that there is a rapport between his people and the gods, that the people perform their part of ceremonials correctly so that the gods, in turn, will do their part and see that the seasons follow each other in order, that the rain comes for the crops and animals multiply in their hunting grounds. The *cacique,* who serves for life, is supposed to be so busy with all of this that he would have not time for such plebeian tasks as cultivating his own fields or harvesting his own crops and these necessary pieces of work are carried on for him by his people, under direction of the "chief of the Indians" who is commonly known as the war captain. Indeed, one energetic young *cacique* incurred the general wrath of his people by going out to gather wood for himself and was strongly reprimanded by the war captain for his crime.

The war captain, as his name implies, formerly took charge of the protection of his village from enemies, human and supernatural. Now that Pueblos, Navajos, and Apaches are friends, his protection consists principally in seeing that the pueblo is guarded from intruders at the time of secret dances, since the presence of strangers would counteract the religious efficacy of those dances, and of seeing that the village is protected from witches. Periodically most of the pueblos conduct a ceremony for chasing all witches and evil from the district, a sort of cleansing of the atmosphere comparable to a municipal clean-up of criminals. In some pueblos the war captain has one assistant, in some he has more, but he and his chief assistant are thought to be not merely men but representatives of *Masewi* and *Oyoyewi,* the twin war gods, who originally led the people out from the underworld, taught them to fight the evil *katcina* spirits encountered in their wanderings, and finally directed them to settle their villages at specified sites, each claimed to be at the center of the world. These twin war gods now live in the mountains and keep a protective eye out for danger to their people, for which they are paid by shrines where offerings, such as prayer plumes and carved wood or stone images of themselves, are placed. Through the centuries, the chief priest and the war captain, with the aid of assistants and of societies organized to deal with the weather, with curing, with war, hunting, etc., directed the destinies of their villages. Then the Spaniards came; there was war and pillage and conquest and the introduction of a new religion which merged with the old until now the pueblo variant of Catholicism is claimed by the eastern pueblos as the "Indian religion" in contrast to protestantism or to any new cults. But to the Spanish, although their own priests might be explorers as well as converters of souls, Indian priests were not the type of men with whom to deal on questions of tribute, submissive government, etc. Hence, in 1620, the King of Spain sent a decree to the custodian of New Mexico and in it ordered an election to be held in every pueblo each January first. At this time "a *gobernador, alcaldes, fiscales,* and other ministers of the Republic" should be freely chosen by the Indians themselves without any Spanish officer being present at the elections.

"Elections" were not familiar to the pueblo people; their officers had been selected either by societies, by society leaders, or by councils of leaders, or they had been appointed directly by the chief priest. Thus, doing their best to follow out the strange new orders, secular officers were selected or were appointed in each village, the manner of their designation varying according to the old customs of providing officers in that village.

These secular officers officiated for one year and could be re-"elected," although usually with at least one year intervening between the two terms of office. Their roster usually included a governor, his lieutenant or assistant, a group of "captains" or sub-assistants, a small group of *fiscales* whose chief function was caring for the mission churches, helping the Catholic priests, and burying the dead, and sometimes a "ditch boss" whose special duty was seeing that the irrigation ditches were opened at the proper time in spring and were kept clean through the crop season. These are the officers whose "election" on each December thirty-first or January first still brings up a series of non-secret dances, open to the public at each pueblo. They are responsible throughout the year for the behavior of tourists, for contact with the United States government, and for collecting photographic fees for building fences around the farm lands!

When Lincoln was president he presented each pueblo governor with a silver-headed cane of office, which is handed down from governor to governor within the pueblo. Otherwise there is no symbol nor compensation for his office or duties; he reaps no honor nor rewards, and a friend of mine once told me that she had wept when she heard that her brother had been appointed to the office "because it will be so much hard work for the poor boy." My inquiry disclosed that the "poor boy" was already forty-two years old, apparently not too youthful to bear the ardors of office holding, but the job is one of thankless negotiations and of more or less troublous and tactful responsibility, neither sought nor desired by peaceful persons whose culture provides no prestige for individualistic political careers.

The social and governmental systems of all the pueblos, while agreeing in a few characteristics, differ considerably from village to village but can be grouped into two large divisions, eastern and western, and into several smaller divisions, each taking in the pueblos speaking dialects of a single linguistic stock. It seems probable the people of the modern Arizona and New Mexico pueblos are descendants of several groups of peoples who drifted into the Southwest at various prehistoric times, settled themselves into villages and adopted a sedentary agriculture life, and continued each to speak its own dialect and to follow its own system of town organization.

In the centuries that have passed since their first settlement here, contacts with their neighbors and the slow growth dependent upon changing conditions and environment undoubtedly have modified both their dialects and their social systems, but the grouping is still apparent. In the western pueblos we count the Shoshonean-speaking Hopi villages, Zuñi, which speak Zuñi, the Keresan-speaking Acoma and Laguna, and Tewa-speaking Jemez; and the eastern group includes Tewa-speaking Taos, Sandia, and Isleta; Tewa-speaking San Juan, Santa Clara, San Ildefonso, Tesuque and Nambé, and Keresan-speaking Cochiti, San Felipe, Santo Domingo, Zia, and Santa Ana. It is noticeable in this classification that there are Keresan villages in both the eastern and the western pueblos, and fundamentally these have a basic social structure; the division is based on the superstructure of western pueblo traits adopted by the western group of Keresans who settled at some distance from their conservative eastern relatives.

The people of the eastern pueblos are divided into two large groups known to anthropologists as moieties, such as the "Summer People" and the "Winter People" in the Tewa villages and the "North Side people" and the "South side people" in Taos. The officers of one take charge of the pueblo government for one half the year and then, with a ceremony of transference, turn the affairs over to the officers of the other for the remaining half. Each set of officers consists of a *cacique* and his right hand man and left hand man.

Second in importance to the moieties are the societies of "doctors"—medicine men who function in curing the diseases of individuals by sleight-of-hand tricks and administering herb brews accompanied by appropriate ceremonies for chasing out the witch who is causing the illness; and for obtaining the aid and good will of the animal spirits who have power for curing. Other minor societies exist, with ceremonial and ritualistic functions.

In the western pueblos there are marked differences in secular, ritualistic and clan systems, and the religious hierarchy of the clan system conducts both religious and secular affairs. Too, more freedom is allowed white visitors in watching certain religious dances.

Jemez is a borderline pueblo with about an equal amount of influence from the East and from the West. Clans own the corn fetishes, considered to be the most sacred possessions of the pueblo, and marriage into either mother's or father's clan is frowned upon. Dancers in the large ceremonies are divided into two *kiva* groups.

Government is by a religious hierarchy consisting of the *cacique,* two assistants, and the "Fathers," a group composed of the ex-governors. The presence of the *cacique* is an eastern trait, but his council of priests is western. The secular government is chosen annually by the hierarchy and is directed by it.

We who visit the Río Grande pueblos today will be told that the governor prohibits our taking pictures, that the governor sets the price on pottery, that the governor has told them that they must not talk to the whites about their customs, their ceremonies, or the ways of the old people. The governor speaks and the people obey. But the *cacique,* occupied with meditations and prayers for the good of his people is not too far removed to remember that he it is who is responsible for them.

THE FUNNY MEN
Eric Knight

ERIC KNIGHT was the British author of the best selling novel, *This Above All*. He visited and lived in the United States for many years and often visited New Mexico. When World War II broke out, he joined the American Army and was a member of a group of officers who were killed when their plane crashed while enroute from the United States to Africa. For more about Eric Knight see Peter Hurd's story, "Cow Pasture Polo" in this volume.

How the legend of Indian lack of humor ever got started is hard to imagine. Anyone familiar with Indian life can tell you that humor runs higher in the pueblos of America than among the skyscrapers. Moreover, Indian humor and the humorist surpass the status given in white civilization. It is part of the communal life; it has a semi-religious rank, and the *koshare,* or village clown, is an honored and powerful person. As the official humorist he has extraordinary powers that are no less than those attained by famous jesters in medieval courts. He is beyond many of the village laws.

His is the official humor; but there is another humor unsuspected by the white tourist: the mass humor of the village. And because the Indian has learned to be secretive, it is possible for a whole village to promote a joke, prolong it hour after hour with a straight face, and send the victim away none the wiser.

Jesse Nusbaum, senior archaeologist of the National Park Service, brought back one of the best reports of the huge mass jokes played by the Zuñi. A learned man had visited the Zuñis to save for posterity their chants and songs. But, generally, when he faced them with his recording instrument, the bashful Indian could get out no more than deep breathing and a couple grunts before the record ran out. At the end of the season, with almost nil results, the learned man had an inspiration. He played them a record to show what he wanted. Then he said he would return the next year to go on with his work.

He returned the next year, full of hope. The Zuñi greeted him with a curious glint of the eye. They dragged him to a seat of honor, and the pueblo whirled in holiday fun. The drums throbbed and everyone danced. Then, suddenly, the pueblo's *koshares* dragged out a packing case not much more than two feet square. On one side they attached a huge kitchen funnel. On the other side they attached an automobile crank. Gravely and vigorously they whirled the crank. They approached the horn and yelled into it in wild and various tones. They ran back from the machine and waited.

And then, from the machine, there came, oh wonder of wonders, the same words that had been shouted in. The village doubled over with mirth. Daring braves dashed out and shouted sentences into the horn. Back came the same sentences in the same tones. The fun went on, after the Indian manner, for hours.

For the Zuñis had solved this whole matter of sound-recording. If the white man wanted to have them shout into a horn and have the horn give the same words back, they had a perfect way.

They'd merely jammed into the space of that box the smallest man in the village, and through the sweating afternoon he echoed any and all phrases shouted in. In fact, sometimes, he surpassed any machine the white man had. If a question was shouted in, and the crank turned, the box didn't repeat the question. It gave the answer.

The Zuñis were surprised and delighted. The white man was merely surprised.

This element of humor, possessed to such a high degree by

the allegedly unhumorous Indian, seems to be almost a necessary part of his life. At least the Indian community finds humor such a necessary part of living it honors a really funny man, exalts him to a special position, and even frees him from ordinary labor in order to be free to think up more funny things for them. It sustains him in comfort.

Nor is it to be thought that these comedians, the *koshare*, are merely silly buffoons. The Indians have men of incredible skill and wit. Their humor is penetrating, and because of their lack of properties, often inspirational and impromptu. While as pantomimists the greatest *koshare* rise to the height of artists. It is no misstatement to say that among white men only such great pantomimic artists as Chaplin can rank with them. Some day they will be "discovered," and erudite critics will be applying the word genius to such outstanding *koshare* as Joe Crazy Horse of the Zuñis or that John Bunny of the pueblo Indian world, Agapito of the San Ildefonsos.

Joe Crazy Horse, or Loco Joe, won his first title with one of his most perfect acts—a piece of pantomime that ranks high in the world. One day, with the Indians waiting to be amused, Joe found as his only prop an idle wagon. The strength of the Indian *koshare* humor is its ability to improvise humor on the homely objects nearest at hand. So Joe stepped between the empty shafts and lifted them. He began to dance a portrayal of a horse. The horse grew, as in true artistry, not from any old horse, but to a personalized and particular horse. This one was stubborn. It wouldn't go. It shook its head and plunged and bucketed. The Indians roared.

And then Joe lifted it beyond humor alone, and began dancing the pathos and tragedy of a bewildered horse. Under his portrayal, the onlookers felt the anger of the driver, the bite of the descending lash—all the tragedy of a bewildered and tired old horse became part of the onlookers' own knowledge as Joe danced that now-famed act of ballet-pantomime.

And perhaps the greatest joke of all was that Joe was investigated by white men in search of case notes on Indian mental weaknesses. It was in one of these research quests that so puzzle the Indian that the two researchers went voyaging to study the percentage of weak-mindedness among Indians. They heard the name Loco Joe and pricked up their ears. A man nicknamed Loco must surely be mildly mad, at least. Imitating horses? People laughing at him? Surely a man to be placed under more tender care than being a laughing-stock.

They went in search of Joe and found him. In one-half hour they no longer doubted Joe's sanity. With a mental brilliance, a scorn and a wit that surpassed their own, he had them doubting the sanity of what they were doing.

Agapito, the plump one, has been famed as a dominating artist in the district around Santa Fe for as long as the oldest white residents of that town can remember. And to see this great Indian *koshare* prance into a sunbaked *plaza* on festival days, garbed only in loincloth and cap, and without any other prop but the homely things of an Indian village, keep a village rocketing with laughter for hours, is a great experience.

White humorists, with a two-hundred-thousand-dollar production behind them, and retinues of gag men to provide material, can entertain for a half hour. Agapito with nothing but a piece of string and his own wit can put on an act for five hours without stopping. He can keep it up until you are weary with laughter and weak from it, and must go away or fall over from your exhaustion.

Last year Agapito put on a noted performance at San Ildefonso that lasted over five hours. Agapito's two assistant *koshares* held the stage. And then the plump figure stepped from the ceremonial *kiva* and struck an attitude. And at that moment you knew the stage was his.

It was that magnetic, instant control of an audience by a great artist—an electrical sort of thing that dominates the audience mind immediately. Only very great artists do it, and they do it only occasionally. I have seen Jane Cowl do it. In the London Paladium I have seen Gracie Fields walk in and with a lift of her shoulder tie a British audience down tight. Many years ago in the People's Theatre in Philadelphia I saw a little man—who then had never faced a movie camera —named Charles Chaplin, of the Karno Komedy Kompany, do it.

From that moment on, Agapito danced and pantomimed and burlesqued till the shadows were low. Even the ceremonial dance gave way to his afternoon of greatness.

There is nothing as futile as trying in words to chronicle humor created at a past time in a technique that depends little on words. I cannot tell you how funny and great Agapito is, nor exactly why. But he is.

From the first moment, when he stopped his slow advancing dance and suddenly took a bite from his necklace, which you then saw was concocted of white man's doughnuts, he was an unending flow of pantomimic virtuosity. He parodied red men, white men, tourists, neighboring Spanish-Americans. He was alternately a bully, a hector, a white woman seeing an Indian for the first time, a sly fool, a humble human.

It was as if all life flowed into him, and he twisted it a little and warped it a little and then passed it on to you so that you then saw it anew—the pathos and ridiculousness and outrageous silliness of life.

And its mark of greatness was the universality of it, for his humor was as outrageously appealing and understandable to the handful of white people as to the great ring of Zuñis, Navajos, and other visiting Indians that mingled with his own San Ildefonsos.

His humor is, if you wish it in military terms, an attack on unlimited objectives through endless utilization of the element of surprise.

A chicken wandered across the dusty square. Agapito's aides chased it in the heat, and he got a chair from a house and lolled there until they caught it. The chicken was an idea. A pot was brought. He killed and cooked it, and suddenly gave a rendition of a white man at home. From nowhere came a copy of the *Saturday Evening Post*. Agapito pantomimed a plump stay-at-home beside his fire. He coughed. Thumbed the pages. The crowd waited. Agapito's eyes turned sidewise:

"George Washington," he suddenly announced in English, and then scanned the page more closely. "United States of America. Fourteen hundred and seventy-six."

The Indians rolled. He had read them a story in foreign words, but with the skill of an artist he had used no foreign words beyond those they understood. It was quite a story—although no humorist in that magazine has ever quite reached the bland and delightful point of combining history with a fusion of the dates 1492 and 1776.

At this point the village cow wandered into Agapito's "home." They became cowboys. The cow was chased behind a building. The crowd waited. The expectation was that the three comedians would reappear leading the roped cows. But not Agapito. Humor is eternally an element of surprise. When they reappeared they were *Penitentes,* carrying a cross, and the *Saturday Evening Post* was now a book from which one of the men read the chant he sang.

For hour after hour Agapito carried on without let-down. It was a great feat. Imagine yourself set down before a crowd without one comedy prop, imagine that crowd to contain people of greatly varied linguistic stocks, imagine that someone said to you: "Now—go on. Be funny. Make us laugh!" Then you understand.

It ended when the shadows were long and the squaws reminded him that humor is only part of hospitality. They brought food and set it before his feet—rows of pans of food and fruit and bread. Agapito became host. He coaxed from the crowds the shyer visitors, the San Domingos and Apaches and Navajos. He bade them eat as they knelt before the rows of food. He exhorted them to carry away in their hands the lavish supply of his pueblo that they could no longer squeeze into their stomachs. He was comedian and host.

Later, at sundown, the day over, he walked slowly to his home. He said he was neither hot nor tired. His eyes twinkled and his stomach still shook as he laughed. But I believe he could hardly have lifted his old, plump body through one more routine.

It was a day of days of Indian humor. And that same sense of humor lives on through the year. Long after white visitors have gone and summer is over, the Indians talk of them, parody them, laugh about them. They act them out, imitate their peering into the windows of homes, the agitated squealing of white women rushing to buy a bargain piece of pottery.

It is then that Indian life is best. The season of dances somehow purifies the village. The small bickerings of the pueblo are forgotten. After the dances the people are tired, empty, forgiving. They go back to quiet routine ways—but always their door is open to the *koshare* who may walk in any evening to entertain them. And, believe it or not, the strange antics of the white people they have seen during the summer provide much of the fun.

One of Agapito's famous visits many years ago was at the height of the Hawaiian craze in America. From somewhere Agapito and his aids secured straw hats. They wore white pantaloons as tennis trousers. With guitars held like ukuleles they sang—any jumble of words in English that had meter. But the main refrain, according to Mrs. Gustav Bauman, was "any rags any bones any bottles today."

The next year American youths in white flannels sent the Indians into stitches at memory of Agapito's parody of ice-cream-panted individuals.

Mrs. Bauman, then the school-teacher at the pueblo, and a resident there in one of the homes, was always the butt of an endless joke of Agapito. For she was then unmarried—and even a most warped Indian eye could see she was quite comely. Nothing could puzzle an Indian more; that a good-looking woman should stay unmarried is not for a man to understand.

It was endless sly fun for Agapito. He would pick up a photo of the school-marm's father.

"Ah, your husbin'?" he would suggest.

"No, I have no husband."

The waiting Indians always thought it quite funny. But one night Agapito enacted it again with aplomb. After the question and answer, and his pantomimed expression of surprise, his eyes glistened mischievously. The people waited. He pantomimed careful scrutiny of the picture—the stern photo of the aged man with beard.

"Ah," he said. "Now I un'erstand. It is your son—your little boy."

The story of the schoolteacher's little boy with a beard was chuckled over and handed round the village. And the fact that the teacher had been included in a joke by Agapito made her part of the pueblo. From that time on she found lessening resistance to the idea of a white woman instructing their children.

The stories go on. The unending humor of the red man is known to those in Indian affairs. They can tell stories into the night. The japes and jokes of the Indians. The time the Indians at a ceremony, in parody of the white man's archaeological craze, dug up a carefully planted pottery article of little beauty but well-known utilitarian worth, and paraded with it before the whites, shaking their heads as their eyes glinted, and saying sagely: "Veree old—ah, veree old!" The stories are endless.

The Indians are very funny people.

*Joe Crazy Horse died December 19, 1945, well past the age of 90.

NAVAJO BILL OF FARE
Ruth F. Kirk

RUTH F. KIRK is a rural defense information specialist with the Office of Civil Defense Mobilization in Washington. During her residence in Gallup she had a rare opportunity to study Indians first hand and has written dozens of magazine articles about the Indians, some ethnologic studies published by museums, and lectures which were presented to a variety of audiences. She is the widow of John Kirk, of Gallup, well-known Indian trader.

Navajo Indians are people. So much interest has been evinced in them as beautiful feather-covered dancers, or swarthy sincere weaver of rugs, or as worshippers of strange gods, that we are prone to overlook the simple, essential fact of their humanity.

Even in the basic matter of food, a Navajo is different from a white man. Some of the difference is a matter of necessity rather than choice, since many of our favorite foods have never been sampled by the Indians, but even with similar ingredients his methods of preparation and his taste vary from ours. If a Navajo housewife were to patronize one of our meat shops —which is unlikely as she raises her own sheep for meat in close proximity to her desert home—she would probably order "the toughest cut, please," because an Indian believes the tough meat is more satisfying, more nutritious, than the tender. If she were to go on a buying spree and select tenderloin steaks, she would expect her family to turn hungry soon after the meal. From the beginning, the Navajo has been a farmer. His name originated from a word meaning "planted fields," and rude as were his methods he has since prehistory been successful in growing corn, squash and melons. Corn is his staff of life.

He plants the seeds in hills, so the tiny growing plants will shade each other from the burning rays of the southwestern sun. Corn in rows would never have thrived. As the new corn sprouts, it sometimes needs thinning and the Indian, hungry for greenstuffs after a long winter of scanty dried foods and meat, is glad to thin out, and consume, the tender new plants. They are boiled and eaten as greens. Perhaps the Navajo equivalent to Popeye enjoys his corn sprout greens and becomes a superman thereby.

Green corn is eaten at all stages, being gathered for roasting —stalk, leaves and all—by the time it is a couple of feet or so in height. Soon after, the stalk becomes too tough to be edible, although Indian children love to chew the stalk as we might nibble sugar cane.

Tiny new ears, cob and all, are boiled and eaten whole, or cut into stew, to tickle Indian palates, and as soon as the kernels form, good old-fashioned roasting ears are enjoyed as heartily by Indians as by anyone. The ears are either boiled or roasted, the Indian fashion of roasting the corn in the husk being particularly delicious as it retains all the flavor of the corn.

This roasting is done in a pit of the same type as used for other native cooking. The hole is dug large enough to accommodate the quantity of food to be cooked, then a fire is built in the pit, for a sufficient time to heat the earth thoroughly. Into this are laid the ears of corn, fresh and sweet from the plant, row upon row until the pit is filled. Over it all is laid hot earth or sand, and a fire kept going overnight or even longer. To keep the fire hot enough to cook the bottom layers of corn and still not to scorch the top is a trick requiring real skill and proves the mettle of the Indian cook.

A whiff of the luscious corn fragrance as the pit is uncovered and better still a taste of the sweet green corn after its covering husk is removed, is payment enough for the long vigil of its cooking.

Many other delicacies are made of the green corn. One especially good dish is "green corn mush." The kernels, bursting with juice, are cut from the cob and ground by hand. The *metate* for this grinding must be placed in a receptacle as the corn is so fluid and fresh it overflows the rim of the grinding stone. Mashed to a soft pulp, spoonfuls of the green corn are put into corn husks and slowly baked; a wonderful dish!

By now the reader is supposed to have his mouth watering and at this very point he should feel the need of some salt. Very well, he may have it, for Navajos like and use salt. In early days they traded with the Zuñi Indians for the native product which was obtained from the salt lake south of Zuñi village. And with the coming of white man and trading stores, salt is a staple item of trade. The Indians usually salt their food after it is cooked.

In pre-Columbian days, before the White man introduced pots and pans, the Indians boiled their food in baskets. This sounds most difficult, but the pitch covered basket held water satisfactorily and while this container could not be placed over the fire, the system of heating rocks and putting them into the basket brought the water to a boil. As the rocks cooled, they were removed from the basket, and freshly heated ones dropped in until the food was sufficiently cooked.

Most of the recipes for preparing corn have evolved further; through methods of roasting and subsequent sun-drying, the food is preserved and may be kept for use many months later. The various *tamales* of green corn, also corn roasted in the husks, may be laid in the sun until completely dried out, after which they will keep all winter.

The first observation made by the average visitor to a Navajo *hogan* is, "But it's so bare; there's nothing to eat!" Sometimes the remark is gospel truth and there is literally nothing to eat, especially at the end of a long winter when the tribe lives on the fringes of hunger if not in its actual grasp. But even when liberal quantities of foodstuffs are available, a visitor is likely to find the cupboard bare, all the reserve being stored in pits in the ground, to be brought out as needed.

These storage pits are excavated to the necessary size, often as large as dugout cellars, and then fires are built in them to dry out the earth, thus protecting the food from moisture. Linings of cedar bark give additional protection, and a roof of brush and earth is built over the cache. It is becoming increasingly popular to build entrances like we use in our dugouts, with a doorway "like a coal mine" as one informant described it. The older form of pit had an end section of the roof constructed in such a way some of it could be removed to provide ingress and egress, but the real doorway is of course much more convenient.

Not only are the prepared corn foods stored in the pit, but the dried corn kernels, corn on the cob dried, and all other corn products; also dried melons and squash are added to the pantry. Every Navajo with a corn patch has also some melons and squash, and of late even wheat is being cultivated by them. The squash are eaten from their first appearance as tiny green things all through their development until maturity, at which time they are cut into strips and sun-dried for storage. Dried squash is later boiled in water, seasoned with salt and sugar and tastes very good. Whole melons may be stored by wrapping them in weeds to protect them from being bruised or mashed. Indians who are fortunate enough to live near the peach orchards also dry the peaches and not only are they great delicacy but they are valuable trade goods, as a gunnysack full of dried peaches is worth several sheep in trade, and Indians from every accessible point journey to the Chin Lee country to trade for the peaches.

The blossoms of the yucca cactus as well as its fruit are used for food, as indeed are many other wild seeds and plants. A meal of boiled white yucca blossoms might not sound so exciting to a white man, but the Indians enjoy it, and the dried and ground blossom, made into puffs and roasted, is a great delicacy when it is used the following winter boiled into a thick gravy or syrup.

Sometimes the storage pits run empty too soon, and hunger

stalks the Indian camp. They have certain limited resources then, such as an unpalatable flour pounded from dried corn cobs, but usually they turn out to look for extra work (not always to be found) or to persuade the Indian trader to give them still more credit even though the last notch of his indulgence has already been reached. So distressing has been the plight of many of these Indians during the bad years that the Government has had to extend relief in the form of food supplies to countless families. With the decrease in the number of sheep owned by the Navajos, their problems of food shortages are urgent and difficult of solution, but it is hoped that an increase in their agricultural effort can aid them, so the future will hold less hungry winters for these good primitive people.

Before the coming of the Spaniards, the Navajos depended on venison for meat, as there were no buffalo in this mountainous region. Corn and venison, together with such wild blossoms, seeds and roots as the people gathered, comprised the diet and it was not a bad menu in those days, either.

With the advent of sheep, the Navajo took very naturally to a pastoral life, and mutton soon augmented venison as his meat. But even today, Navajos like venison on those rare occasions when it can be had, and some interesting eating habits have come from this ancient heritage. As for instance their method of preparing deer pemmican. Strips of deer meat, jerked and dried, are pounded to a powder which is stored away. When it is needed, it is boiled with water to make a gravy-like dish, not very tasty but most nutritious. A little of this pemmican added to a scanty pot of stewed corn makes a satisfying meal.

The method of preserving meat by "jerking" it is a heritage from olden times. The meat is cut into strips and then each strip is taken by its two ends and actually stretched, or "jerked," after which the strip is hung to dry in the sun. This jerking process gives the meat a hard rind which is impenetrable to the bite of flies. Great lines of jerked meat may be seen near any Indian dwelling after a butchering season, and so covered with flies that it seems impossible the meat should be edible. Yet a bit of washing is all it needs to make it clean, and a few minutes over the hot coals renders the stiff black stuff pliable, after which it needs pounding and cooking to render it edible. It is a superb solution to the problem of keeping meat during warm weather without ice.

With the increasing importance of sheep for meat and a corresponding decrease in the number of deer available, the Navajo has naturally become very fond of mutton. Having determined which animal he wants to butcher, the Indian goes about the necessary business in a most expeditious fashion. A slit throat is a matter of a single gesture and all the blood is carefully saved. The skinning is accomplished skillfully and quickly and scarcely is the animal disembowelled than a section of his ribs is roasting over the fire. Freshly butchered meat, cooked while it is still warm, is much more delicious than when it is cooked after cooling. Nothing makes much worse chewing than an old sheep, killed in the summer time when the flesh cannot be frozen, and cooled before cooking.

Indian campsite meals are nearly always broiled meat, but even here there is variety, as flesh barbecued on a stick has an entirely different flavor than that roasted in the coals.

Store bought flour is only one modern luxury indulged in by the Navajo. He loves coffee and sugar as well. He enjoys potatoes and onions and has learned also to like beans and *chile*. Canned tomatoes are a special luxury and that he can find his old favorite, peaches, all ready to eat in a can is a never-ending source of delight, especially on those rare occasions when he finds himself in funds for its purchase.

Indians take a page from the Turkish book in making coffee, for they like it best very thick and very sweet. The sugar is put in when the coffee is made, both ingredients undergoing a good boiling before the coffee is served. Cream is seldom used, most Indians preferring the thick black effusion as it comes from the pot.

Navajo Indians do not care for fish nor duck but they like prairie dogs and will eat horseflesh. Goat meat is interchangeable with mutton; in fact is often preferred. Goats are always run in the herd with the sheep. Not only do the Indians believe this helps keep the sheep in good health but goat milk is valuable (probably more for tiny lambs than for humans, although some babies get it, too), but the meat is considered a real delicacy.

Often an Indian trader will buy butchered lamb from the Navajos. The meat is very well flavored, entirely different than corn-fed packing house lamb and in the opinion of those accustomed to its grass-fed flavor it is better. On these carcasses, the lamb has a stubby round bit of tail showing, but often the Indians bring in a carcass with this tail bit amputated. That means it is a goat, not a sheep! For the flat shape of the tail is the only way to distinguish between a goat and a sheep after the animals have been dressed, and in order to disguise the fact that it really is goat, off comes the tail! Needless to say, the white trader insists on having a tail *in situ* and that tail a round one.

Since a meal should properly end with dessert, so a description of Indian foodstuffs should end with a tale of their sweets. No longer do the women use the "saliva" method, patiently chewing corn to turn its starch to sugar, then spitting out the mouthful to chew another, until a sufficient quantity has been worked to make into sweet cakes. That custom always has left me tottering between horror at its uncleanliness and sympathy with the jawwork of the poor woman who had to do the chewing. But nothing really has come along to take its place, because desserts as we know them are not found on most Indian menus. Watermelon is popular and the Navajos even raise a white-coated variety that keeps in storage nearly all winter, so they can have melons in February as well as in season. And they have the dried peaches from their ancient trees. Piñon nuts are a favored treat, and the average weight of the Navajo Indian tribesman will increase about ten pounds each during a Fall that brings a piñon nut crop, because they eat so lavishly of these toothsome, rich little nuts. Navajos like candy and a trip to the trading store usually includes on the want list a sack of penny candies or some candy bars. But the crowning glory of trading store delicacies is pink soda pop, which is really ambrosial, the drink of the gods.

So from corn to mutton to melons does the Navajo eat; from the tender sprouts of green corn in the spring to the lean meals in late winter when the storage pits are emptying and the last available sheep has been consumed; from the dawn of history pemmican to white man's wonderful soda pop. So has gone the evolution of Indian menus from the foodstuffs at hand. Only one thing has remained the same, now as then, and this sad truth is summed up in the answer given me when I kept asking a Navajo friend about foods to eat during the late winter. She said, "Well, there isn't much. You know Indians always eat better in the summertime."

FOLKWAYS

PEOPLE OF THE SOIL
Elizabeth Willis DeHuff

ELIZABETH WILLIS DEHUFF has written and lectured widely on Indians and other New Mexico subjects for many years. She is the author of several books. The list includes: *Say the Bells of Old Missions, Taytag's Tales, Taytag's Memories, Swift Eagle of the Rio Grande, Five Little Katchinas, Two Little Hopi, Hoppity Bunny's Hop, Toodle's Baby Brother.* She was born in Augusta, Georgia, but taught school in the Philippine Islands before moving to New Mexico and after many years in Santa Fe returned to Georgia to make her home in Augusta.

When modern life seems too nerve-racking and hectic in its complexities, the best tonic is to drive a few miles from Santa Fe and step back, in that short distance, several centuries. Nowhere else in the United States can be found an indigenous peasantry, living much as their ancestors did when they settled in *Nuevo Mejico* in 1598.

Those settlers who followed Juan de Oñate brought with them their wheat, geraniums, alfalfa seeds, sheep, cattle, horses, burros and their simple manner of living. The long six months' journey from Mexico City and the two months' trip from Chihuahua, the nearest Mexican city, across desert wastes infested with hostile Indians, shut these settlers off from the outside world and allowed their language and their customs to crystallize. Visitors now from other sections ask, "How could those early Spaniards ever settle in this bleak, arid land?" My answer would be, "because of its similarity to the interior of Spain." Because of a nostalgic reaction, this area probably appealed to them more than a more lushly vegetated section. Humans like what they have been accustomed to.

Nowadays, into that static more changes are coming with better roads and automobiles, bringing contact with the outside, but even now the change is slow; since change among an agricultural group of people on small farms is always slow. Still speaking Spanish, as it was spoken in Spain in the sixteenth century, they answer one's, no doubt to them "foolish," questions politely. "Why do you thresh your wheat this way?" Patiently the answer comes, "My grandfather threshed it like this. His grandfather threshed it like this, so I thresh it like this. It is the right way." They are content with the old ways, until outsiders come driving up luxuriously in a fine automobile. Then they have a moment of envy and discontent. But with the passing on of the automobile, the desire for innovations and for any other life but their own passes, too.

Linked closely with this simplicity of life is an eager curiosity and gracious cordiality. They usually welcome visitors.

Since each room of a home has an outside door, opening either upon a long *portal,* or flush with the hard-packed clay ground outside, one doesn't always know upon which door to knock to gain entrance. But no matter whether it is the door of the bedroom-parlor, or of the kitchen-dining room, the one who opens the door bids the visitor, "Enter! Enter! Seat yourself!"

You will find the women busy. They are a hard working group. If it is the harvesting season, and that is the most interesting season to visit them, there will be only one woman in the house. The others will be out-of-doors helping to pick up the cut wheat, throwing up the straw on the threshing floor to separate the wheat grains, winnowing the wheat by throwing it from a basket, washing it, spreading it to dry. Or they may be cutting open squashes or peaches to dry on the ground in the continuous daily sunshine; stringing pungent red *chile* peppers to hang on the house wall to dry; husking corn; stripping freshly butchered mutton or beef to dry into

charque (which early cowboys mispronounced into "jerky");
or mudding the house wall before winter sets in.

The one woman found in the house, will be equally, if not
so strenuously, busy preparing the family's food. After she
has asked you to seat yourself, she will quietly go back to the
task in hand, whether it be assorting dried beans to put on
to boil, spanking balls of dough—flour, water and salt and, if
she's lucky, a little lard—from hand to hand into round, flat
tortillas, or roasting *chile* peppers to place in a cloth, sprinkled
to dampness, to steam off the tough membranous-like skin.
And how delicious these green *chiles* smell while steaming!

If, however, the task is not so urgent as a *tortilla* on the stove
lid about to scorch, or beans that must start boiling immediately, she may seat herself stiffly on the edge of a straight chair
opposite you, with hands folded in the lap of her full home-
made cotton skirt, or it may be the much-faded skirt of a
store-bought house-dress. Always the hair is covered with
a wrapped cloth or tucked under a boudior cap.

Of course, you are a woman visitor. Otherwise, you would
have been directed outside to where the men were working.
But since you are a woman and have been invited to enter
and be seated, you are asked, "How is your husband?" If
you must reply that you have no husband, your hostess will
cluck her tongue and shake her head sadly in sympathy that
you are one of the unfortunate unmarried. She would like
to ask why, but instead you feel that she is looking you over
to draw her own conclusions, discovering for herself your
old-maid ear-marks. If you speak Spanish and she speaks no
English, she will next ask you about your family, where you
live, what you do—since you are not married—and so forth
and so forth. She is really interested. But if you do not speak
Spanish, she will try to converse with you, especially to find
out why you are there, with her shoulders, her hands, her
head and her lips, using all the signs she can think of. Then,
if you do not understand, she goes to call some one who speaks
English, as interpreter.

The visitor is lucky if for some obvious reason—like a broken
automobile—she has to spend the night.

After the supper of beans, with mutton or dried beef stew, with *chile* pepper sauce, bread and coffee and a conversation consisting of questions and answers, you will be given the best bed in the house, often the double bed of the man and woman of the house. They will probably sleep on a pallet of mattress and blankets on the kitchen-dining room floor. The young girls of the family will sleep in the other double bed in the bedroom-parlor. They will wash and undress somewhere else. The flowered pitcher and bowl on the Victorian wash-stand is truly for company. You use it gingerly and sneak outside to brush your teeth—for, of course, when you wander from the beaten-path over the roads of yesterday you take a toothbrush and cans of food along. The woolen stuffed mattress is usually deep and comfortable, though when one gets good and warm, she is conscious that babies have slept there many times before.

Being in a strange bed, one sleeps fitfully and all during the night, there are strange soft noises, for all peasant people seem to have a night life of strange silent movements and pilgrim-ages. One wonders, listens for hints to a solution of what one hears, then gives up. Perhaps the continuous fire in the kitchen stove has to be fed; bread may have risen to a point of requiring immediate kneading; relatives may have come to get medicine or aid for the sick. Many things may have hap-pened; one never knows! She is only conscious that there are comings and goings and movings about at intervals all during the night, silent and mysterious!

They arise with the sun. You do, also. Otherwise, you feel ashamed of laziness and find yourself definitely "in the way." The younger men go out to do chores, while the women get breakfast and you are entertained by the old man of the family, who has nothing else to do. He may live in a nearby house with his elderly wife, but either curiosity or the knowl-edge that he is the only leisured host brings him for a chat and breakfast with the stranger.

One wonders how many of their customs came with them and what was borrowed from the Pueblo Indians. But in the case of wheat and its treatment, there is no questions, since they brought wheat with them. Only fifteen or eighteen years ago, there was still a threshing floor on the Camino del Monte Sol in Santa Fe itself, where sheep and goats trampled off the grains. Up the Tesuque valley and in the Mora country, it is trampled by either sheep or horses, who are usually driven loosely around the threshing floor, but recently one enterprising thresher, who apparently did not have enough horses nor sufficient help, drove a span of horses around in harness. He could in that way control and conserve their steps.

This real and indigenous peasant life shows most delightfully at the time of *fiesta,* marriage and death.

Their lives are busy with the routine of wresting a livelihood from an arid soil and saving every scrap and vestige of food grown; but they are not cluttered and nerve-racked by the crowding in of unnecessary excursions, dozens of engagements in different places, upon different themes in one afternoon so for weeks the days are spent in preparation for *fiesta.*

Relatives and friends will drive in for miles to attend and they must be feasted upon the best, even if the family will almost starve for weeks afterward. Since there is not much diversity in raw material, as to food, there has developed a number of ways of using each articles and these ways have become "standard." If wheat is to be baked into ordinary loaves of bread, it is ground at the water-mill into the ordinary wheat flour; but if it is to make a *dulce,* a sweet, for desert called *panocha,* without the use of sugar which is scarce, the wheat grains are moistened and sprouted—to bring out the sugar content—before they are ground. Then the flour, *trigo enraizado,* kneaded into a pudding, must bake slowly in an Indian pot in an outdoor *adobe* oven. The pot sparkles with mica contained in the best, most heat-resisting clay, of which most cooking pots are made.

If blue corn meal is to be used as the thin breakfast mush or *atole,* the grains of blue corn are first roasted and then home-ground on stones, called *metates;* but if the blue corn meal is to make *tortillas* (flat pancakes) for *enchiladas* or to be used in *tamales,* then the outer husk is removed with lime before the corn is home-ground. This makes a smoother finer meal, which is called *harinilla de maiz* ("little flour of corn").

There must be just enough moisture and not too much moisture in the sprouted wheat to make it grind properly, so it requires experts to prepare food for *fiesta*. The methods have been handed down from grandmother to granddaughter throughout the centuries. Unless ground on peasant stones, or baked in peasant ovens, the flavor is impaired. The processes are slow and everything must be prepared in advance so that hostesses may attend the celebration of the mass, which always begins and sanctions all festive occasions.

In earlier days, a groom-to-be among the rich made a trip to Chihuahua or to Mexico City to buy a handsome chest and fill it with materials—silks, brocades, linens, laces, shawls, a Spanish comb, white satin for the wedding dress and a wedding veil—for his bride-to-be. The poorer people found the trousseau near-by, but it was also the gift of the groom.

Today, the trousseau is still the gift of the groom, but it is bought from stores in the nearest town. The groom-to-be accompanies the bride-to-be, her mother and sister and often other members of her family into the general store, where he finds it much more embarrassing to pass judgment upon ready-to-wear garments tried on by his sweetheart, or displayed only to himself and her mother for his approval, especially as to price, than the former purchasing of goods by the metre.

Eight o'clock in the morning is the favorite hour for the ceremony at the Church. On the return home, the procession, afoot, is followed by two or more musicians, gaily playing "fiddle-tunes" upon a fiddle and guitars. A small page stumbles over rough spots in the roadway, as he holds the short, white satin train of the bridal dress up out of the dust. The happy face of the bride looks proudly over her bouquet. The most delightful bouquet I have seen was a bunch of asparagus ferns, bought from a florist, upon whose branches crisp dollar bills were fluted across the center and tied. They made very pleasing poisies as well as practical ones. The elaborate wedding breakfast develops into an all day feast, accompanied by dancing. The musicians seem tireless.

Even death offers an occasion for feasting and singing, mingling joys with sadness, reminding one of how a tiny infant often mixes his emotions and begins to cry in the midst of laughing. The leader of ancient hymns sings lustily and tirelessly all night at the *velorio,* or "wake," in which others join fitfully whenever they can remember the words.

And with it all, there is that genuineness of unfettered simplicity; the closeness to elemental realities in peasant life, which only in New Mexico, of all states, is indigenous.

FOLKWAYS AND FIESTAS
Aurora Lucero White

AURORA LUCERO WHITE LEA was born in Las Vegas. Her father was the late Antonio Lucero, first secretary of state for New Mexico. She has written such books as *The Folk Dances of the Spanish Colonials of New Mexico, The Folk Lore of New Mexico,* and *Los Pastores.* Her latest book is *Juan Bobo,* published in 1962 and adapted from an old Spanish folk-tale, *Bertoldo.*

In New Mexico, *fiestas* coincide with significant dates on the Catholic calendar. All villages observe feasts celebrated throughout the Catholic world, days such as Christmas, Holy Week, Corpus Christi, All Souls' Day, the Day of Kings, etc. In addition there is always the *fiesta* of the *santo patron* in honor of whom the village chapel is named and to whom the village itself is dedicated. If the *santo patron* is San Antonio, the village *fiesta* falls on St. Anthony's day, if San Lorenzo, on San Lorenzo's day.

Each year *mayordomos,* a sort of *fiesta* council, are appointed to take charge of the preparations for the year's *fiesta.* Among other things they take up a collection for the purpose. If the amount raised does not come up to expectations of the council, the *mayordomos* themselves have to make up the deficit out of their pockets. This is a very nice custom for it insures the success and continuance of the *fiesta.*

The *mayordomos* are charged, in addition, with the duty of

repairing and cleaning the village church. The structure being *adobe,* this means that the cracks in the walls have to be filled, the roof repaired, the outside plastered and the interior finished with *jaspe.* The wooden *vigas* are scrubbed, as well as all woodwork and floors. Where there are seats these too undergo the same thorough cleaning. Altar cloths are washed and mended; the old paper flowers discorded for gay new ones, and the *santos* are dressed in their *fiesta* finery.

If there is no resident priest, the homes of one of the *mayordomos* is chosen to serve the *fiesta* dinner and to furnish quarters for the visiting priest and his party. This house, too, undergoes the same going-over as the chapel—the *vigas* are scrubbed, a coat of *jaspe* is given all the rooms, fireplaces are repaired, and the outside is neatly plastered with *adobe* mud. Within, the woolen mattresses are reconditioned. This means washing the wool in *amole* weed and drying it out in the sun, working it with the hands until it is soft. The *chimayos* are also washed in this famous soap weed concoction which gives them a soft, lustrous finish. The *padre* and members of his party, who drive out for the vespers the night before *fiesta* and remain until next day are delighted with their quarters, and well might they be, for many hours of loving and patient care have entered into the preparations.

Vespers are held in the village chapel the evening before the *fiesta. Luminarias* are built around the church and *salves* are fired at intervals just before and during the service, but there is no merry making on *la noche de las visperas* as everyone has gone to confession in order to receive communion on the morrow at mass.

The whole *placita* takes on a holiday air during *fiesta.* Visitors from neighboring ranches and towns always come and often times there are visitors from *la ciudad.* The whole world dresses up for *fiesta.* Those who can afford it deck themselves out in new raiment; the rest make the best of it with old clothes adding a ribbon here, a colored kerchief there, so as not to be completely outdone.

Children are gay in white starched dresses and pink and blue stockings. The older little girls manage to steal enough *colorin* from their big sisters to imprint bright red spots on their cheeks. For the rest a gentle dab of *jaspe* gives them that China doll look. The boys and youth wear brightly colored *camisas,* sometimes, silk, more often cotton. All *caballeros* have an expensive felt sombrero for *fiesta* and the younger ones start emulating their elders early. The young women and matrons wear pink, blue, rose and purple satin dresses. Their make-up is put on a little more carefully than that of the *niña* but, containing the same ingredients, the *señoras* still look like China dolls, a little worse for wear. The babies wear cotton or silk to match their mama's gown and a pleasing mother-daughter pattern is created.

At the house of the *mayordomos* open house is held. Always there is a table stacked with goodies: candy, raisins, cookies, oranges, soda-pop. For the elders there is *vino* or *cerveza.* Dinner is served only for the *convidados* but *todo el mundo* calls after mass and is invited to *pasar a la mesa.* It is the custom to fill one's pockets or handkerchief with *refrescos* as one passes the table, and to manage to get one's self invited to pass as often as possible so that when one returns home the combined *refrescos* of all the family constitute another little *fiesta.*

If members of the choir have accompanied the priest, high mass is sung. The *mayordomo* with an air of earned importance sit in the Church atrium with lighted candles. It is a great distinction to be a *mayordomo* and all *paisanos* covet the honor even though it usually turns out to be an expensive affair. After mass, the *fiesta* dinner is served. Local musicians provide the entertainment, playing, now old ballads, now modern jazz tunes. In olden days the *cantador* occupied a prominent part during *fiesta* but now he is slowly relegated to the scrapheap, the *jovenes* no longer being interested in the old traditional *cantadas.*

After dinner there is a full schedule—dancing goes on at all the *salas,* or at least in as many as there are dance orchestras to provide the music. Very often there are *caballitos* for the children, the *corrida de gallo* and *carreras de caballo* for the oldsters. All the *comercios* carry on a lively business, and in addition *puestos* are set up where *comestibles* are sold consisting of candy, ice-cream, hamburgers, peanuts, pop corn and souvenirs. The ranchers who have no relations in the village camp out and eat at the *puestos*. Needless to say, the children get sticky, the mothers become disheveled, the fathers, having had a *copita* too many become argumentative, and now and then some one receives a knife wound from which he fails to recover.

Being opportunists, the young people dash off to the dances, unchaperoned. Many young persons emerge from the *fiesta* dances engaged, and marry as soon as their poor parents can gather together enough money to meet the necessary expenses for the wedding.

The *corrida de gallo* is perhaps the most picturesque survival of the *fiesta* folk customs and it is still engaged in with the same gusto as in other years. Where still practiced, the *corrida* is still gay, colorful, daring. The victim in a *corrida* is usually an old hen. It is buried up to its neck in sand. Riders dash up to the chicken at full speed, lean out from the saddle and try to grasp it. One of the riders finally seizes the hen and gallops away with it, followed by the others. *Galleros* come from several *placitas* in cavalcades. They place themselves seventy-five or a hundred yards on either side of the hen or rooster. The signal is given and a galloping pony springs from one or both groups. As he comes close to the buried hen, he leans lower then sweeps past it with one swift grab. If he misses, the next rider is signaled and so on until some one is lucky. Sometimes the run is made by a half a dozen riders from both sides. The lucky contestant swings the bird in the air and shouts his challenge. He then flees and the others start after him. His own team swings into action and runs interference charging into the path of their rivals. Sometimes the winner gallops home with his trophy; others, the battle rages on until nothing is left of the poor bird. Once women used to engage in the *corrida* on the day of Saint Ann, and at the little village of Agua Sarca, *galleras* may still be seen engaging in this quaint folk custom, heritage of the Moorish tradition.

Formerly, and when gambling was permitted, games of chance were important features of a *fiesta*. *Monte* and *conquean* were among the favorite card games. *Ajedrez* and dominoes were always popular, and there was always roulette.

Many interesting tales are told in connection with the games of chance when in their heyday *caballeros* lost entire fortunes in a single night and whole *haciendas* exchanged hands with the spinning of a wheel. Women, too, participated and such names as "La Tula" helped make history. The story goes that the lady operated a fashionable gambling salon; that here the elite, including *hacendados* and *militares* rubbed elbows. Needless to say "La Tula" amassed a fortune, which she left to the Church upon her death.

Once each *placita* had its own troupe of entertainers and dancers who performed *autos* and gave *danzas* during Church fiestas. Parts were usually handed down from father to son. The whole village attended the rehearsals, hence the performance became a community enterprise. The night of the play, should an actor bcome stage-struck, the audience took on the role of the prompter. Village women made the costumes, gathered the properties, decorated the *sala* or church, as the case might be. No fee of admission was charged for the performance, and the only remuneration received by the director and actors was the silver offering taken up the night of the play. Of course expenses were reduced to a minimum, the community sharing in the cost of production. The *dueño* of the *sala* made no charge; the kerosene lamps and chairs were loaned by the *vecinos*. In winter each family contributed a few sticks of wood for the rehearsals and again for the play. Each actor furnished his own costume. Plays were nearly always given during the Christmas season, and in the *placitas* where there was no resident priest the performance took on the importance of a church service.

Nowadays it is next to impossible to find persons who remember the old plays with the exception of *"Los Pastores,"* *"Nuestra Señora de Guadalupe"* and *"Los Matachines."* A troupe from Leyba, an isolated community, knows the *"Comanches"*; another troupe from Santa Cruz knows the *"Moros y Cristianos.*" Many years ago the *"Adan y Eva"* play was given at Las Vegas and there are those who remember when the *"Niño Perdido"* was given at Taos. An old woman from Tecolote remembers having seen the *"Tres Reyes"* once when she was a mere child. Although many *viejecitos* have been interviewed no one remembers seeing other plays than the ones listed here. The *"Posadas"* are not included as they cannot be rightfully listed as plays.

Good roads, radios, automobiles have begun to make their influence felt as far as New Mexican *fiestas* are concerned and while these functions still offer "varied, unforgettable, poignant pictures of the people," the traditional features: *autos, danzas, corridas,* etc., are in danger of disappearing unless folklore enthusiasts come to the rescue.

DIALOGUES OF DON PLÁCIDO
F. M. Kercheville

F. M. KERCHEVILLE is a professor of Spanish at the University of New Mexico. He is the author of numerous textbooks on Spanish and has conducted radio courses in Spanish and written for a number of education journals. He has written numerous books, essays, short stories and poems and for a number of years wrote a series titled, "Don Plácido" made up of kindly philosophizing and whimsical conversation. He has a Ph.D. from the University of Wisconsin and undertook special studies and research at the University of Madrid, Spain, the University of Chile and at the University of Paris. His home is in Albuquerque.

Great men often go unsung. Like the immortal Cervantes, our mutual friend, Don Plácido, is "old, a soldier, a gentleman, and poor."

Age, mere number of years, means nothing to Don Plácido. He may be seventy or nearing a hundred. There is nothing feeble about him. He is tall, only slightly stooped, and carries himself with pride. To be sure, his face is wrinkled and his hair more than gray. Some may think him a modern mummy. Old and rather dried-up physically is Don Plácido, but he is not dead like an Egyptian *momia*. He is far from being ready to be rolled up and laid on the shelf.

In New Mexico Don Plácido has worked as a *vaquero,* served as a sheriff, school teacher, and superintendent of public instruction in the days when, according to his own words, *"la educación era muy poco pública y menos instrucción,"* (when education in New Mexico was very little public, and less instruction).

Our old friend is a sort of modern Diogenes, interested in all men and all things. However, unlike the original Diogenes, Don Plácido takes a few young men with him and goes searching for the light, whereas the Greek philosopher snatched up a lantern and ran through the streets of Athens looking for a man. The old New Mexican does not boast the ego of the grand old Greek.

Don Plácido is in reality a southwestern Socrates. He has a good education for his day and opportunities. He speaks, reads, and writes Spanish quite well, English and French not too badly. Many good books line the walls of his *estudio*. Don Plácido is sociable and boasts many friends, among them his own good *esposa,* Doña Mariá. If, like Socrates, in his own day, Don Plácido has not been asked to swallow any hemlock, he has calmly drained many a cup of bitterness uncomplainingly. He has drunk even the dregs without becoming sour or bitter toward life or his companions, of the cup. Don Plácido is a peculiar and agreeable mixture of realism and idealism. He is a sort of New Mexican *Don Quixote,* well versed from experience and reading in the lore, the strange haunting beauty, the calm, powerful appeal of the western scene, the deserts and mountains of the southwest, particularly New Mexico.

But enough of this puny praise! Don Plácido does not need it. He will undoubtedly forgive us for this interruption and these meager words of adulation. Upon our last visit to the *casa* of the southwestern sage we left him quietly enjoying his morning *siesta.* Upon returning in the afternoon, Don Plácido chided us for allowing him to go to sleep in the presence of friends. His own words follow:

"*Señor amigo mío,* why did you not awaken me? I love my *siesta,* but not in the presence of my young friends. To sleep in the presence of company is not the way of a *caballero,* and I have always tried to be a gentleman. Forgive me, my friend, you have known me long years, and the way of a friend is to forgive. For my discourtesy to you I shall try to atone by telling you a good story.

"For the truth of this story I will not say. But this I know: it will make you smile and be happy within, and a good story and the happiness within do not always depend on the very truth. *Aquí tiene usted la historia,* here's the story:

You must know, my young friend, that many, many years ago our people lived along the banks of the Río Grande. In the north, between Taos and Santa Fe, many people lived by fishing from the river. The Río Grande was the home of many nice, big *truchas,* what you call trout. You know the mountain peaks near Santa Fé are named Truchas Peaks. Maybe there are also many trout there in the mountain streams. Perhaps, *yo no sé,* I do not know.

For many years our people lived on fish from the Río Grande, and then there came a time when the people forgot to fish. Soon all the people forgot that the Río Grande was the home of fine *truchas.* Years passed by and no one fished at all. The *truchas* were forgotten completely, *absolutamente.* One day, not so many years ago, an Anglo, a tourist on the road between Taos and Santa Fe, stopped to fish. He caught many fine trout. He drove into Santa Fé with the fish, and our people saw the *truchas* and asked him where he caught them. He said, 'from the Río Grande. People then rushed to the river to fish, like to California. It was a fish-rush, *señor,* greater than a gold-rush.

One man, Pancho Pescado, went fishing every day, *todos los días, mañana y tarde.* He was crazy, *fanático* about fishing. He loved *truchas.* He would have only trout. Pancho loved to fish, *señor,* like some men love wine or a beautiful woman. He was *loco* from fishing. Finally Pancho became too old to fish. No one would take him to the Río Grande. *Pobre diablo,* poor devil, he could not walk. He was old and *cojo,* what you call in English crippled. For him *la vida,* life, was fishing, so when he could not fish, he became melancholy, *muy triste,* very sad, and he just sat down and started to sleep the last long *siesta.* That *siesta, tarde o temprano,* sooner or later, we must all take.

And so Pancho Pescado, as his *amigos* called him, died. All his friends came to the *velorio* to watch over him. All of them were *muy triste,* very, very sad. Pedro, another fisherman, his best friend, would not believe that Pancho was dead. He said he was only bored to death, and that was not real death. Pedro said he had heard of men making like they die, what you call playing 'possum. So Pedro, the real friend, begins to try to raise Pancho from the dead. He talks to him, blows his nose, calls him many bad names like the one that means billy goat, but Pancho Pescado will not come back to life. Then Pedro stops and thinks very deeply. That's when one really thinks, *señor.* Suddenly Pedro's eyes brighten. He runs home and gets his fishing pole, brings it back and put it in the hand of his dead *amigo.* At first the pole dropped from Pancho's hand. But the second time it stayed. Some people say the fingers moved and held the pole. I do not know. This is only a story, you know. But Pancho was still dead.

Pedro then ran to the neighbor's house and borrowed a gold fish from the pool in the yard. He placed the little fish in Pancho's left hand. The fingers moved, but Pancho Pescado stayed dead. Finally, Pedro ran to the meat market that sells fish packed in ice. He bought a Río Grande *trucha,* a nice fine one. He came back and put it in Pancho's hand in place of the gold fish. Then he went over and gave the fish-pole a jerk and made a noise like a fishing line cutting through the waters of the Río Grande. Pancho Pescado suddenly opened his eyes and sat up quickly on the straight boards on which he lay. *"Vámonos a pescar,* Pedro, *vámonos a pescar,* come on, let's go fishing, Pedro," Pancho shouted and jumped to his feet, crippled as he was. This is the story of the resurrection of the fisherman, Pancho Pescado.

Now, my young friend, this story may not be true, but many people say the beautiful *truchas* in the rivers of New Mexico are fine enough to almost bring a real fisherman back to life from the dead. I, myself, have seen the sunshine of New Mexico bring men back from the dark shadows of *la muerte.* Trout and the sun are wonderful. Miracles still happen in New Mexico.

THE LITTLE LIGHTS
THAT BURN ON CHRISTMAS EVE
Margaret Abreu

Biographical information about MARGARET ABREU is given with the article, "First Printing in New Mexico," earlier in this volume.

The origin of *las luminarias,* or festival lights, used at Christmas and during *Fiesta* in Santa Fe, dates back to that holy night
of long ago when the shepherds tending their flocks kept the
watch and lighted fires for warmth, protection and light. These
fires called *luminarias* were burning brightly when the angels
appeared to the shepherds bringing them tidings that the Christ
Child was born.

So today at Christmas, that world festival, *luminarias*—as
lights instead of fires—adorn patio walls and even the roofs on
Christmas Eve in preparation for midnight services in most
churches in New Mexico.

The *luminarias* are a legacy to the Spanish-speaking people
of New Mexico, from Spain and Mexico, the latter since the
time of Cortez. The early *luminarias,* however, were the stacks
of pungent *piñon* wood, laid criss-cross, and the center filled
with pitch kindling, to be lighted at the moment they were
needed. These little fires were laid and later lighted around the
homes along the streets and even on the flat roofs. The Spanish
women later added—besides Christmas Eve—the feasts of Our
Lady of Guadalupe and Saint Anne to be honored with use of
luminarias.

But the happy, *fiesta*-loving Spanish women dreamed of a
better way to embellish the *fiestas,* religious or otherwise. Had

they not heard their mothers and grandmothers tell of the traditions of Spain in story and legend? Now that the men had become rich in New Mexico with their vast flocks of sheep or cattle, now that they owned *haciendas* larger than any feudal possessions, now that they were able to obtain cloth, velvets and silks, via the Chihuahua caravans, the women also longed for the Chinese lanterns, which their grandmothers said had come from China and Arabia into Spain.

The *luminarias*—the wood fires—were fine; they had served the purpose of light, warmth and color. But the dream of lanterns lingered; had they not heard for generations about the *fiestas,* the *Navidad,* or nativity, the *velorios,* and the *meriendas* of old Spain and Mexico, when the lanterns were hung from trees in the plazas and *patios* and lent romance to a festival. Tales were told in long winter evenings as they were seated before the warm blaze of the fireplace. The women reminisced about early *fiestas* in Spain and later in Mexico, and the young people loved to hear especially about *La Fiesta de la Raza.*

This *fiesta* was a very special festival in Spain. It had been celebrated, so legend ran, since time immemorial—not in honor of some hero who had lost his life in battle, not in reverence of some saint who had performed a miracle, not to commemorate a date of some patriotic significance, but a day set aside for special rejoicing and exultation in the mere fact that Spaniards were Spaniards and of no other nationality. In supreme egotism the people of Spain delighted in proclaiming the fact that Spanish blood flowed in their veins.

And so the women sighed for the *luminarias* that would give only a beautiful light and not a fire, that would be only gay and fragile, that would add romance to a *fiesta,* a *navidad* or a *tertulia,* a party. Their young hearts thrilled to romance. Romance, like *Raza,* is not easy to define let alone translate; it is a thing of the spirit rather than of philology; it is a glow, a feeling and a yearning like nostalgia.

Finally, ever seeking an ideal, women found the long-looked-for *luminaria.* They found it in the trading places when the freight wagons came from Chihuahua, Mexico.

The caravans brought to Santa Fe among other things, China

dishes for the *gente de razon,* the well-to-do people. These dishes had been shipped to Mexico from either the Philippines or China. They had been carefully wrapped in layers of paper to insure against breakage. It was in this paper that the women found the materials for their *luminarias.* This was no ordinary paper. It was silk-like and transparent, made in China in polychrome; and placed against a light, it showed myriads of bright colors. Since it was used for wrapping, it must have been the discards of fine paper in the shops of China. Be that as it may, the *luminarias* came into being. The women were delighted and disappointed at the same time with the finished article. Delighted because it resembled the Chinese lantern, disappointed because it could not be hung. The paper was fragile, and string and wire were not to be had.

Nothing daunted, the women decided that the new *luminarias* need not be hung. Were not their *tapias,* patio walls, an ideal setting for the new decor? Were not their roofs flat?

Gently the paper had been smoothed out with loving hands, and cut into different shapes, tall and round like a can, square as a box or fashioned as an inverted lamp shade. It mattered not. The ladies stuck a precious candle in the bottom of the lantern and surrounded it with a mound of sand.

All during the time these New Mexico women were looking for an ideal, something akin to a miracle was taking place in their hearts. Their mothers before them had known privation, disillusion and nostalgia; they had suffered much, these daughters of *hidalgos* ("some-one-who-is-somebody") —the *conquistadores,* those fearless conquerors who had wrested from the aborigines an arid wilderness and secured from it that social well-being which is the true heritage of a brave and noble people, the heritage of culture. And that miracle which had nothing of the supernatural, was the simple, yet joyous discovery that the *luminarias* in their lovely transparent colors were *not* the colors of China, but of their own new homeland. The lovely hues showing through the light of a little candle and making the lanterns glow, were not the porcelain blue of a Chinese vase, but the lapic lazuli blue of the Santa Fe sky; the yellows were not the gold of Chinese embroider but of the aspens in the mountains around Santa Fe; not the roseate of a Chinese silk tapestry but of the blood-red sunsets on the Sangre de Cristos. And the dream of a very special *fiesta* in Spain was beginning to dim, for they had not crossed the Rio Bravo for all time and was not Spain so very far away?

Then an earth-shaking event took place in old Santa Fe: the American Occupation traders from Independence and from Saint Louis and the brown paper sacks found their way into the Capital.

Mere men could find a practical use for the paper sacks; not so the women. At long last they found a sturdy and practical component for a new *luminaria*.

For almost a century, the *luminarias* made of paper sacks, a handful of sand and a candle have been used in Santa Fe. At Christmas, at *fiesta* and at cocktail time. They grace our homes from roofs, walls and the paths leading to the very door.

At business places, electric light bulbs have replaced the candles. But in the homes, let someone mention a party, or a barbecue or anything festive, and someone runs to the grocery store for paper sacks.

Las luminarias, as little fires, are still used in the villages especially on the Eve of Our Lady of Guadalupe, the patroness of the Americas and for special processions. But the paper-sack *luminarias* have come into general use.

(Perfectionists, we always have with us. Twenty years ago, someone brought up the question that *luminarias* were merely the little fires and not the lanterns. Someone else decided that *luminarios,* with "o" were the lanterns. Later someone coined the word *farolito* for lantern. *Luminaria* is a feminine noun, not a masculine one. It means "festival lantern." *Farolito* is the diminutive of *farol,* a lantern, from the common variety to a lighthouse lamp. The Spanish-speaking people called the little fires *luminarias* because they gave light or illuminated the area where they were used. When the lanterns came into use they correctly used the name *luminarias. Farolito* is the modern version preferred by some English-speaking people. Spanish-speaking people prefer *luminarias.*)

The sight of a *luminaria* brings a smile of sheer joy to the young women of today. They, unlike their mothers, never heard of the special *fiesta,* so at Christmas time they think only of the *luminarias* for Christmas Eve decorations before going to Midnight Mass, *la Misa del gallo,* for the carols and the treats, and later for the collation of the chocolate as they open their gifts.

For Christmas Eve in earlier days, the children set up on a window sill the *Nacimiento* (crib) representing the scene at Bethlehem, using little figurines of clay that had originally come from Spain, which were used from year to year. After it was arranged the children would bring presents to the Child Jesus—candy, paper flowers, piñon nuts, fruit. They did not receive their own presents until January 6 since they believed *Los Reyes Magos*—the Magi—brought their gifts as they traveled to Bethlehem following the star.

Since Christmas Eve was a day of abstinence or meatless day, yet a time for cooking and preparing food for *El Dia de Navidad,* the homes of the Spanish people were redolent with the fragrance of spices, mixing with the scents of cooking of corn for *posole, tamales* and *empanaditas,* all made with meat. So after midnight Mass and the new day, the ladies partook of a small collation of chocolate and *biscochitos.* Not so the men and the youngsters; a dish of *posole,* a cup of coffee and an *empanadita,* fried meat pastry, completed their pre-dawn breakfast before retiring for the little sleep left to them. For Christmas dinner, of course, there would be the *gallina de la tierra,* the chicken of the region, as the turkey was called. Already they had forgotten the Spanish name for turkey, the *pavo.* Accompanying the *gallina de la tierra,* there would also be served *calabazitas,* or baby squash, with green *chile,* which had been dried the previous Spring, also *queso añejo* or the preserved goat's cheese. A side dish of *tasajos* or the dried musk melon whose precious seeds they had brought from Spain, or the sauce made from the *orejon* (big ears), which consisted of dried apples or pears. And, of course, more *posole.*

It was a sumptuous dinner, the makings of which had been carefully planned and prepared for six months—for this was indeed a festival day, a day of rejoicing and celebration.

TEN MINUTE TOUR
Earl W. Scott

EARL W. SCOTT is the author of numerous short stories and articles and is a former instructor at Highland University. For several years he worked for the State Tourist Bureau and State Highway Department, retiring a couple of years ago. The past two years have been occupied in running down background on material for a long-projected novel, *Melody Lady*. His home is at Seton Village, Santa Fe.

"The stop is Santa Fe. Ladies collect your mitts and fans— Gents your six guns. This is the end of the Trail."

It was perhaps with some such announcement as this that the stage driver pulled up his lathered six-mule team in front of the Fonda back in the seventies.

Even in those times there must have been many a traveler desiring to make the most of his stay, be it for hours or days, in the nation's oldest capital. For many years tales of this old *adobe* city, nestling at the end of the Santa Fe Trail, had drifted eastward beyond the Allegheny Mountains to whet the appetites of the curious and stir the blood of adventure.

And there would have been much to see. What a ring-side seat it would prove if a modern tourist could be whisked back on some magic carpet and ushered for a short hour to a *Plaza* bench in that fabulous frontier era. The cavalcade of an expanding America would have milled about him. Creaking schooners of traders, skin-clad trappers, soldiers, Indians, scouts and dark-eyed *señoritas*—Spaniard, Frenchman, Englishman, American, all intent on their own affairs. Much of what they saw is still here.

With that in mind, a number of ten minute tours on foot are suggested for the visitor, with the old *Plaza* as headquarters.

First to see is the Palace of the Governors on the north side of the square. From this single-storied, rambling *adobe* structure, centuries of laws were dispensed, battles fought, treaties signed. Here Zebulon Pike was imprisoned and Lew Wallace wrote much of *Ben Hur*.

Its many rooms are a treasure house of priceless native blankets, beads, documents, pottery and implements of war—symbols of every tribe and creed that went into the building of this great Southwestern Empire.

The intelligent traveler has long since proved to himself the wisdom of the words, "To observe is to learn." Time spent in browsing about this old Museum can well be an education in itself. Development of the life and culture from the earliest Tewa tribesman to the inhabitants of our day can be traced from arrows to *ollas*, so carefully preserved here beneath glass. Ancient grinding stones jostle exquisite silver bracelets of modern Navajo design. There's a wealth of antique ordnance when wars were young—pistols, daggers, spurs and armor. The library of records and yellowing script alone is a challenge to history or book lover.

A twelve-foot table shows a physical map, a clay replica in miniature of an Indian pueblo, complete from communal-house to *kivas*. Wall murals display scenes from the surrounding country, termed the most interesting fifty mile square in America.

Truly color and atmosphere may well be absorbed in the Palace of the Governors as background for jaunts about the surrounding city.

Less than a mile northward lie the crumbling walls of Fort Marcy. This one-time barrack of American occupation overlooks the city from a spread of low lying hills.

Westward, across the Taos road, in the very teeth of the sinking sun, the Cross of the Martyrs throws its lengthening shadow. This noble monument to enduring faith was erected in memory of the brave *padres* who lost their lives in the Indian uprisings.

All over town are interesting examples of traditional architecture—some very old, and like the Presbyterian church, and the National Park Service building, some built in recent years.

Short blocks south of the *Plaza* on College Street and beyond the Rio Santa Fe stands the tiny church of San Miguel with its treasure of old Spanish bells. These sturdy buttressed walls have weathered the snows of centuries. The high slotted windows suggest preparation against possible attack and faded altar paintings have been pierced by enemy arrows.

Nearby stands the "Oldest House," a one-time dwelling, originally constructed of puddled *adobe* (wet mud poured into skin-stretched forms, before the making of sun dried bricks became the order of the day).

Almost a stone's throw to the south stands a second dwelling shaded by a line of venerable trees. Old timers tell how the one-time notorious desperado Billy the Kid, clambered into these sheltering branches to attempt the life of the Territorial Governor, Lew Wallace. How, but for the timely breaking of a dead limb the world might well have lost one of its greatest stories, *Ben Hur*.

There are several thoroughfares in the City of the Holy Faith, well worth exploration. Palace Avenue, San Francisco Street, Agua Fria and by all means Canyon Road. But a stroll up the *Acequia* path is suggested preferably at sunset or under white moonlight.

The *Acequia Madre* (Mother Ditch) is likewise centuries old, built back when the snows were younger on the towering Sangre de Cristo peaks to the east. It has long nurtured the many lovely patio gardens for which Santa Fe is famous. *Adobe* walls line its banks where huge cottonwoods stand guard. While the more modest lilacs and willows make drooping shadows across the singing water. Here if anywhere the gentle spirit of the old town lives again. You may be forced to step aside for three hurrying burros, prodded into greater effort by some hastening Manuel. Groaning under their huge saddle-stacked loads of freshly gathered piñon wood, their tiny hoofs bite red dust from the rut-worn path as they make for the distant *plaza*.

Perhaps Manuel in passing may touch his battered hat brim and murmur a greeting of *"Buenas Noches, Señor."* You answer as courteously, realizing you have made way, not for tomorrow, but an almost forgotten yesterday.

If it chances to be springtime, you find many golden blooms of Castilian roses spilling in a yellow flood over *patio* walls. Those tiny tinkling bells, sounding across the greening fields, announce the arrival of a goat herd on distant Atalaya Hill.

So finally the *Acequia* path bisects Canyon Road and turning left you make for the Plaza. Soon on your right loom the twin towers of the Cathedral, with the benevolent statue of Bishop Lamy bowing entrance at its doors

Santa Fe has long been a mecca for artists and artisans from every part of the world. If chance offers, try the galleries of the Museum of Art. Study the oils, etchings and pottery, choice offering of these merchants of beauty. See the blanket weavers and silversmiths working at their trade in the shops around the square. There'll be dark-faced Indian women, in squaw boots and blankets, offering Santa Clara and Domingo pottery for sale under the shelter of the Palace *portal*.

For some time you may have noticed the figure of an old man sitting calmly on a bench, close to the granite marker, near *Plaza* center. His hair is gray, and his eyes wise with many years of living. Fronting him, on the sidewalk, is a slowly growing heap of tiny hulls, some of which crunch loudly under the feet of passers-by. You pause, watching. Periodically he reaches into a pocket to thrust a handful of the objects into his mouth. Time passes, but what is time to Señor Ascension Lujan—just one more *mañana* among so many others. He munches contentedly, spitting fresh hulls onto the walk.

Noting your interest he smiles offering you a handful of his treasure. "But what are they?" you ask, accepting his gift, and frown at the brown objects in your palm.

"Piñones, amigo," he grins, "with your teeth you crack the leetle shells and you have a fine meal, no?"

"Right." you follow his example, deceived by his deftness. You gulp and choke, much to his delight, chasing the elusive kernels about your mouth with a balky tongue-tip, but to no avail. You are finally forced to give up in disgust, realizing there can even be science in mastering a piñon nut. You mutter a halting *"Adios"* as you turn away, just to get the feel of the world and not to be outdone by your new-found friend. You are recalling now the sweeping vistas of green, viewed from the bus windows as you approached the town. Those hillsides of orchard like growth had been termed *piñon* trees by a fellow passenger.

"You may boast about Iowa corn," he'd offered, "these folks found a wide trade in *piñon* nuts before the war. Shipped 'em as far away as South America and Russia."

Thinking of these things as you stroll away you discover your steps slowing haunted by the memory of the granite marker close to Ascension's bench. There'd been words chiseled there. You return to read.

Leafy shadows, from nearby trees stir restlessly across the face of the gray stone. The sentence leaps at you.

END OF THE SANTA FE TRAIL

And as you sense the import of that simple notation, history starts building pictures in the evening shadows about you. A troop of blue-clad horsemen sweeping into the square, a jangling wagon train urged on by sweating bullwhackers whose cracking whips and shouting cries lift echoing to the low hung stars. Somewhere there's string music and words, not English, hummed softly. The spell is heightened, then broken by the nearby clanging of the Cathedral bells.

Reluctantly you turn, walking slowly toward your hotel. Surely you saw these things or was it the spirit of the Ancient City weaving its moonlight spell?

At the curb you turn. The *Plaza* is peopled only by whispering trees and the solitary figure of a bright-eyed old man, munching *piñons* on a bench.

OLD DAYS IN OLD ALBUQUERQUE
Julia M. Keleher

JULIA KELEHER was born and reared in Albuquerque and the early history of the town has been one of her chief interests. She received her B.A. and M.A. degrees at the University of New Mexico and did graduate work at New York University and the Breadloaf School of English. She returned to the University of New Mexico to become an assistant professor of English. She has written numerous magazine articles and co-authored *The Padre of Isleta* with Elsie Ruth Chant. She retired from the University in 1959.

The sixty-year struggle of Old Albuquerque to retain its identity and individuality is drawing to a close. Slowly, but surely Old Albuquerque is being encompassed on all sides and soon there will be but one Albuquerque, a merger of the Old and New Towns.

For centuries Albuquerque maintained the even tenor of its way, its *plaza* teeming with life, its church of San Felipe de Neri built before 1707, standing as a landmark and sentinel of spirituality from the Sandia mountains to the Río Grande. The coming of the railroad in the spring of 1880 marked the beginning of the end of the importance of the old town of Albuquerque. The railroad station, more than two miles away from the *plaza*, assumed its rightful place as the most important factor in the life of an area which extended long distances in every direction. Within a year after the completion of the railroad into Albuquerque station, merchants and business men began to desert the Albuquerque that had carried on for so many generations. One by one business men moved into the new village, bit by bit the *plaza* of the old town began to fade into the background. There was a bitter struggle, carried on for years over ownership of the name "Albuquerque." The old town clung with tenacity to the name. The post office department decided that all mail addressed to Albuquerque should continue to be sent to the post office in the original town, and that mail destined for the new town should be addressed New Albuquerque. To avoid confusion, people began to address letters to Old Albuquerque. Thus was born the name that has clung to the old town until the present day. Gradually the New Albuquerque was dropped and just Albuquerque was substituted, but not until after many communications had been addressed to the Post Office Department in Washington and many government officials had their say as to the rightful ownership of the name Albuquerque.

Time was when the Albuquerque of the old days was the trading center for the people up and down the Río Grande Valley. Bernalillo, it is true, was an important place, because of the residence there of many *ricos,* the Oteros, Pereas and others, with their *haciendas* and headquarters for untold thousands of sheep. Tomé, down the Río Grande in Valencia county, was a thriving town, but complained every now and then to the Spanish, Mexican and even American civil and ecclesiastical authorities that Albuquerque was trying, in the language of the present day, "to hog everything." Albuquerque was headquarters for many years, under Spanish, Mexican and American rule, in turn, for soldiers and dragoons, and for army supplies. Horses and drivers of stage coach lines changed at the end of the run in Albuquerque, and every few days wagon trains arrived in Albuquerque from the Missouri river with great loads of merchandise destined for the town merchants and for traders on the Río Grande as far south as Mesilla and for the Mexican towns of Chihuahua and Durango.

Everything for Albuquerque was changed with the coming of the first railroad train on April 22, 1880. The official name of the railroad company that built into Albuquerque was "New Mexico and Southern Pacific Railroad." Right-of-way men had come into Albuquerque for the railroad, expecting to locate a depot and transportation facilities adjacent to the existing town. Difficulty was encountered in obtaining at a reasonable price a tract of land adequate to accommodate the railway facilities. Franz Huning, one of the earliest of the settlers in the Río Grande valley, had purchased a tract of land, which can now be described as running from Laguna Boulevard to Tenth Street on Central Avenue, and from Central Avenue south to the Río Grande Park and to the east bank of the Río Grande itself. It was on this tract of land that Franz Huning hoped the railway terminal facilities would be built. However, the right-of-way men and location engineers selected at reasonable price tracts of land in places then considered a great distance from the center of business in Albuquerque. The New Mexico Town Company was incorporated by railroad promoters. Lots were sold on Railroad, now Central Avenue, in the eighties at what appeared to be rather high prices; for example, inside lots between Fourth and Fifth Streets were sold at one hundred sixty-five dollars for twenty-five feet. Sixty years have demonstrated the wisdom of those who bought lots on Railroad Avenue, as prices have increased a thousand and more per cent.

It was originally contemplated by the promoters of the railway line into Albuquerque that it should be extended immediately to Guaymas, on the west coast of Mexico, the closest salt water to Albuquerque. On the very day that the railway came into Albuquerque, W. R. Morley, with the high sounding title *Ingeniero en Jefe de la Compania del Ferrocarril de Sonora,* was in Guaymas, laying plans for the construction of the line into the Republic of Mexico.

The coming of the railroad into Albuquerque called for a celebration. Citizens turned out in great numbers. Perhaps many sensed the railroad meant oncoming declines in property values in the old town, and visioned the fate that has subsequently overtaken Old Albuquerque. On April 22, 1880, at noon, to welcome the coming of the railroad, the procession was formed in the *plaza,* at Old Albuquerque to be sure, for there was as yet no other Albuquerque. There were many men on horseback. Quite a few of the horses were bedecked with saddles and bridles ornamented with silver. Every available carriage was in the procession, the ladies riding in them being attired in their most becoming costumes. Over the dusty road to the railroad line the procession wended its way, headed by the Eighth United States Cavalry Band. Appropriate speeches were made at the "depot grounds" and the program continued until after dark when a huge display of fireworks lighted up the skies for miles around. The first railroad train, once it reached Albuquerque, was turned around and traveled north again to Bernalillo, sixteen miles away, to give free rides to all who could climb aboard, with the return trip accomplished without mishap. The committee in charge of the celebration consisted of W. C. Hazeldine, chairman; Santiago Baca, Francisco Chavez, Franz Huning and E. S. Stover.

With the enthusiasm generated by the coming of the railroad, Albuquerque station became more and more the important place in the world of business and commerce in the Río Grande Valley and as Albuquerque station increased in importance "Old Albuquerque" became of less and less importance. The first New Mexico Territorial Fair was held in Albuquerque, October 3 to October 8, 1881. The officials of the fair were as follows: E. S. Stover, president; Franz Huning, José L. Perea, Ambrosio Armijo and M. S. Otero, vice presidents; W. K. P. Wilson, treasurer; M. T. Thomas, secretary; H. R. Whiting, corresponding secretary; with an executive committee composed of W. C. Hazeldine, S. Baca, N. T. Armijo, T. Hughes and E. Madden. The resources exhibited at the fair included minerals, cattle, sheep, hogs, fruits, poultry, grain and vegetables. Governor Lionel A. Sheldon attended the fair and remained all week. Col. Robert G. Ingersoll, then at the height of his fame as a lecturer was scheduled to attend the fair, but failed to put in an appearance. The fair was held in Old Albuquerque on a large tract of land west of what is now known as Río Grande Boulevard, just north of the golf course of the Albuquerque Country Club.

The Albuquerque of the old days was a colorful and interesting place. The county of Bernalillo was an empire in itself, embracing the territory now shown on the map as Bernalillo, Torrance, Sandoval and McKinley counties. The transportation of freight in and out of Albuquerque was almost entirely by oxen trains. Oxen and mule trains were on regular schedule to Los Lunas, Belen, Las Cruces and Mesilla. Prominent merchants in Albuquerqué before the coming of the railroad included Charles Lewis, Franz Huning, Stover, Crary & Co., Henry Springer, Louis Ilfeld, Ed. Spitz, Thomas F. Keleher. The eastbound oxen trains carried wool, hides, pelts and minerals. The incoming trains carried merchandise and government supplies. There was a well established custom that business was carried on as usual on Sunday as well as on week days. The Albuquerque *Review* was the principal paper published in the town during the seventies, with the late William McGuinness, father of M. J. McGuinness, now an Albuquerque attorney, as editor. On June 19, 1875, the *Review* was printed on manila wrapping paper in order to impress delinquent subscribers with the importance of paying up.

For many years there stood in Old Albuquerque a rambling *adobe* building just west of the old Bernalillo County Court House, pointed out as "the old General Sheridan residence." This legend had its origin in the fact that Miss Rucker, a daughter of Major Daniel Rucker, was born in the house when he was stationed in Albuquerque. Miss Rucker, grown to young womanhood was married to General Phil Sheridan in Chicago on June 2, 1875.

Albuquerque was the home for many years of José Manuel Gallegos, who died on April 21, 1875. He was educated for the Roman Catholic priesthood, and officiated as curate at the church in Old Albuquerque for some years prior to 1865. Entertaining a preference for political life to church work "Padre" Gallegos held many important positions in the Territory. He was several times in the Territorial legislature, was elected speaker of the House at Santa Fe, and was twice elected to serve as delegate in Congress from New Mexico in Washington.

Albuquerque was pretty much isolated from the world of rapid communication until July 24, 1875, when a telegraph line was built into the *plaza* from Santa Fe and continued on to Socorro, Fort Craig, Fort McRae and Fort Bayard. One of the first telegrams sent out over the wire was by J. M. Perea, of Bernalillo, who closed a deal by telegraph with a Colorado dealer for 24,000 sheep. The prices, interesting to sheep growers of today, were, for ewes, $2.40; for lambs, $1.50; for wethers, $1.87. In the days between 1870 and 1880, hundreds of emigrants passed through on their way west.

Thomas D. Post was a most popular man because he operated Post's Exchange, for many years a landmark, known in the years of Old Town's decline as San Felipe Club. Tom Post's Exchange was rated as a most excellent hotel, where most of the stage drivers stopped and gave over to the latest gossip.

The Río Grande was frozen nearly across at Albuquerque on Christmas day in 1878. Teams were obliged to travel to Isleta to cross over the river. Tom Post talked about building a pontoon bridge across the river for the accommodation of the public, but the New Mexico sun soon asserted itself and a pontoon bridge was not required.

The last stage coach that carried mail from the east into Albuquerque, by way of Las Vegas, Santa Fe and La Bajada, arrived in Albuquerque on April 19, 1880. On June 18, 1880, from the banks of the Río Grande, a crowd of people said *adios* to A. M. Conklin, proprietor and editor of the *Advance,* a weekly paper published in Old Albuquerque. Conklin decided to move to Socorro and finding it difficult to obtain transportation for his printing office and household effects, decided to build a boat and go to Socorro by water. O. Burlingame built the boat for Mr. Conklin. The river craft was named "The Advance." Conklin, Burlingame and outfit floated down the river by day, ran ashore at night and camped, just like Mark Twain would have had them do. Conklin and his printing outfit arrived in Socorro safely and he started the Socorro *Sun,* but his career was abruptly terminated when he was killed in a church there on Christmas Eve, 1880.

The old days in Old Albuquerque are gone forever. But the romance and the glory that once belonged to the Albuquerque that was will never pass away.

THE ROSWELL STORY
Frieda Bryan Hyatt

Frieda Bryan Hyatt lives at Ruidoso and was a former editor of the *Bowie Texas News*. She has been a correspondent for numerous Texas newspapers, and has been writing magazine articles for several years. An original play which she wrote was presented at the Texas Centennial and in twelve other towns. After commuting between Bowie, Texas, and Ruidoso for five years, Mrs. Hyatt and her husband, Samuel, are now permanent residents of New Mexico.

Lady Luck has played a big part in the establishment and growth of Roswell. Way back before there ever was a town, five tiny streams of water poured out of the dry hard soil. They formed an oasis for thirsty cattle crossing the range in this hot country. This was six miles from the present site of Roswell.

In those days, cattle was the chief source of income. In the 1860's unfenced land stretched as far as the eye could see. The Goodnight-Loving Trail was well-known by 1865.

Indians, like cattle, knew the importance of the precious water at this spot. The Mescalero Apaches and the Comanches beat a path to the streams in the wake of thousands of buffalo that came this way. The abundance of water in a mild climate made an attractive combination for others on the move. This "natural" appealed to a gambler of note, one Van Smith who moved from Omaha, Nebraska, to Santa Fe. He could not resist the chance for a sure thing.

Van Smith put up a couple of buildings. They were made of *adobe* which in this dry climate were substantial enough. One of his edifices served as a sort of inn. When a post office was opened in the community Van Smith managed to have it named for his father, Roswell Smith. The latter never saw the town but the name stuck. Lady Luck smiled on the new community. In contrast some men from Missouri who had laid out a site a few miles southwest of Roswell saw their infant, Missouri Plaza, die soon after birth. Oblivion came because there was not a sufficient supply of water. But at Roswell the water flowed and the town flourished.

In 1877 Captain J. C. Lea and his wife purchased Van Smith's holdings. Included were several hundred acres of land that now make up the center of Roswell. This was a happy circumstance for the future of Roswell, for Lea was a man who looked ahead. He was also a born developer. He had ditches constructed to lead from Spring River to small tracts of land. The precious water enabled vegetables to be successfully grown on the land. Feed for cattle and horses thrived under this arrangement. Cottonwoods were hauled a distance of 50 miles and planted on the sides of the ditches. The area became a place of beauty. Thus chance made Roswell a beautiful city later on.

Even in those early days the trees were very noticeable. One visitor who would not have been thought of as particularly tree-minded back in 1877 was George Coe. This little man took a leading part in the Billy the Kid saga and fought side by side with the Kid at the Blazer Mill battle, skirmishes at Roswell, and the famous fracas in Lincoln town.

In his autobiography Coe wrote: "Back in the year 1877 Roswell was a town of six small trees growing on the west side of the main road, and two small houses. One house was a residence and the other served as a store and post office. On the east side of the main road there were a few native huts made of mud sticks and gunny sacks."

By 1885 a plat of the tiny community was finished. In 1891 Roswell was incorporated as a town with its citizenry totaling 400. Another farsighted developer hit town. This was E. A.

Cahoon who showed up in 1890. He was a thrifty New Englander, used to railroads and to money. But he landed in this
western hamlet via buckboard, having left the nearest railroad
175 miles distant. Cahoon clicked immediately with the fortunes of Roswell. He brought money with him. Cahoon and
cash appeared under the clear New Mexico blue sky as a sign
which read: "First National Bank."

For the next 40 years both played a large part in Roswell's
economy. The bank was operated on vision, courage, and good
judgment. It was a good business any way you looked at it. One
of Roswell's leaders today says with pardonable pride: "The
biggest thing that has happened to Roswell is its growth." He
is right. Figures tell it plainly.

The city had a population of 2,049 in 1900; 6,174 in 1910;
twice this number by 1940; just short of 45,000 today. Retail
sales went from $7,817,280.00 in 1940 to nearly 82 million dol-
lars today. Wholesale sales jumped to twice what they were in
1950 with the figure crowding $43,000,000 this year.

In Chaves County, of which Roswell is the county seat, agriculture accounts for $32,000,000. This is nearly a $10,000,000
gain over the year 1957. Building permits in 1961 soared to
nearly $14,000,000; postal receipts hit $601,198; the three
banks in the city had deposits just under $53,000,000.

Non-agriculture represents well over $48,000,000 income to
residents of the county.

Permanent government facilities lead with Walker Air Force
Base pouring in over $15,000,000 a year into the city. Twelve
Atlas ICBM Installation sites swell this figure considerably.
The way Roswell's economy has worked is very fortunate for
its future. Diversification puts the city on a good basis. In 1920
agriculture and livestock accounted for the income of the majority of the citizens. Today these occupations make up a third
of the earnings. A nice balance, for the rest comes from government, the petroleum industry with its exploration and development offices; legal, medical, and banking activities; wholesale
and retail trade for this part of New Mexico.

Two new silhouettes on the architectural skyline are elementary school buildings with no windows. They are air conditioned the year around.

Oil flows in Chaves County to enrich its people, and Roswell is one of the chief benefactors. In 1950 a little over 48,000 barrels of the precious fluid were produced. The figure is 5,000,000 barrels a year now. There are 79 major and independent companies, independent consulting geologists, and lease brokers in Roswell. The industry brings in over $6,000,000 a year to the employees.

With an elevation of 3,600 feet and an average summer temperature of 77 degrees, outdoor living is enjoyed in Roswell. Homes boast beautiful *patios* and there is much outdoor entertaining. There is a large array of outdoor play equipment, three large city pools, two well-equipped country clubs, an outstanding library.

Roswell has earned an enviable reputation in its work with youngsters. Civic workers make this a year-round program. The National Little League Baseball Championship was won in 1956. A trained executive is in charge of the Chaves County Memorial Youth Center. The structure is valued at $200,000. There are two other smaller centers in the city. Arts, crafts, tap dancing, theatre, swimming, and games serve to keep the youth occupied in a healthy way. Summer projects culminate in a grand finale on the youth center grounds. Each fall a Halloween celebration is staged. Children take part in costumes, bands, and floats. The Roswell Sertoma Club, along with radio station KGFL, sponsor the Golden Gloves program. Regional and State tournaments for this slugfest are held in Roswell. The Roswell Optimist Club, The Roswell Daily Record, and the Valley Chevrolet Co. promote the annual soap box derby held on July 4.

Planning on the part of the residents is shown in the wide streets and the beautiful buildings. It is also shown in the Golden Age Club for men and women over 60. It is good for the members and for Roswell. A child or an adult need never say: "There isn't anything to do." In this city that started because of a good meeting place of water and land there is always something to do. Bottomless Lakes Park is 10 miles east. The name came from the early day cowboys' fruitless efforts to determine their depth. They tied their lariats together and never could reach bottom.

South of Roswell 106 miles is Carlsbad Caverns National Park. To the west 70 miles is Ruidoso with its race track, towering pines, ski run, and exhilarating climate. Sixty miles west is old Lincoln town, center of Billy the Kid's escapades.

Bob Crosby achieved the distinction of being the world's champion cowboy. His personal belongings are on display in the city museum. Here also are collections of paintings by famed Peter Hurd, old and modern artists, the Goddard Rocket Tower, and other historical exhibits. Dr. Goddard is known as "The father of the modern rocket."

South of the city is the Oasis Ranch, site of the largest arte- and Roswell youngsters have won hundreds of blue ribbons for sheep and other entries.

The oil business is a gamble for many but Roswell citizens have put as much certainty into it as possible. One evidence of this is the handsome eight-story Petroleum Building. Roswell business men put up the capital for it. Other modern buildings have been financed by local citizens to house offices of oil firms. People are downright neighborly in Roswell. They greet you; make you feel at home. And they are church-minded. The city has 76 churches to prove this.

The horse helped Roswell get its start, just as it did most western towns. Without the horse the herds could not have been moved along the long cattle trails that threaded the region. Today the horse still gets top billing from a lot of people in Roswell. The Pecos Valley Horsemen was established in 1947. Chaves County Sheriff's Posse is another organization for horse lovers. Both groups have brought riding honors to their community. New Mexico Military Institute's cavalry unit gained fame until it was discontinued recently. The N.M.M.I. has turned out thousands of sturdy leaders in military, business, and cultural activities since it was set up in 1891. Fifteen buildings occupy its vast campus of 47 acres.

Interwoven with the everyday life of Roswell's citizens, just as it has an invaluable place in this country's safety, is Walker Air Force Base, of the Strategic Air Command. At Walker is the 509th Bomb Wing, the 6th Wing, the 812th Air Base Group, the 4036th USAF Hospital and several attached units from other commands.

The base was re-named in 1958 for Brigadier General Kenneth N. Walker of Cerrillos, N. M. This hero was posthumously awarded the Congressional Medal of Honor for heroic flying in the South Pacific. Walker's famous drill team and drum and bugle corps has thrilled thousands at the Eastern New Mexico State Fair. The 150-member Rod and Gun Club, the SAC Aero Club, auto show-sponsoring Dusters drag race club, Explorers Club, and the Riding Club add to the outdoor attractions of Southeastern New Mexico.

Roswell has come a long way since the time when only cattle, water, and empty land greeted the eye.

MY NEIGHBOR IS AN ARTIST
Lorraine Carr

LORRAINE CARR (HUDDLESTON) IS a radio reporter and commentator in Santa Fe and is author of the best selling book, *Mother of the Smiths,* published in the late 1940's. Besides novels, she has written articles and short stories for a number of magazines. Although born and educated in Texas, the granddaughter of the famed Texas Ranger, Joseph Milton Hanna, Lorraine Carr, having lived in Taos and Santa Fe for the past thirty-two years, is a long-time New Mexican.

Taos is one of the most colorful spots in our nation and has long been the mecca for artists from all over the world. For many years I lived among the artists of the Taos colony, and they were friendly, interesting neighbors.

Yet when I have casually remarked to southern friends that my neighbor is an artist the statement could invoke no more consternation had I said that blood-thirsty Apaches who coveted my scalp lived to the left of me and to the right of me.

One austere friend took great pains to relate to me tales she has heard concerning "them crazy artists." In her estimation they are indeed a queer sort, clannish, unfriendly, high hat, sissies, softies and utterly lacking in hospitality. Not only are they of little value to a community, but . . . . it was then she tugged at my sleeve and whispered: "Don't you know that genius and lunacy are well known to be next door neighbors?"

Yes, she truly believes my neighbor to be a lunatic dressed in a velvet smock with a beret pulled cockily over one eye.

He paces his studio floor in a sort of frenzy, waiting, so it would seem, for an intrusion that would permit him the pleasure of hurling a sketch box at her nose, or to chase her down a narrow street, flourishing the hind leg of an easel dangerously over her head.

True, I've seen my neighbor pace the floor in a sort of frenzy, for the more vital the painter's art, the greater his "madness"; I have heard him swear profusely, simply because a picture would not "click"; I have seen him crawl about the studio on all-fours, squinting, first his right eye, then his left one; I've seen him cup his fist into a miniature telescope through which he might view, unobstructed, the inverted canvas, and hoping, thereby, to determine if he had put enough light on the rump of a little bear cub. And, more times than once he has commanded that I, too, crawl about the studio floor on all-fours, and I have obliged him by my indulgence in such crazy antics, and have shared with sincerity his anxiety over the predicament of the little bear's rump . . . . but even so, I knew this neighbor was not a lunatic. He was a genius. And, if on the morrow he should pass me on the street and fail to speak, I would say to myself. "His mind is full of his work," for I have learned such men and women are usually inconvenient friends.

I have learned, too, that art is not a sentimental affair. It is an activity, a continuous labor that often requires the strength of a bull and the patience of Job. The very word "artist" no matter if it be writing, painting, dancing or music, denotes supreme self-sacrifice and the ability to give oneself up, unreservedly, for the world and for the service of humanity. Genius has always been and will continue to be solitary, repressed, suffering—and misunderstood.

My neighbors are men and women of national and international fame, many of whom have lived tragic, intense, and extravagant lives. Nevertheless, they are not queer, clannish folk, but human beings the same as you and I. When faced with an emergency the efficiency and heroism demonstrated by them often exceed the same efforts of the layman.

In the old days in Taos there was no means to fight a fire

other than the tedious bucket brigade. Taos is the third oldest village in the United States and many of the old *adobe* buildings, older than the Constitution, are ready fire traps. So in days gone by most any night we might hear the "all out" call, which was the ringing of the old church bell in quick, irritant peals. We always piled out of bed, no matter how deep the snow, grabbed our buckets and went on the run. Soon the cry of *fire* spread over the sleeping village. Down La Loma and up Kit Carson street came fat men with the tails of their nightgowns flapping in the brisk north wind; down narrow crooked streets came old men with their long underwear showing beneath heavy overcoats; old women and young, Anglos and Spanish dressed in pajamas or outing flannel gowns under bathrobes came with their buckets. Yes, all of us ran with all our might. For the house of Pedro, the wood-hauler, was on fire.

There was no thought of highhattedness. I have seen my neighbor, Kenneth Adams, rush up to the old well, whence came the water supply for our buckets, and relieve Maria, the washwoman, now wearied from continuous letting down and drawing up of the bucket.

Adams has stood at the well drawing water until his hands were blistered by the rope . . . . and his hands, mind you, are symbols of skill and efficacy, hands that had painted a picture that has won a Corcoran Prize. Nor did he work more diligently or exhaustingly than Emil Bisstram or Victor Higgins, one a Guggenheim Fellowship man, the other a high critic who has served on the Corcoran jury. Yes, these three artists fought shoulder-to-shoulder alongside José, the *adobe* maker. Their faces were grimy with soot and cinders; their hands red and chapped; their sockless feet shoved into unlaced shoes were mired down in snow and slush; their long underwear was wet to their knees, and was no different as I could see from the suit worn by José, and all of it likely a Montgomery Ward brand.

Or take the case of Blanche Grant and the late Buck Dunton who were at outs for a dozen years or so. Once I dared ask Dunton about an old grudge that would hold so long. All he said was: "No woman is going to tell me where I can build my privy." In the old days in Taos the plumber was like the fire engine: there wasn't any. And it seems the stubborn Dunton had built his outhouse on the rear of his property line which was much too close to Miss Grant's studio for nasal comfort to say nothing of the pangs that must have pierced her artistic heart.

I took sides with the woman painter but Dunton blurted out: "Well, it's my back yard and it's my privy and by God it's going to stay there." Well, knowing this big game painter as I did I felt certain the small structure would remain right there. Miss Grant evidently shared my opinion for she planted a huge bed of hollyhocks around the unsightly edifice. The crimsoned blossomed plants attained a height of ten feet and she painted them on a canvas that sold for five hundred dollars.

Now take E. L. Blumenschein, often called the high critic of the colony. He was as well known in New York City as in Taos. Blumenschein's smallish, delicate stature might have suggested a softie or a sissie. He was indeed a great artist, exceedingly painstaking, and painted with such vigor and intensity that it has been said he would pause at his work only if Jesus should come. But if you stuck a smelly old fishing creel under his nose, he'd ask, "Are they biting?"—and drop his brushes and in two shakes be headed for the Río Grande. Blumenschein was no sissie. In mid-winter he stood the livelong day with the snow knee-deep, casting a frozen line into the water. Never have I seen such ecstasy in any countenance as that which a worm writhing in agony with a fish hook probing its bowels has wrought in his.

Once while O. E. Berninghaus was busy painting the *adobe* house of a native family, he was suddenly distracted by the wailings of the mother. The artist could not understand a word of Spanish, yet the fluent manipulations of her hands indicated that her little boy had fallen into the old well, the diameter of which would permit the immersion of a small elephant. He dropped his brush and directed the mother to fetch a rope in a hurry. But in face of the emergency she had rushed into the house to pray. The artist believing a rope to be more needful than prayer hurried out to the barn-yard to find one. While he snaked the dripping boy from the well, the mother was yet muttering, full speed, words of imploration in front of the image on the wall.

Bert G. Phillips was one of the oldest and most beloved in the Taos art colony. In the early days when Taos was lawless, ugly and uncouth, two strangers from goodness knows where, halted their horses beside the high *adobe* wall which connects the old Penitente Church, used by Phillips as a studio, with the *adobe* house in which he lived.

"Now what do you think is over that wall?" one of the strangers asked.

"A firing squad," answered his companion who was mindful of recent gunplay and bloodshed.

Over the wall Phillips, busy at his easel, had heard the remarks. He paused from his work for one brief second to glance at the sun. If he put aside his brushes for a few minutes the changing shadows would necessitate his recalling the model on the morrow; that would mean more money for posing, and Phillips had but little cash. But this beauty inside the *patio* was all he had to share with the strangers over the wall. It was his hospitality.

Phillips opened the blue gate that permitted entrance to the *patio* in which he was working and called out loudly: "Come right in, gentlemen."

The two strangers, who probably could not identify a sketch box from an oil cup, looked up to see a young man dressed in paint-smeared smock, with palette in hand. They roared with laughter: "Oh, one of them damn crazy artists."

"Come right in," again Phillips invited them.

The two men viewed with suspicion any act of friendliness in the Taos country, so with their hands on their hips ready to draw they stepped inside the blue gate. They found, not a bullet-ridden wall as they had anticipated, but tall trees, green grasses and overhead bits of sky as blue as turquoise; even the sunlight that filtered through the trees looked like gold. Over in one corner of the *patio* sat a bronze-faced Indian girl among a mass of tall, crimsoned hollyhocks. She wore a purple dress with a darker purple shawl about her shoulders and was busy beading a strip on a piece of white buckskin.

One of the strangers gasped as he removed his hat. "Well . . . . Well!"

" 'Tis a pretty sight" the other stranger commented as he, too, removed his hat in gratitude.

J. H. Sharpe has been acclaimed the greatest painter of the American Indian. So great is his fame, national and international, that people who journey to the village of Taos to view his work sometimes tremble when they lift the latch on the gate that leads to his famous studio. Yet, Pablo, the wood vendor, would slap Sharpe's back most heartily and call out: *"Buenos días mi amigo,"* for the wood vendor had learned that great folk are simple folk.

My neighbors have been great men and women, yet just human beings who live, eat and sleep in a way no different from your way or mine. I have helped Nicaloi Fechin gather the wild plums from the trees around his studio; Leon Gaspard and I have fed the rabbits together and have gathered in the eggs; Frank Hoffman's old jersey cow kicked the bucket out of my hand when I was helping him do the milking; I've dressed John Young-Hunter's infected hand when he was afraid he might never use it again; Joe Fleck and I have often fought over the water in the irrigation ditch to see who would water the apple trees; Dorothy Brett and Eleanor Kissel and I usually talk about blue teacups and such things as we have on our shelves . . . . I believe that none of my neighbors consider his or her art a badge to a higher cast. To them art is a reality, a reality which, without a doubt, has cut its path insomuch as it has tended to annihilate separateness and to unite in one feeling all the population of the village, the characters of which are exceedingly different.

Many will argue the physical aspects of the Taos Country has played a part in the bringing about a feeling of brotherly love among the folk of the village and the artists. Taos is surrounded by mountains that have defied any railroad to burrow through, consequently the country is so remote from the busy world that all have turned to each other to share a common inspiration.

Perhaps my neighbor, the artist, has surrendered to the scene which has patterned his art in that it is a vigorous, home-grown quality. His life has also been patterned. In the vill-age of Taos, Pedro, the woodhauler, lives in a mud house with hollyhocks growing against the sunbaked wall. Likewise the artists' studios are made of mud. The *adobes,* perchance, have come from the same sunlit field in which Pedro's *adobes* were molded. Perchance the hollyhocks growing against the studio wall were seeds from Pedro's garden.

In the old days in Taos the butcher, the baker, the candle-stick maker could look upon a painting that was a masterpiece, for in those days the art was displayed in the barber shops, the cafes or any place around the *plaza.* Of course any num-ber of people who would pause at the window of the village hardware store in which a masterpiece was displayed might gaze first at the pitchforks and shovels that were to the right of one of Joseph Imhof's lovely paintings, or they might try to see the price tag on a washing machine which was just to the left of a Martin Hennings aspen painting.

The village folk were far richer because of this art. Even though it was often but the flicker of an eye or an arrested glance as they went about their mundane affairs, inevitably they were touched by this wealth of beauty, this hospitality of my neighbor . . . the artist!

RATON: GATEWAY

R. H. Faxon

R. H. FAXON is secretary of the Navajo Trails Association and manager of the Walsenburg, Colorado, Chamber of Commerce. He is a former newspaper reporter, publisher and political writer, and lived for many years in Raton before moving to Colorado. Born and reared in Kansas, he studied at Washburn College, Topeka, and was active in civic and state affairs, and served for a time as private secretary to a U.S. Senator.

Raton is the gateway, the open door into New Mexico. Its hail and farewell have greeted thousands upon thousands of visitors to the Sunshine State, and it glories in its responsibility.

Located in the northeast corner of the state, not far from the Texas line, almost literally on the Colorado line, its situation is peculiar, pleasant, obligatory. On the main line of the Atchison, Topeka & Santa Fe Railroad, on three great federal highways, served by two great motor companies— Santa Fe Trailways and Southwestern Greyhound Lines, it is, indeed, Main Street, over which marches constantly, restlessly, pleasantly, rapidly, slowly, as the case of human nature may prescribe, a host of strangers to find welcome in a strange land.

Cultivating to the utmost its spirit of hospitality and concern for the welfare of the visitor, it feels it is best serving its great state and the public by this more or less single quality— keeping open the gate for friendly welcome to strangers, to incomers, a kindly good-bye to outgoers.

Raton is not a "tourist city" in the best sense of the word in the Western vernacular. But it does stand as sentinel at the gateway to one of the finest regions of the State, and indeed, to the West.

At its door is Capulin Mountain National Monument, one of the eight National Monuments of the State, and the most perfect extinct volcano on the North American continent. Its elevation is approximately 9,000 feet. On U. S. Highway 64 and immediately adjacent to U. S. Highway 87, thirty miles east of Raton, it is reached by these admirable roadways; and over them thousands upon thousands of visitors go to view this wonderful scene. Winding to its top is a government-built road, six per cent grade, safe, wide, a beautiful drive. At the top is ample car-parking space, and then the visitor walks down a winding pathway to the bottom of the crater, a distance of some 500 feet, there to view the cauldron where, thousands of years ago, was mixed the molten mass that spewed from the rim of the bowl and wound its way undulatingly down the side and over the valley—a ribbon-like tracing that the eye can follow in all directions. From the top of this splendid mountain on a clear day—and practically every day is a clear day in New Mexico—one may view five states—New Mexico, Texas, Oklahoma, Kansas and Colorado. The mountain is symmetrical, beautifully-perfect, and its name, Capulin, mean "cherry," given in the not always fanciful way by Spanish and Indian to mountains and rivers and towns and plains by the early explorers because of its resemblance to the cherry, with the slight dip at the top, discernible from considerable distances, not unlike the base of the cherry where the stem attaches.

On Johnson Mesa, right in Raton's back yard, 1,500 feet higher than the town, a rich farming, dairy, and stock country, there is, at the north rim, the phenomenon known as Ice Caves. These are an underground glacier, have been authenticated by geologists, and will be developed by Raton as a scenic point of beauty and grandeur.

Nearby, on the west end of Black Mesa, are the petroglyphs, the pictures carved in rock in pre-Columbian days, some long before that, Doctor Renaud of the Department of Archaeclogy and Anthropology of University of Denver says, and he has investigated them and has written a monograph on them. They, too—perhaps some day to be a small state park—are of educational value in this region.

Raton is justly famed for its magnificent Raton Pass, at an elevation of 8,500 feet, from Trinidad on the Colorado line, the road ascends gradually, in beautiful curving, to the state line, thence upward, with panoramic view of *mesas,* valleys, wonderful verdure and tree and plant life, the Sangre de Cristo range to the westward with its eternal snow-clad peaks. Shortly, the town of Raton, nestling in the valley, at an altitude of something less than 7,000 feet, bursts upon view. This scenic drive over Raton Pass is one of the really grand and impressive things about the entire Western country.

Down in the valley, now climbing to heights above, curving around as does the scenic drive itself, and at the top passing through a long tunnel is the main line of the Santa Fe Railroad over whose route a battle was fought between the Santa Fe and the Denver and Rio Grande in 1879, when the Santa Fe won and became New Mexico's first railroad as it entered what is now the town of Raton.

Now along the line of the railroad, now along the line of the scenic drive itself is the old Santa Fe Trail that, from Columbia, Missouri, then Independence, and Westport Landing, now Kansas City, through Kansas, across the corner of Colorado, and into New Mexico, over "The Pass," carried the hardy pioneers from 1821 onward. The old Santa Fe Trail, through what is now Raton, southward through Cimarron and "The Gap" immediately south of Cimarron, with the old "Dry Cimarron" route from Dodge City into Colfax county and Wagon Mound, the two lines converging near Fort Union finally ran into Las Vegas, thence to Santa Fe, "The End of the Trail," winding up at the *plaza* and the Palace of the Governors.

So Raton is rich with its history. Wootton tollhouse still standing, now a ranch headquarters; old Willow Springs Ranch, right in Raton; old Clifton House immediately south of the city, where the travelers used to seek sanctuary and rest in the days of the wagon-trek—these embellish and enrich the country with memories, and with now partly-spoliated places which may be reconstructed in the not far-distant future to remain as monuments to brave pioneers. Old Fort Union, southward, is another place where safety was sought and refuge taken in those old days; and that, too, is a reconstruction possibility.

Now, over the old route of the old Santa Fe Trail, the route of the railroad, the route of the scenic drive, with airplanes darting overhead, the whizzing motorist goes over famous U. S. Highways 85-87. It is indeed an epic in transportation.

Raton is a city of somewhat under 10,000 population. It is sightly, clean, winsome, attractive. Its shops, its fine hotels, its beautiful homes, attest the best in modern life.

Famous for its conventions, its hostship to trade and professional groups not only of the state but of the Rocky Mountain region, Raton has become the meeting-place, the crossroads, the hostel.

All the comforts, all the pleasure, all the culture of fine modern life are afforded in this town of Raton, gateway into New Mexico.

Daily the hundreds of travelers pass through. Some tarry for a length of time. Some pause for refreshments, for necessities, and for information regarding the gay pleasure spots farther along, in Cimarron Canyon, at marvelous Eagle Nest and superb Red River, at quaint Taos, or at Springer and Wagon Mound and Las Vegas, thence into Santa Fe, America's oldest city; Albuquerque, the metropolis; Gallup, the Indian capital, Socorro, Hot Springs, Las Cruces, Carlsbad, Clovis, Roswell, Tucumcari—all the other wonder-spots of a wonder state.

But Raton bids them enter, bids them goodbye; as you who travel restlessly or pleasantly, fast or slow, will see, presently —for, soon or late, you must pass through Raton and over its Pass or eastward through the lovely plains and valley into states in that direction.

Raton: Gateway!

FROM CONQUISTADOR TO METROPOLIS
Fremont Kutnewsky

FREMONT KUTNEWSKY is a business journalist who came to New Mexico in 1928 as an advertising solicitor for the *Albuquerque Tribune*. He later managed an advertising agency and for ten years was field advertising manager of *New Mexico Magazine*. He has contributed articles to the Magazine every year since 1941. In 1955 he joined the Magazine staff at Santa Fe and spent five years doing editorial and circulation promotion work. He retired in 1960 to take up free lance writing. His home is in Albuquerque.

In 1935 the City of Albuquerque celebrated its fiftieth anniversary with a three-day jubilee, complete with parades, carnivals and street dancing.

Twenty-one years later, in 1956, the city celebrated its 250th anniversary with still more elaborate fanfare.

This could be confusing if you're not familiar with the city's history. There have always been the two Albuquerques—since 1880; Old Albuquerque, clinging serenely to its fine old Spanish ways and flavor; and New Albuquerque, the ambitious, worldly offspring, which appropriated the name, and finally annexed the parent community.

Three generations of mailmen have had their headaches over the two Albuquerque post offices. Old Albuquerque stubbornly held on to its postal independence, even after it was surrounded by New Albuquerque's growth.

The quaint old community, with its beautiful San Felipe de

Neri Church where services have been held every Sunday since 1706, and its gas-lit *plaza* ringed on three sides by curio shops, artists' studios and Spanish restaurants, is one of the most remarkable tourist attractions in the West.

And so, metropolitan Albuquerque, 61st largest city in the United States, was the second crop off an old vine, created by railroad builders who feared to lay their rails too near the meandering Rio Grande. Not that the old Spanish Villa wanted the railroad and its threat to thriving stage lines and related employment.

An Anglo resident, Franz Huning, owned suitable land on the mesa two miles to the east. He welcomed a deal with the New Mexico & Southern Pacific railroad (now the Atchison, Topeka & Santa Fe). The rails reached the site in the spring of 1880. According to an employee of the railroad at the time, the first depot was "an aggregation of old boxcars." He said there wasn't a building in the townsite, but the first merchant was there with a stock of merchandise in the open, which he sold at "two-bits a drink"—beer or whiskey.

The original Villa de Alburquerque, founded in 1706, served throughout Spanish and Mexican rule as a way station on the Chihuahua Trail. This route, later known as El Camino Real, was a 500-mile-long lifeline connecting Santa Fe and colonial New Mexico with Mexico and the mother country, Spain. It was a long, lonely and dangerous route, following the river most of the way.

The villa was founded by acting Provincial Governor Francisco Cuervo y Valdez. He was replaced the following year by a regular appointee of the King, but while he had the opportunity he chose an excellent spot for a future city. It was sixty miles south of Santa Fe, on the banks of the Rio at a wide place in the valley, flanked on east and west by easy passes through mountain ranges, and where the river was fordable.

Old Indian trails had criss-crossed here. It was in the heart of a once populous pueblo civilization. The trails of the earliest Spanish explorers, Coronado, Espejo and Oñate, crossed here in the 16th century, all at different times.

The villa's first century was a quiet one. Local families intermarried. Few residents left, few newcomers came in. It was a charming, impressive community in 1806 when Lt. Zebulon Montgomery Pike, of the United States Army, saw it. The lieutenant and his party had lost their way, they said, while exploring President Jefferson's big bargain, the Louisiana Purchase lands. They built a stockade and ran up the stars and stripes on Spanish territory, and were "invited" by a detachment of Governor Joaquin Alencaster's dragoons and mounted militiamen to "come with them."

At Santa Fe the governor was courteous, but sent the entire party on to Chihuahua, Mexico, to appear before the commandant-general. Spain was fearful of the aggressive force of the Yankee's westward push across the continent.

Pike was pleasantly entertained both at Santa Fe and Albuquerque. After his release he wrote a book about his travels praising New Mexico as eloquently as a modern chamber of commerce. The book stimulated American efforts to establish trade relations with New Mexico across the Great Plains. These efforts were rebuffed as long as Spain controlled New Mexico. The Spanish settlers were forbidden to trade with any other country than Spain.

When Mexico won her independence in 1821, Yankee traders and their wagonloads of merchandise were welcomed with open arms. In the heyday of the Santa Fe Trail some of the caravans came on to Albuquerque.

New Mexico was admitted as a Territory of the United States in 1851, and soon waves of emigrants heading for California passed through. Supplying and re-outfitting the covered wagon trade became a profitable business.

The railroad reached New Albuquerque in 1880, putting an end to stage coaches as expected, but bringing new business in the form of construction payrolls, the purchase of timber and supplies, the arrival of investors and enterprisers from the east. The railroad brought merchandise for the stores and carried wool, hides and mineral on the back haul.

For the next fifty years the railroad shops and divisional payroll were Albuquerque's mainstay. Local business men were careful to play ball with railroad officials. Both sides agreed on a non-wide-open town. A minute man posse of merchants backed up the town marshal in keeping gamblers and gunmen out, and these for the most part learned to give Albuquerque a wide berth.

One marshal, Milton Yarberry, got too free with his own gun, killed a couple of men, one over a woman. He was tried and condemned to be hung at the Old Town courthouse. Engraved invitations to the hanging were issued. A lot of excitement was generated and there were threats of a lynching.

However, the hanging went off without a hitch—almost. At the last moment it was discovered that nobody in authority knew how to prepare a rope for a hanging. A hurried search revealed that one man, Major Bernard Ruppe, druggist, knew how. He soaked the rope the night before, then showed the sheriff how to make the noose. Elfego Baca pronounced it a "very nice hanging."

Major Ruppe was New Albuquerque's handy man about town. He knew everything and could do everything. For example, when the first death occurred in New Town there was no undertaker. Major Ruppe did the embalming.

He collected money from storekeepers and saloonkeepers to pay the salary of the town's first marshal, to buy firefighting equipment for the volunteer firemen, to buy instruments for the band, of which he was an enthusiastic member. He was a doughty, fearless character. At times he cooperated with the authorities in making arrests. His title of major was the result of militia duty.

One of the first merchants to set up shop in New Town was Thomas F. Keleher. He had driven an ox team from St. Louis to Fort Union in 1865 with supplies for the soldiers. In New Mexico he bought buffalo hides and shipped them to Russia. Keleher's leather store at 406 West Central was carried on by Tom Keleher, Jr., after his father's death. Tom's cousin, Will Keleher, became one of New Mexico's most prominent lawyers, and in recent years has written several books on phases of New Mexico history, including "Maxwell Land Grant," "The Fabulous Frontier," "Violence in Lincoln County."

M. P. Stamm was taking a load of butter to Socorro, a larger and more promising town than New Albuquerque in the early 1880's. Some booster in Albuquerque persuaded him to sell it there. He did, and remained to found a successful produce business.

Stamm was a great buyer and seller of real estate. He subdivided Terrace Addition and gave space for Highland Park in the midst of it to the city. Highland Park has just about disappeared beneath the new Pan American Freeway (Interstate Route 25), between Gold and Silver Avenues.

Another prominent early resident was Edmund G. Ross, from Lawrence, Kansas. He had been a United States Senator, the man whose one vote saved President Andrew Johnson from impeachment. President Cleveland appointed Ross governor of the Territory of New Mexico in 1885.

Adolph Harsch opened a bakery in one of the first buildings in New Albuquerque. He branched out into a prosperous sideline—bottling and selling water from Coyote Springs, at the foot of the Manzano mountains. The water was mineral and had a strong, unpleasant taste, but old-timers thought it wonderful as a chaser after whisky. (In the 1930's this industry was revived briefly by M. R. Buchanan, proprietor of the Albuquerque Ice Co. Buchanan carbonated the Coyote water, somewhat softening the flavor. He sold the water in syphon bottles.)

Bernard Rodey, who started as a stenographer with the railroad company, studied law and became a prominent lawyer in Albuquerque. He was elected to Congress from New Mexico, and later was appointed federal judge in Puerto Rico. Still later he was attorney for the Territory of Alaska.

The funeral parlor situation was cleared up when Oren W. and Henry Strong, on their way to El Paso, driving an ox team, lost one ox. They stayed at Albuquerque, started a furniture and wagon re-outfitting business, to which was added an undertaking department. The family is still in the business—Strong-Thorne Mortuary.

Although New Albuquerque was imbued with the westward-ho spirit of enterprise and wanted very much to outdo Old Town, the two were on friendly enough terms. A leisurely horsecar line connected the two communities. For some years

Old Town retained the county court house and jail. It was there that Yarberry was hanged. Territorial Fairs were held in Old Town about where Rio Grande Boulevard reaches the Albuquerque Country Club's golf course.

In those early days a number of mining men thought that there might be rich gold, silver, copper, zinc and other ores in the Sandia and Manzano mountains. They spent considerable money trying to find them.

Their projects petered out, but a real gold and silver strike was made forty-five miles to the north and across the Rio Grande at a place called Bland. A rush to the area in 1893 shot the camp's population as high as 3,000. A Denver newspaper called Bland a "new Cripple Creek." Silver-conscious miners named the place after Richard P. Bland, of Missouri, a free-silver candidate who ran against William Jennings Bryan for the Democratic presidential nomination in 1896.

Before Bland played out it had a hotel, two banks, a newspaper, an opera house and stock exchange, all crowded into a canyon only sixty feet wide. They had to blast out the walls of the canyon to make room for a stamp mill and a boarding house. To Albuquerque merchants and livery stable owners, Bland was a bonanza long to be remembered.

But the free-silver Democrats lost out. The country went on the gold standard with McKinley. Silver was demonetized, its price fell, and with its fall went Bland. Some activity continued there until 1916, and several attempts have been made since to revive the camp. (It's a ghost, but privately owned, and fenced off.)

By the turn of the century Albuquerque was riding high. Its railroad shops employed two or three hundred men. Cattle and sheep marketing gravitated to this railhead. Wool and hides were warehoused and auctioned.

The Albuquerque Commercial Club built a three-story brownstone building at Fourth and Gold Avenue, where the Simms building now stands. The N. T. Armijo building went up at Second and Central, also of brownstone shipped in from Flagstaff, Arizona.

In 1899 the San Felipe Hotel at Gold and Fifth street burned down. The Elks Club bought the site and built a club house and an opera house. Weber and Fields and Lillian Russell were featured on opening night in 1904. A special train was run from El Paso. It was a sell-out with tickets $5.00 to $20.00 according to the late Roy A. Stamm, who was a ticket-taker.

In the early years of the 20th century Albuquerque residents had not gone in for home beautification with lawns or flowers. Chester T. French, a mortician, gave them the start. He raised a beautiful yard of dahlias and morning glories at his location across from the high school at Broadway and East Central. People came from miles around to see his flower garden, the first in town. He gave away tubers and packets of seeds to all who would plant them, and taught children how to grow flowers. For a quarter-century no civic banquet was held without its free bouquets of dahlia blooms from French.

If Albuquerque is now a city of beautiful residential grounds, French is due considerable credit for his pioneering.

In the 1930's, Mrs. Albert G. Simms brought Cecil Pragnell, an internationally known landscape gardener to Albuquerque to beautify Los Poblanos, the Simms' country home on north Rio Grande Boulevard. Pragnell remained to preach and teach beautification as county agent for a number of years. After retirement he was retained by the Baptist Assembly in the Sangre de Cristo Mountains east of Santa Fe, and has made a show place of the grounds there.

After 1920, with population up to 15,000, Albuquerque indulged in another building spree. The Franciscan Hotel was financed by local subscription; also between 1923 and 1925 the First National Bank and the Sunshine buildings went up.

In 1927, aviation was the talk of the nation. Charles A. Lindbergh electrified the world by flying solo from Roosevelt Field, New York, to Le Bourget, France. The Army made a first flight to Hawaii. The Government cleared the way for commercial aviation by turning air mail over to private carriers.

Albuquerque was one of the first cities in the west to bid for a commercial airway. Frank G. Speakman and William Franklin organized Albuquerque Airport, Inc., leveled off a field on the southeast mesa (about where Sandia Base headquarters are now), hung up a wind sock and were in business.

In order to publicize the field and prepare the way for air lines that they were sure would come, the partners engaged Art Goebel, a young man from Belen, N. M., who had made a national reputation as a cross-country flier, to survey an air route from New York City to Los Angeles.

Art made the course in 18 hours, a record at the time, and came up with five reasons why Albuquerque should be on any transcontinental air line between the two cities:

(1) shortest route, New York to Los Angeles; (2) no exceptionally high mountains on the way; (3) severe winter weather could be avoided; (4) plenty of open spaces for emergency landings, especially in New Mexico and Arizona, and (5) more favorable all-round weather than any other cross country course.

Armed with these facts, the partners mailed circulars to every flier in the country whose name and address they could obtain. They sold out to James G. and T. Thornton Oxnard, from Amarillo, Texas.

The Oxnard brothers wanted to start an air line between Denver and Mexico City, but were blocked by an untimely revolution across the border. They settled for Albuquerque, formed a new company, improved the field and in 1929 wangled terminal connections for Western Air's transcontinental passenger service. The schedule called for daylight flights between Los Angeles and Kansas City, Mo., combined with a night trip by rail to New York City. Across the continent in 48 hours was big news then.

Varney Air Lines (later, Continental Air Lines) established a line between Denver, Colo., and El Paso, Texas, forming junction with Western Air at Albuquerque. Through mergers, Western Air became Transcontinental & Western Air and still later, Trans World Airlines—or TWA.

Just as the big depression hit eastern centers hardest the Government gave Albuquerque a lift by starting construction on a

Federal Building and the Veterans Facility on the southeast mesa.

At the same time work got under way on a ten million dollar flood control, drainage and irrigation project in the middle Rio Grande Valley.

A growing number of federal agencies, several regional in scope, soon overflowed the post office and new Federal Building and spread out over the city in thirty or forty locations. This helped to keep rental values of commercial property steady. Government payrolls overtook the long-time standby, the Santa Fe payroll, in providing income for local families.

After the Golden Jubilee of 1935, celebrating fifty years as an incorporated city, Albuquerque took a rosy view of the future. The Chamber of Commerce was re-organized. Plans were laid for a municipal airport and state fair grounds—via WPA financing.

Members of the Jubilee Executive Committee whose work now hitched Albuquerque's wagon to a star were: Mayor Charles Lembke, ex officio chairman; Arthur Prager, chairman; John P. Murphy, manager; H. B. Hening, W. H. Black, Leslie Briggs, John Flaska, Oscar Love, W. J. White, Maurice Osoff, Pete Matteucci, Ross Salazar, August Seis and Frank D. Shufflebarger.

Former mayor, Clyde Tingley, was in the governor's chair at Santa Fe (1935-1939) but he participated in the planning and promoting of the airport and fair grounds.

Major A. D. Smith, an old-time army flier, manager of the Transcotinental & Western Air terminal on the west mesa (now Cutter-Carr Air Field) conceived the idea that Albuquerque would be a logical location for a big air base. He selected a site (the present airport site) and promoted the idea.

George A. Kaseman, president of the Albuquerque National Bank, and a former railroad man, aided Smith by optioning 888 acres of mesa land preliminary to the city's sponsoring a WPA project to build the port, Smith then persuaded his employers, TWA, to advance $100,000 of lease money.

Smith's long-standing friendship with Major General Henry

H. (Hap) Arnold helped Albuquerque boosters to see the right people in Washington. All details of the plan were cleared with the Army—in view of the possible future air base.

All worked out just in time. Construction started in 1939, the year war broke out in Europe. The United States got involved by supplying the western allies with arms, equipment and supplies. The Army decided to place an air base at Albuquerque, and hangars, buildings and runways were rushed to completion. The base was named Kirtland after an Albuquerque soldier of World War I.

In the spring of 1941 Col. Eugene L. Eubank and his command, the 40th Heavy Bombardment Group—B-24s—were transferred from March Field, California, to Albuquerque. They were hardly settled when orders came to fly to the Philippines by way of Hawaii. War broke out, and the mass flight had to detour by way of Australia. Col. Eubank was cited for his performance and promoted to brigadier-general.

The availability of a well planned and equipped airport undoubtedly had its effect on the officials who decided to locate Los Alamos high in the Jemez mountains. Carco Air Service established a 20-minute shuttle service between Los Alamos and Albuquerque, making possible the necessary contacts between scientists hatching atomic bombs and their colleagues and government officials in various parts of the country.

Shortly after the war, certain secret activities began at the site of the former Oxnard airfield in Albuquerque. Albuquerque people began quitting their jobs and taking work "out on the base," and soon the facility was called Sandia Base.

It was apparent that big things were going on out there. Million dollar buildings, truckloads of material always headed that way, stepped-up activities among local steel and sheet metal fabricators, machine shops, furniture and fixture plants were the indicators.

Eventually it came out: Sandia Base was there to convert nuclear explosive packages into usable weapons. It consisted of Sandia Laboratory, in charge of Sandia Corporation, non-profit subsidiary of Western Electric, and a field headquarters for the

Laboratory's one customer, the Armed Forces. Officers from all branches—Army, Navy, Air Force and Marine Corps—were stationed there to cooperate in the design of weapons, learn their make-up, train teachers to teach others to handle the weapons, and produce manuals.

At the close of 1961 approximately 7,100 military and civilian personnel were employed at Sandia Base and its subsidiary, Manzano Base, in the Manzano mountains.

Kirtland A. F. Base, hardly a stone's throw away, got the assignment of a Special Weapons Command. This unit adapts planes to carry and crews to drop A-Bombs, and participates in all field tests. A center for nuclear weapon research and development was installed at the base, and is now the Air Forces' "Nuclear Center."

Albuquerque's population doubled from 1940 to 1950, and doubled again from 1950 to 1960. Housing pushed out on the northeast mesa closing a six-mile gap that had existed between the city and the Sandias, and moving the center of population from down by the railroad tracks to out near the fair grounds.

At the present rate of growth, Albuquerque's metropolitan population of 275,000 will reach 375,000 by 1970.

A.C.F. Industries, Inc., a subsidiary of American Car & Foundry, bought and enlarged a plant in Albuquerque and rapidly built up to 2,000 employees.

Downtown the Simms Building, the new Federal Building and the Bank of New Mexico Building filled out the metropolitan skyline.

Out east, the new Western Skies luxury motor hotel and the new Four Hills Country Club enhanced the city's attraction for conventions and tourists. Back in Tijeras Canyon the Ideal Cement Company put up a large cement plant, and real estate subdividers are luring residents up into what were picnic areas a few years ago.

The University of New Mexico, whose pueblo style campus is a show place in Albuquerque, enrolled 8,000 students in the 1961-1962 term. City and parochial schools enrolled 65,000.

The Federal Aviation Agency has built a $3.6 million regional air traffic control center north of the city limit and will move its Kirtland Base staff and additional personnel into it in 1963.

The city's hospital facilities were enlarged by completion of the Methodist Bataan Memorial Hospital and Lovelace Clinic and Baird Memorial Research Laboratory out near the Veterans Hospital, the Ruth Hanna memorial addition and a new wing at Presbyterian Hospital and the new Bernalillo County-Indian Hospital near the University. Ten Albuquerque hospitals admit 40,000 patients annually.

Will the Southwest continue to attract new population? If it does, no other metropolitan center is in a better position to serve it. Albuquerque has no sizeable competitor within 250 miles in any direction.

ERNIE PYLE
CALLED ALBUQUERQUE "HOME"
Maurice Trimmer

MAURICE E. TRIMMER is bureau manager of United Press International in Santa Fe, where his main job is covering the State House legislative sessions and political campaigns. He has been a New Mexican for four years. The article on Ernie Pyle, which was chosen for inclusion in this anthology, was his first contribution to *New Mexico Magazine*.

Ernie Pyle had wandered through every state and several foreign countries when he decided to build a home at Albuquerque in 1940.

The skinny, little World War II journalist had been a traveling reporter for five years when he realized he needed "a sort of home plate, that we could run to on occasion and then run away from again."

"We lived constantly in hotels or on boats . . . we have been sick in hotel rooms all the way from Alaska to Santiago, Chile," he wrote in a New Mexico Magazine article of January, 1942, entitled, "Why Albuquerque."

By "we" Ernie meant himself and his wife, Jerry, who traveled with him on his early journeys. She waited for him at Albuquerque during his wartime writing, from the London blitz to a ten-mile square island in the Pacific called Ie Shima, where he was killed.

They slept in 800 hotels in six years and traveled 250,000 miles before they drove in stakes at 900 Girard Southeast in Albuquerque.

Ernie wrote later ". . . if we can have only one house—and that's all we want—then it has to be in New Mexico, and preferably right at the edge of Albuquerque where it is now.

"We like it because our front yard stretches as far as you can see, and because old Mt. Taylor, 65 miles away, is like a framed picture in our front window.

"We have seen sunrises so violently beautiful they were almost frightening, and I'm only sorry I can't capture the sunsets and the thunderstorms and the first snows on the Sandias, and take them east and flaunt them in people's faces."

A fellow newsman once said of Ernie: "No other journalist ever evoked such mass affection as was accorded him during his meager tenure as a national figure." But Ernie became used to eulogies.

During World War II more than twelve million Americans read his frontline stories six days a week. He wrote more about privates and patrols than generals and battles.

He won the Pulitzer Prize in 1944.

The University of New Mexico awarded him an honorary Litt.D degree and Indiana University, his alma mater, gave him its first doctorate of humane letters.

Harvard University planned to present him a third honorary degree June 28, 1945, but he was killed by a Japanese sniper on Ie Shima April 18 that year.

His columns were published in two best sellers—"Here Is Your War" and "Brave Men." His prewar writings of humor and pity later came out in "Home Country." He took his published success in stride.

Hollywood made a movie of his life, "The Story of GI Joe," for which he served as a consultant but never lived to see.

The farm boy from Dana, Indiana, was a personal friend of world leaders, celebrities and generals, but preferred to live with and write about ordinary people who sometimes did extraordinary things.

". . . he has a compassionate comprehension of the American

soldier . . . that only a man very like Lincoln could possess," Brig. Gen. Donald Armstrong wrote in reviewing Pyle's "Brave Men."

His compassion was not superficial. He had a natural disgust for pretense and phonies. He was shy. His personal life was shadowed by the illnesses of his wife, who suffered from sometimes dangerous nervous and emotional difficulties much of the last ten years of their marriage.

He was born Aug. 3, 1900 on a farm outside Dana, the only child of Will and Maria Pyle. As a puny, red-haired youngster, he learned to plow at nine, fed the hogs and horses and helped build corn bins. He never liked farming.

When he got to Indiana University, he didn't know what he wanted to study. Another farm boy named Paige Cavanaugh, said, "Well, why not sign up for journalism. At least you don't have to add and subtract. It sounds like a pipe."

Ernie found a career and a friend. Some of his most humorous writing is found in his lifelong correspondence with Cavanaugh.

While at college, he made his first long trip of a lifetime of traveling. He accompanied the school basketball team to Japan. He returned to school but quit a few months short of graduation to accept a job with the La Porte, Indiana, Herald in January of 1923.

In a few months Ernie was offered a position with the newly-founded Washington Daily News and quickly accepted to begin a twelve-year stint on Washington and New York papers. There were interruptions for the trips that later were to become part of his job.

In 1926 he and Jerry, a civil service clerk from Minnesota he had married the year before, set out to drive "around the rim of the United States." They crossed New Mexico, which they "loved at first sight."

They again headed south in the winter of 1934-35 to try to find warmth and sunshine to dry out a severe attack of influenza Ernie couldn't shake. During a stop at Albuquerque, Ernie called the late E. H. Shaffer, editor of the Tribune. Their meeting sparked a warm friendship between the two families that helped draw the Pyles to Albuquerque when they decided to tack down a "base."

When Ernie and Jerry reached the West coast they signed up for a three-week trip on a freighter back to Philadelphia.

Upon his return his newspaper asked him to write some newspaper articles about his trip. Officials of the Scripps-Howard newspaper chain, for whom Ernie worked, liked the stories and agreed to Ernie's request to "go where I please and write what I please."

"It's just the kind of job I've always wanted and I hope I can make a go of it," Ernie wrote a friend. He was 35.

Crisscrossing the continent, he stopped often at Albuquerque.

When he and "that girl" visited New Mexico in 1938, they were well-known and considered home folks. They had dinner with Governor and Mrs. Clyde Tingley.

By 1940 Ernie and Jerry began looking seriously for property in Santa Fe or Albuquerque.

"We were like trees growing in the sky, without roots," Ernie wrote later. "So at last we decided to acquire a base . . . just some definite walls in a definite place that we could feel were ours."

Ernie finally picked the Girard Avenue location. He arranged for the building of a simple, $4,000 house on the land, which at that time was far from any other houses, with a 65-mile view and quail and rabbits as visitors.

Before the house was finished Ernie sailed on November 16, 1940 to London to cover the blitz. It was his first glimpse of the war he was to hate increasingly.

He returned to Albuquerque for a few months in 1941. Jerry was sick and he cared for her and worked at odd jobs around the house. It was during this time he wrote:

". . . we like it here because you can do almost anything you want to, within reason. In four months, I haven't been out of overalls more than a half dozen times. And I go to the Alvarado Hotel's swell 'Cocina Cantina' always in my overalls and nobody raises an eyebrow."

On December 7th the Japanese bombed Pearl Harbor and

about seven months later Ernie was back in England, this time with American troops. He followed them into North Africa and Italy, where he wrote probably the most widely-printed dispatch of World War II—the death of Capt. Henry Waskow in the mountains near San Pietro. The Washington Daily News devoted its entire first page to Ernie's description of unnamed soldiers saying goodbye to their young captain.

Later Ernie was to cover the Normandy invasion and follow his beloved "dogfaces" into Paris.

When he returned home in the latter part of 1944, he was tired and sick of war and death, almost too weary to enjoy the honors that awaited him. He posed for the famous sculptor Jo Davidson. Life magazine sent Lincoln Barnett to visit Ernie at Albuquerque. He quoted Ernie as saying:

"I dread going back and I'd give anything if I didn't have to go.

"I can't bear to think of not being here. I like to be alive. I have a hell of a good time most of the time."

A few weeks later he was on a Navy plane headed toward the Pacific. He joined an invasion landing on Okinawa. He said afterward it would be his last landing. A few days later on April 16 an assault was made on an outlying isle, Ie Shima. Ernie went in 24 hours later. He slept that night in a cluttered, abandoned Jap dugout.

The next day he accepted an offer to ride in a jeep with some officers toward the village of Ie. A few hundred yards short of the village a machine gun opened fire in the tall grass. The men in the jeep dived into a ditch. Ernie raised his head to see if the others were all right. A bullet pierced his left temple. He never made a sound.

When news of his death reached the public, letters and telegrams from generals, journalists, officials, soldiers and their families were stacked inside the little house on Girard.

Jerry's health failed rapidly after that and she died November 23 at St. Joseph hospital in Albuquerque.

The heirs to the estate conveyed title to the house to the city in 1947. A branch public library opened there October 11, 1948.

The house looks much the same on the outside as it did when Ernie left. It has become a sort of shrine as well as a neighborhood library. Visitors come in taxi cabs, between trains, and tourists pull up with trailers, to look at the house where Ernie Pyle lived and walk quietly through the small rooms.

A Norwegian reporter came by. "This is like going to church," he said.

In a glass case in the front room are the Jo Davidson sculptured head, a pair of sun goggles and the wide-rimmed, western hat Ernie wore so often when in Albuquerque.

"I don't know why," a librarian told columnist Hal Boyle, "but it is the empty hat that affects them emotionally. They see it and start to cry."

Albuquerque has four times as many people now as when Ernie saw quail and rabbits in his front yard. His sagebrush-spotted mesa is covered with houses that shut off the view of the far mountains. If Ernie were alive today, he probably would look for another couple acres at the edge of town where he could see "halfway to the Pacific Ocean."

A soldier who was at Ie Shima recalled his last conversation with Ernie years later in a newspaper article:

"Ernie said the island landscape reminded him of the landscape around his home near Albuquerque. He and an officer agreed they liked New Mexico better than anywhere else."

THE ATOMIC AGE

OPEN CITY
Betty Shouse & Marjorie Miller

BETTY SHOUSE and MARJORIE MILLER collaborated on the chapter "Open City" while they were employed in Los Alamos. Betty Shouse was a school librarian in Los Alamos and is now a librarian at Roswell Public Library. Marjorie Miller now lives in Santa Fe and devotes considerable time to the dramatic arts.

The gates to New Mexico's secret atomic city are open. This is a long step from the urgent secrecy of the war years when residents were known only by a box number in Santa Fe, and even many of those working in Los Alamos did not know what was going on in the technical area.

The original establishment, which was similar to an army post, is indeed a far cry from today's pleasant city of some 13,000 residents.

The remote Los Alamos Mesa was acquired by our government in 1942 for secret scientific research. This area of the 7,400-foot high Pajarito Plateau had been occupied by the exclusive Los Alamos Ranch School for Boys, Dr. J. Robert Oppenheimer, original director of the project, remembered the boys' school at Los Alamos and suggested it as a possible site—one of several locations in the Southwest that had been considered for the new laboratory.

It was decided that the weapon research, Project Y, of the Manhattan District, would be located here because of the secrecy and safety provided by the isolated plateau. This pine-covered shelf of the Jemez Mountains would also offer the advantage of an ideal climate for favorable working conditions the year round.

At that time, too, it was believed that the fifty-odd buildings of the school would provide adequate accommodations for the scientists and their families who were assigned to the project! In 1957, only a few of these original log buildings remain. The largest is the Lodge, the pleasantly rustic hotel for consultants and visitors to "the Hill." The Lodge is "rustic" in appearance only. North of the Lodge is "bathtub row," so called because these attractive log homes once contained the *only* bathtubs in this war-born city.

Early in December, 1942, the first construction crews arrived. None of these men knew just what they were building. Nor did anyone realize there might be any connection between this work and Oak Ridge or the other phases of the huge Manhattan District Project. The cost and size of this gigantic project had to be kept secret. It was the job of the Manhattan District's Counter-Intelligence Corps to keep the war's most important classified project completely under wraps. The C.I.C., however had little chance of keeping the existence of the Manhattan District entirely a secret. It was too big. The C.I.C. men were so cautious that they found themselves investigating each other.

One of the C.I.C.'s biggest problems was handling the top scientists. These men began arriving in April, 1943, and included many American scientists and many Europeans with international reputations: Enrico Fermi from Italy, Niels Bohr from Denmark, John von Neumann and Edward Teller from Hungary, James Tuck and Sir James Chadwick from England. A sort of bodyguard was assigned to each of the nuclear scientists. The duties of these young intelligence officers ranged from a "man Friday" to guardian. The personalities of the C.I.C. men were matched with their wards. For example, J. Robert Oppenheimer's man couldn't be a conversational flop or not know one end of a horse from the other. Enrico Fermi, whose English was far from perfect, had an Italian-speaking

American, John Baudino, for his aide. Their relationship was most congenial. In time Baudino got to know more about the atom than he wished. Fermi would often introduce him to his fellow-scientists as "My colleague," and say, "Soon Johnny will know so much about the project he will need a bodyguard, too."

It is a supreme tribute to the C.I.C. that the secret was so well kept, but they had many bad moments. A Cleveland reporter who had spent a vacation near Los Alamos hurried home to write an excited story entitled "The Forbidden City." He said, "The Mr. Big of the city is a college professor, Dr. J. Robert Oppenheimer, called the 'Second Einstein' . . . (A) widespread belief is that he is developing ordnance and explosives . . . others . . . will tell you tremendous explosions have been heard." The C.I.C. hushed this in a hurry.

Meanwhile the Laboratory was continuing to grow. In January, 1943, the University of California was chosen to operate the Laboratory. By July, 1943, there were some 1,900 people on the post (this included construction workers and military personnel). The total population by the end of 1943 had reached 3,500, and by December, 1944, it had leaped to 5,700. This was far from the original estimate of only 100 scientists and their families.

People down in the Rio Grande Valley below were wondering what was going on up on "the Hill." Various stories floated about. Some said a space-ship was being made; others suggested the real purpose was the construction of windshield wipers for submarines.

The men involved in Project Y were much too concerned with the importance of their work to be aware of much else. Their theoretical studies had proved the feasibility of a nuclear fission bomb and experiments had confirmed it. The big step lay ahead—an actual field test.

The bleak, desert area of the historic *Jornada del Muerto* (Journey of Death) 50 miles southeast of Socorro in south-central New Mexico, was chosen as the test site. Trinity Drive in Los Alamos later was named in honor of the code designation for this operation.

Preparations for the "Trinity" explosion were begun early

in the spring of 1945. Final assembly of the first atomic bomb took place in an abandoned ranch house on the night of July 12. The unit was elevated to the top of a 100-foot tower two days later. Following this was much tedious instrumentation before the final detonation could take place. Pre-dawn July 16 all was ready. Signs of a coming thunderstorm threatened to delay the important test, but near 4 o'clock in the morning the weather cleared. At 5:30 there occurred the detonation of the world's first nuclear fission bomb, with an estimated forces equivalent to 20,000 tons of TNT.

The secrecy of the preparations had been so carefully accomplished that not a single newspaper identified the historic event. So it was not generally known until it had been followed by Hiroshima and Nagasaki and the end of the war that Los Alamos scientists had accomplished the successful construction of an atomic bomb.

The war's end brought a period of doubt and anxiety to Los Alamos. There was a great exodus from "the Hill" and the population suddenly began falling as rapidly as it had risen. By October, 1945, Oppenheimer himself, feeling that he had accomplished his mission, departed to devote his time to other areas of scientific endeavor.

As his successor, the present director, Dr. Norris E. Bradbury, was appointed. Dr. Bradbury had first been assigned to an important post at Los Alamos in 1944 after an outstanding academic career in several universities. Taking over the post-war operation of the Laboratory was a difficult task. It was commonly believed at that time that Los Alamos would be abandoned as a surplus war plant. On the contrary, Dr. Bradbury felt that Los Alamos should have a prominent place in the future of this country's atomic energy program. So firm was his conviction that a strong nucleus of interested scientists and technicians stayed on to develop eventually the most powerful array of atomic weapons of any country in the world.

The newly-created Atomic Energy Commission took over on January 1, 1947, and many long-range plans were soon under way. The University of California also had agreed to continue to operate the Laboratory. Building was begun in earnest for a permanent city. Many new housing projects were started, as well as extensive facilities for research. The chief purpose of Los Alamos was still to be in the field of atomic weapons, but there has been outstanding progress in many allied fields including physics, chemistry, metallurgy, mathematics, and biology. The booklet published for the Los Alamos open house in 1955, calls the Los Alamos Scientific Laboratory "the most significant institution of its kind in the United States."

Today's visitor to "the Hill" may be more aware of the town itself than of the laboratory. The laboratory facilities have been moved into permanent buildings in the new "Tech Area," on sites to the south of Los Alamos Mesa. The scientist whose office once was a converted broom closet now works in more spacious, if less historic, quarters.

The town no longer has the raw, bare look of a construction camp when new housing was continually being built. The Russian olives and pines have grown larger, the green lawns and pastel-colored houses blend with the pine-covered *mesas*.

Traditions are being established. Los Alamos high school celebrates its homecoming each fall with colorful floats, a game at Sullivan Field, and a homecoming dance. Several thousand children start to school each September, many of whom were born in Los Alamos. Each season brings familiar pleasures. There are the annual fall jaunts into the aspen basin above town. The Little Theater group chooses its plays for the coming season, repairs flats, and sells season tickets. The skiers bring out their skis in anticipation of ski weekends at Los Alamos' ski run of nearby Santa Fe Basin. The Gay 90's curtain goes up on the annual midwinter melodrama produced by the faculty of the Los Alamos schools as a fund-raiser for student scholarships. Summer means picnics at Bandelier National Monument, only a scant 15 miles away or swimming at Ponce de Leon, some 60 miles away, near Taos. The pattern of living is much the same as in any pleasant suburb or small city.

The gates of New Mexico's secret city have been open since 1957. A drive-in moved into the pass office that once guarded the entrance. Now the familiar words "meet me at the gate" merely mean "let's have a cup of coffee and a hamburger."

THE SPACE AGE
Excerpts from Articles

CONTRIBUTORS to the chapter on research of the Space Age who have
not been previously mentioned in these biographical notes are Steve
Lowell, George F. Meeter and Russell Tinsley. Steve Lowell is a former
member of the Associated Press staff in Albuquerque, now assigned to
the AP office in Seattle, Wash. His home is in Bellevue, Wash. George
F. Meeter is an information writer at Holloman Air Force Base. His
home is in Alamogordo. Russell Tinsley was stationed at Holloman AF
Base during his military service and was attached to the public relations
office. He is now living in Texas, and is a free lance writer for outdoor
magazines.

SPRINGBOARD TO SPACE

When man ventures into outer space, not all his boost comes
from rockets. A large part of it comes from a sprawling laboratory on the New Mexico desert.

A military Disneyland sprawls under the rampart of the
mighty Sacramento Range of south-central New Mexico. Here
the Air Force carries on fantastic experiments to help us into
space.

The big military laboratory not only produces amazing test
tools for the future but men whose names will live in flying
history because of the use they have made of those tools.

Lt. Col. David Simons, Capt. Joe Kittinger, 2nd Lt. Clifton
McClure will forever be remembered in man's story of flight.
It was in the summer of 1957 that Kittinger soared to 96,000
feet in a balloon gondola to pave the way for an even higher
flight—to 102,000 feet, the fringe of space, made by Simons.
Later, Lt. McClure ballooned to 99,600 feet.

And rocket sled tracks and Col. John Stapp will never be forgotten in annals of air and space. Back in 1954, Stapp sped 632 miles an hour down a Holloman track to be stopped in a little more than one second. That was to test the effects of ultra-rapid acceleration and deceleration on humans, like a rocket pilot would experience when he blasted off.—*Steve Lowell.*

NUCLEAR SPACE ROCKETS

As far back as 1947, Dr. Stanislaw Ulam, of Los Alamos, outlined a way to propel a rocket by a series of small nuclear explosions. (Dr. Ulam is the man who provided the basic calculations for the H-Bomb.)

Now that idea is being studied at Los Alamos and at General Atomics in California, to find out how effectively such a series of small atomic explosions could be directed to get the most push from certain amounts of exploding material.

Each small explosion would give the rocket another shove forward. Ulam says he believes this system might provide several times more push for each pound of propellant than would a nuclear reactor-type rocket engine.

It appears that Los Alamos will continue as a brainy beehive of activity, hatching nuclear rocket and ram-jet engines and developing other peaceful applications of atomic energy. Ulam indicates there is plenty to do.

"For instance, there is Project Sherwood," he says. "It is concerned with controlled thermonuclear reactions and would make the energy of fusion available for peaceful power output."

One group at Los Alamos broke away from concentration on nuclear problems recently and came up with an idea for a solar sail.

They say that if they were directed to they could rig a sail made of thin plastic coated with aluminum. It would be carried into outer space in a rocket, would unfold there, and then the "pressure" of the sunlight reflected from the metal-coated sail would push it around space.—*Steve Lowell.*

Sandia Base is the home of Sandia Laboratory, Field Command Headquarters of the Armed Forces Special Weapons Project, and Headquarters for the Atomic Energy Commission's Albuquerque Operations Office. Together, these agencies pump an annual payroll of $79 million into the economy of New Mexico and exert a strong and dynamic force on the community.

This tremendous growth at Sandia is the direct result of the nation's nuclear weapons program, and it hints at a story of scientific achievement which is only partially revealed because of security. The Base has grown from a minor installation with a few dozen people to a complex organization of 14,000. From a few war-built barracks type buildings, Sandia has grown into a city in itself—comparable, say, to one with a population of 25,000—with business buildings, laboratories, homes and barracks.

The Base is under dual occupation—a civilian and military agency sharing an important weapons assignment.

On the civilian side is Sandia Laboratory, the major ordnance engineering laboratory for the Atomic Energy Commission's weapons complex, operated by Sandia Corporation. On the military side is the Armed Forces Special Weapons Project, representing the "customer" for the AEC's ordnance products.

Sandia Laboratory shares with the Los Alamos Scientific Laboratory and the University of California Radiation Laboratory the responsibility for designing and developing the weapons which comprise the nation's atomic arsenal. Los Alamos and Livermore Laboratories are engaged in nuclear research that produces the nuclear explosive device. Sandia Corporation scientists develop the device into a usable military weapon. This includes designing fuzing and firing systems, guidance and control mechanisms, and other components and circuitry which make up the intricate electronic and mechanical weapon system. In addition Sandia designs the casing or "shape" in which to house this complicated gadget. It also has the responsibility of evaluating the performance of nuclear devices at far-flung test sites and of carrying on studies to assure the safe operation of aero-space nuclear systems.

A weapon design starts as an expressed need of the Armed Forces. The military sets the requirements and makes its needs known to the AEC, whose laboratories also keep the military planners advised of possible future capabilities of nuclear explosives to facilitate long range planning.—*Fremont Kutnewsky.*

WHITE SANDS MISSILE RANGE

White Sands Missile Range is the rocket and guided missile test center in New Mexico.

Here was developed the Nike, the electronically controlled 1,000-miles-an-hour guided missile which is America's new defense weapon against atomic-bomb-carrying jet planes. The Nike missile searches out its target in the sky and explodes automatically at a pre-determined radar contact.

Here also have been developed American rockets with speeds of 5,000 miles an hour, multi-stage rockets, and other experimental missiles that are still in the secret stage.

—George Fitzpatrick.

AERO MEDICAL LABORATORY

At Holloman Air Force Base near Alamogordo, the Aero Medical Field Laboratory uses Chimpanzees for studies in space biology. The Laboratory makes strict application of American Medical Association rules for handling animals.

Each chimp is taught to carry on task in the partially simulated "space" environment of the plastic-enclosed contour couch. After ordinary performances are stabilized, the "graduate" training takes place, perhaps in a more highly evolved electronic-paneled test chamber, or within the "space capsule" itself where, fastened in his couch, the animals learns to perform more complicated tasks. . . .

By such devices and schooling—and by actual aircraft flights under the same careful supervision—are developed a wealth of factors which help to accumulate the knowledge of how man himself can and must respond in any given space environment.

—George F. Meeter.

SUNSPOT, NEW MEXICO

Crowning the Sacramento Mountains of south central New Mexico at 9,200 feet is the Upper Air Research observatory where the Air Force has erected the world's largest instrument for observing the constant behavior of the sun. The instrument is a highly sensitive 16-inch coronagraph that is twice the size of the next largest one at Pic du Midi, on the French border of the Pyrenees Mountains.

The observatory is located at Sac Peak, about 17 miles south of Cloudcroft. It is one of eight laboratories of the Geophysics Research Directorate of the Air Force, Cambridge Research Center, Mass., of the Air Research and Development Command. It is supported logistically by Holloman Air Development Center, 50 road miles away.

The observatory has been in operation since 1947. The community has been aptly known as Sunspot, New Mexico, since a post office was established on the peak in 1953.

The importance of the Sac Peak Observatory to the Air Force is shown by the fact that within recent years geophysical research has established that active phenomenon on the sun such as sun spots, flares and prominences create disturbances to the earth's magnetic field with resulting disruption of all types of communication.

Until recent years, man gave little or no thought to the sun's behavior, accepting it as a necessity of life. But with the invention of delicate, modern devices which are vulnerable to small solar disturbances, study of the sun became very important.

—Russell Tinsley.

ACKNOWLEDGMENT

The selections in this volume were copyrighted at the time of their publication in *New Mexico Magazine,* as follows:

"Lament for La Bajada," by Kyle Crichton, March, 1935; "Autographs in Stone," by Evon Z. Vogt, May, 1935; "Down the Río . . . in Boats," by Harvey Fergusson, May, 1935; "House of the Dons," by Ann Nolan Clark, February, 1936; "Party for a Lady," by Myrtle Andrews, April, 1936; "Dialogues of Don Plácido," by F. M. Kercheville, September, 1936; "Raton—Gateway," by R. H. Faxon, June, 1937; "The Title of Doña Sofia," by Beatrice Chauvenet, August, 1937.

"Art in New Mexico," by Ina Sizer Cassidy, April, 1939, and December, 1944; "Roadside Geology," by E. R. Harrington, January, 1939; "Pueblo Politics," by Florence Hawley, August, 1939; "World's Greatest Wonder," by Keen Rafferty, October, 1939; "The Magic of Water," by Wilfred McCormick, October, 1939.

"From Sagebrush to Spruce," by Ross Calvin, January, 1940; "People of the Soil," by Elizabeth W. DeHuff, June, 1940; "The Miraculous Staircase," by C. Chavez Lowe, June, 1940; "The Beefsteak Trail," by N. Harry Champlin, March, 1940; "Medicine Water," by Betty Woods,

March, 1940; "Folkways and Fiestas," by Aurora Lucero White, March, 1940; "The Funny Men," by Eric Knight, June, 1941; "Southwest Crusader," by Dudley C. Gordon, October, 1941; "Navajo Bill of Fare," by Ruth Kirk, June, 1941; "Titan of the Range," by Agnes Morley Cleaveland, December, 1941.

"Old Days in Old Albuquerque," by Julia M. Keleher, January, 1942; "Don Quixote of the Six-Shooter," by J. Frank Dobie, May, 1942; "Boyhood Bucks," by S. Omar Barker, November, 1942; "My Neighbor is an Artist," by Lorraine Carr, December, 1943; "Poet on Horseback," by Lewis D. Fort, February, 1944; "Neighbors to the Sun," by Irving F. Hand, February, 1944.

"Cooking Secrets of Mesilla," by Miguel Hambriento, October, 1945; "Interview with General Sheridan," by Grant Maxwell and Fred Kirkpatrick, August, 1945; "Letter to the Editor," by S. Omar Barker, June, 1945; "You Can Choose Your Climate," by Cleve Hallenbeck, January, 1946.

"Ten Minute Tour," by Earl W. Scott, August, 1944; "A-D-O-B-E Spells Contentment," by Dorothy L. Pillsbury, June, 1947; "The Kingdom of New Mexico," by Fray Angelico Chavez, August, 1953; "Forgotten Army Post," by William S. Wallace, September, 1955; "New Mexico Was Our Fate," by Conrad Richter, March, 1957; "The First Territorial Governor" by Calvin Horn, June, 1957; "Open City," by Betty Shouse and Marjorie Miller, January, 1958; "Roundup of the Waters," by Lawrence Clark Powell, February, 1958; "The Space Age," excerpts from articles, March, 1954; January, 1957; February, 1959; March, 1959; July, 1958; "Sun and Sanctuary," by John L. Sinclair, December, 1959.

"The Little Lights That Burn On Christmas Eve," by Margaret Abreu, December, 1959; "Formula for Gracious Living," by George Fitzpatrick, January, 1960; "Ernie Pyle Called Albuquerque 'Home,'" by Maurice Trimmer, October, 1960; "From Conquistador to Metropolis," by Fremont Kutnewsky, October, 1960; "Glorieta Baptist Assembly," by Olen C. Jeffries, July, 1961; "Shalam . . . Land of Children," by Lee Priestley, December, 1961; "The Roswell Story," by Frieda Bryan Hyatt, May, 1962; "Cow Pasture Polo," by Peter Hurd, October, 1962.

This is the fourth volume to be published under the Horn & Wallace imprint. All new matter has been set in Linotype Baskerville, the typeface used in the original 1948 edition. The text paper is Potlatch Tillicum Offset. The binding cloth is Holliston Payko, coppertone.

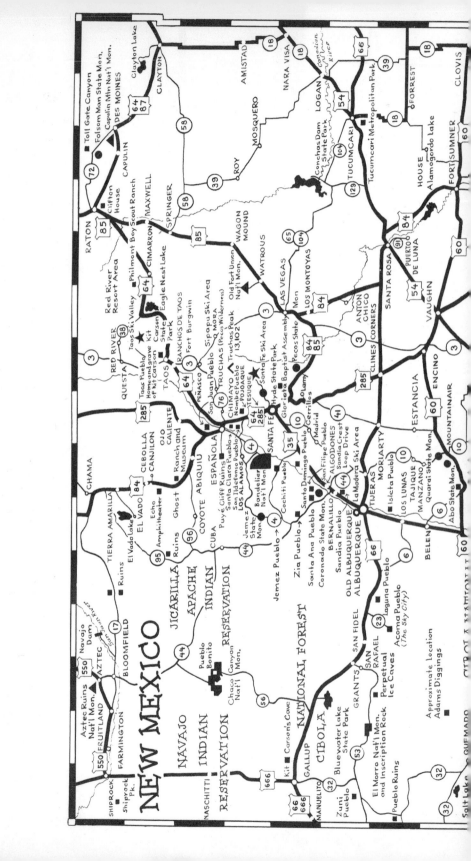